MASS PARDONS IN AMERICA

MASS PARDONS IN AMERICA

REBELLION, PRESIDENTIAL
AMNESTY, AND RECONCILIATION

GRAHAM G. DODDS

Columbia University Press

New York

Columbia University Press

Publishers Since 1893

New York Chichester, West Sussex

cup.columbia.edu

Library of Congress Cataloging-in-Publication Data

Names: Dodds, Graham G., author.

Title: Mass pardons in America : rebellion, presidential amnesty, and reconciliation / Graham G. Dodds.

Description: New York : Columbia University Press, 2021. | Includes bibliographical references and index.

Identifiers: LCCN 2021003024 (print) | LCCN 2021003025 (ebook) | ISBN 9780231200783 (hardback) | ISBN 9780231200790 (trade paperback) | ISBN 9780231553780 (ebook)

Subjects: LCSH: Pardon—United States. | Clemency—United States. | Amnesty—United States. | Executive power—United States. | Presidents—United States. | Government, Resistance to—United States.

Classification: LCC KF9695 .D63 2021 (print) | LCC KF9695 (ebook) | DDC 345.73/077—dc23

LC record available at https://lccn.loc.gov/2021003024

LC ebook record available at https://lccn.loc.gov/2021003025

Cover image: "Pardon," from *Harper's Weekly*, by Thomas Nast (1840–1902). Credit: Minneapolis Institute of Arts, MN, USA. Gift of Charlotte Karlen / Bridgeman Images

Cover design: Lisa Hamm

FOR OLIVER AND JULIA

CONTENTS

ACKNOWLEDGMENTS

This book has evolved over many years, and many people have helped along the way. And since the initial idea for this study was to combine two separate areas of my research agenda—unilateral presidential powers and governmental actions for political reconciliation—the many people who helped with my many previous projects in those areas also helped with this one, even if they didn't know it at the time.

I presented early versions of several of this book's chapters at various academic conferences over the past few years, during which I benefited from the comments of numerous discussants, other presenters, and audience members. Rogers Smith, my dissertation adviser of long ago, gave me characteristically generous and helpful comments on the project over wine at a café in Paris. Richard Ellis provided sharp, insightful feedback on my framing of the Civil War pardons. Jeffrey Crouch provided guidance regarding some of the many constitutional and legal issues about the pardon power. Anne Flaherty helped with information about Native Americans. Michelle Belco apprised me of some resources on Jimmy Carter. The historians Stephen West, Jason Opal, and Leonard Moore made helpful suggestions about relevant secondary literature for a couple of the cases discussed. And my sister-in-law, Elizabeth Kimball, pointed me toward relevant literature on rhetoric.

In every step of the publication process, the staff at Columbia University Press was highly professional, encouraging, and helpful. In particular, Stephen Wesley showed early interest in the project, and his input along the way was consistently quick and smart. And Annie Barva's editing was very thorough and careful.

In the years it took to write this book, I have benefited enormously from the encouragement and companionship of a wonderfully diverse group of colleagues and friends. But the support of my family in Canada—especially my wife, Amy—and of my relatives in the United States—especially my mother, Diane, and my sister, Melissa—has been fundamental and essential. This book is dedicated to my beloved children, Oliver and Julia. May they inherit a world that embraces the spirit of forgiveness and reconciliation that is the subject of this book.

MASS PARDONS IN AMERICA

INTRODUCTION

The President . . . shall have Power to Grant Reprieves and Pardons for Offenses against the United States, except in Cases of Impeachment.

—U.S. CONSTITUTION, ARTICLE II

It is the determination of the ultimate authority that the public welfare will be better served by inflicting less than what the judgment fixed.

—JUSTICE OLIVER WENDELL HOLMES, *BIDDLE V. PEROVICH* (1927)

G erald Ford is not generally considered a great or dramatic president. For many, he is memorable only for his pardon of his disgraced predecessor, Richard Nixon. Others might remember him mainly as the frequent butt of jokes on *Saturday Night Live*. Ford even encouraged the public's view of him as simple and unremarkable: upon being sworn in as vice president, he said, "I am a Ford, not a Lincoln," using the automotive pun to suggest that he was an unassuming public servant who harbored no aspirations of political greatness. But in one respect, Ford showed both an aspiration to use the great power of the presidential office for a pressing national purpose and a knack for political drama.

When Ford ascended to the presidency in August 1974, American military involvement in the war in Vietnam had been over for a year, but the wounds of the long and controversial war remained raw. Countless Americans had protested or resisted the war over the years, and government had responded to its citizens' defiance with sternness and force, at times with deadly results. Hundreds of thousands of Americans had violated Selective Service draft laws, and tens of thousands had deserted from the military during the war. Tens of thousands of Americans were in hiding, and perhaps a hundred thousand more were in exile abroad while wanted by authorities.

Ford responded to this lingering strife in a determined and dramatic fashion. Just ten days after he became president, he went to a convention of the Veterans of Foreign Wars (VFW) in Chicago and bravely told the thousands of veterans assembled there that he had come to embrace a policy they abhorred: he was going to implement a program of "earned reentry" and clemency, whereby Vietnam War draft evaders and military deserters could come home or rejoin society by undertaking a term of service, after which they would be free from prosecution and punishment. Ford's VFW speech explicitly invoked the Christian values of mercy and forgiveness, and he carefully sought to distinguish his policy from the more radical alternative of an "unconditional blanket amnesty," but the dismayed veterans greeted their commander in chief's announcement with stony silence.

One month later Ford gave a televised address to tell the American people that the time had come to enact his clemency program. He spoke for six minutes and carefully reiterated many of the same religiously tinged arguments and explanations he had made at the VFW. He said, "Reconciliation calls for an act of mercy to bind the nation's wounds and to heal the scars of divisiveness."[1] Ford dramatically concluded his speech by signing his clemency proclamation and two accompanying executive orders as the cameras rolled, thereby instantly bringing into being what he hoped would be the means by which the country could finally heal the terrible divisions of the Vietnam War and move toward its bicentennial with a restored sense of unity.

Ford was not the first president to use a mass clemency, pardon, or amnesty to try to reconcile with a large and aggrieved group of

Americans who had strongly resisted their country, nor would he be the last. Indeed, seven of the three dozen people who had previously served as president had also issued mass pardons or amnesties in response to significant domestic resistance, insurrection, and even outright rebellion, and Jimmy Carter would do so just twenty-eight months after Ford did. These actions ranged from a conditional pardon for a select few to a blanket amnesty for all. Some built upon earlier actions, and some were intensely controversial. Regardless of their differences, these mass pardons and amnesties enabled presidents to help heal major political ruptures and to achieve significant political reconciliation.

This book examines these little-studied but important and often dramatic presidential actions. It analyzes how presidents have used both deeds and words—proclamations of mass pardons and persuasive rhetoric—to reconcile with Americans who opposed their government.

PARDONS

Among the few powers that the Constitution explicitly gives to the president, one of the best known is the pardon power. Many Americans might not be attuned to the intricacies of other unilateral presidential tools such as executive orders, presidential memoranda, and signing statements, but most people are aware of pardons, if only because of recent presidents' ceremonial pardons for Thanksgiving turkeys, Ford's pardon of Nixon, or the popular speculation over possible pardons that routinely comes up near the end of a president's term.

U.S. presidents have used their pardon power on many occasions over the centuries, issuing tens of thousands of pardons. Only William Harrison and James Garfield issued no pardons, and they served the shortest terms among all the presidents (just 31 and 199 days, respectively). There are many famous presidential pardons. In 1869, Andrew Johnson pardoned Dr. Samuel Mudd, the physician who set the broken leg of Abraham Lincoln's assassin, John Wilkes Booth, and was then convicted of conspiracy to commit murder. Warren Harding pardoned the socialist leader and presidential candidate Eugene Debs, who was serving a ten-year sentence for violating the Espionage and Sedition Acts of 1917–1918. Franklin D. Roosevelt issued 3,687 pardons, commutations, and acts of clemency during his 4,422 days in office.

Richard Nixon commuted the labor leader Jimmy Hoffa's fifteen-year sentence for jury tampering and fraud. Gerald Ford (in)famously pardoned his predecessor for the role Nixon played in the Watergate scandal and pardoned Iva Toguri D'Aquino, better known as Tokyo Rose, for treason during World War II. Jimmy Carter pardoned the folk singer Peter Yarrow, who was convicted of taking indecent liberties with a minor. Ronald Reagan pardoned the NASCAR star Junior Johnson, who was convicted for making moonshine, and the New York Yankees owner George Steinbrenner, who was convicted of making illegal donations to Nixon's reelection campaign in 1972.

In 1992, George H. W. Bush pardoned former secretary of defense Caspar Weinberger and five other officials for their roles in the Iran-Contra arms-for-hostages scandal. In December 2000, Bill Clinton pardoned fifty-nine people, including former congressman Dan Rostenkowski. Several weeks later, on his last day in office, Clinton issued 140 pardons, including ones for his brother Roger, the heiress-turned-terrorist Patty Hearst, and the fugitive financier Marc Rich.

George W. Bush pardoned dozens of people, but for the most part the "compassionate conservative" Bush "wielded the presidential power to pardon people and commute sentences less frequently than his recent predecessors and far less often than earlier presidents."[2] Barack Obama "granted clemency to more people convicted of federal crimes than any other chief executive in 64 years," yet many observers contend that Obama used his pardon power sparingly, if not stingily.[3] And Donald Trump pardoned various conservative political figures, including Joe Arpaio, Scooter Libby, Dinesh D'Souza, Dwight and Steven Hammond, Conrad Black, Pat Nolan, and David Safavian. Trump also commuted the sentence of his campaign adviser Roger Stone. According to the journalist Thomas Edsall, "Trump has wielded his pardon power in ways he evidently believes will work to his political advantage."[4]

A DIFFERENT TYPE OF PARDON

Again, many Americans are familiar with the president's pardon power and with some of the instances in which presidents have used it. However, there is another type of pardon that seldom receives much attention, either from the public or from scholars: mass pardons or amnesties. Whereas most pardons concern a specific individual and a single instance of wrongdoing, mass pardons are directed at multiple people or even large groups, sometimes thousands and thousands of people, and they can address wrongdoing on a great scale.

Because mass pardons are broader in scope, they are potentially more far-reaching and significant than most pardons for just one person. Moreover, mass pardons offer presidents a potent means of bringing aggrieved and alienated groups back into the national community. They can enable the president to reconcile with large segments of society, put a problematic past behind the country, and move the country forward as a united nation. And they arguably constitute a distinct and important type of presidential action.

This book explores this important but little-known type of pardon and examines its use for domestic political reconciliation. It argues that mass pardons can do a great deal of good if the president carefully uses rhetoric to convince both the targeted group and the broader polity that the form of expiation such pardons embody is appropriate and desirable, as is the broader goal of reconciliation.

DEFINITION

The president's power to issue pardons is one of only a handful of significant executive powers explicitly set out in the U.S. Constitution. Article II states, "The President . . . shall have Power to Grant Reprieves and Pardons for Offenses against the United States, except in Cases of Impeachment." But in this as in many other regards, the Constitution's

description is vague, almost to the point of inviting competing interpretations and controversy.[5] Some further background is therefore necessary to begin to understand what exactly the pardon power is and
how it came to be, let alone how it has been used and to what effect.

Chapter 1 covers the historical, constitutional, and political background of pardons in some detail, but an initial way to understand
what the president's power to grant pardons entails is to seek a definition of the term *pardon*. Pardons are one of several closely related actions
that aim to mitigate the stigma of criminal wrongdoing. Amnesty,
reprieve, clemency, and commutation are similar to pardon, and distinctions between and among these acts are often rather imprecise.[6]
Roughly, pardon and amnesty erase both the guilt and the criminal sentence or penalty, whereas reprieve, clemency, and commutation mitigate
the penalty but do not eliminate the finding of wrongdoing. As a law
professor explained it, "The critical difference is that pardons essentially remove the fact of conviction under the law, while commutations
merely reduce the punishment."[7]

For example, in 2007 George W. Bush commuted the two-and-a-
half-year sentence of vice presidential aide I. Scooter Libby but let stand
his conviction for perjury and obstruction of justice. (Eleven years later
Donald Trump pardoned Libby, thereby overturning the convictions.)
And in 2017 Barack Obama commuted the remaining twenty-eight
years of the thirty-five-year sentence of Chelsea Manning for leaking
classified information to WikiLeaks but did not pardon her, in part
because of the seriousness of her crime. Obama explained his reasoning
as follows: "It has been my view that given she went to trial, that due process was carried out, that she took responsibility for her crime, that the
sentence that she received was very disproportional—disproportionate
relative to what other leakers had received, and that she had served a significant amount of time, that it made it sense to commute—and not
pardon—her sentence."[8]

For some, there may also be a distinction between pardon and
amnesty. For example, Jimmy Carter suggested that pardon entails forgiveness, whereas amnesty entails an element of moral acceptance, as if
no wrong were committed. Many people disputed this distinction, but

Carter repeatedly made it. Similarly, in 1973 a *New York Times* article sought to differentiate the terms as follows: "The word 'amnesty' itself is legally ill-defined. It is not in the Constitution. It means granting 'oblivion[,]' a general pardon for a past offense[,] and is generally used to cover a whole class of citizens. Pardon, in contrast, removes only the penalty for a past offense and generally is defined as being offered to a single individual."[9]

Alternatively, pardons are sometimes distinguished from amnesty in that the former generally concern individuals, whereas the latter concerns groups. According to the historian Jonathan Truman Dorris, "As a kind of working definition, the word 'pardon' is commonly applied to a release or act of forgiveness given to an individual; the word 'amnesty' is the appropriate term for a general pardon or a broad governmental policy of oblivion covering great numbers of persons designated in a sweeping category."[10] The constitutional scholar Edward Corwin alludes to a similar distinction: "Pardons may be absolute or conditional and may be conferred upon specific individuals or upon classes of offenders, as by amnesty."[11] However, most presidents have not made precise terminological distinctions in issuing pardons and amnesties. And, as we will see, the Supreme Court has suggested that there is no difference (e.g., *Knote v. United States*, 95 U.S. 149 [1877]). In short, the relevant terminology here is imprecise and inconsistent.[12]

RATIONALE AND REACTION

Regardless of what one chooses to call a pardon or related action, there is the issue of what purpose it serves. Typically, the rationale for granting a pardon or similar action, whether for an individual or a group, is that basic principles of justice or the broader interests of the country are sometimes best served by not enforcing the law, by essentially letting wrongdoers off the hook even though they did something wrong and therefore deserve disapproval or punishment. In *Biddle v. Perovich* (274 U.S. 480, 486 [1927]), Justice Oliver Wendell Holmes explained the rationale for a pardon as follows: "It is the determination of the ultimate authority that the public welfare will be better served by inflicting less than what the judgment fixed." In other words, a pardon aspires to advance justice or public welfare, not just to adhere to the law. Despite the popular view that justice should be blind (to guarantee impartiality by blocking knowledge of the particular individuals involved), blind enforcement of the laws is not always conducive to broader justice. Justice is sometimes better promoted by making an exception and not fully enforcing the law.[13]

The decision not to apply or maintain the normal, full punishment for wrongdoing can be controversial because a pardon constitutes a departure from the norm. Without a compelling reason for departing from standard procedures, a pardon can therefore seem to be an inappropriate exception to the established rules of criminal justice; a pardon can appear to be a wrong that compounds the initial wrong to which it applies. The U.S. House Committee on Government Reform touched on this intuition in 2002 when it gave its report on "clemency decisions in the Clinton White House" the polemical title *Justice Undone*, as if Clinton's clemency grants had wrongly reversed what was right or had wrecked a just status quo.[14] Similarly, after outgoing governor Matt Bevin of Kentucky issued several hundred controversial pardons in late 2019, the county prosecutor Jackie Steele complained, "What this governor did is an absolute atrocity of justice."[15] Also in late 2019, the *New York Times* criticized Donald Trump's pardons of army officers convicted of war crimes, saying the pardons did "injury to the morality of a nation that once held its own to account."[16] Obviously, the perception that a presidential pardon is inappropriate or unjust can hurt the president politically. Conventional wisdom has long held that Gerald Ford's loss (by 2.1 percent of the popular vote) in the presidential election of 1976 was caused largely by lingering public anger about his pardon of Richard Nixon.

How can a president avoid the political damage that flows from the public perception that a pardon was unwarranted? A strategy that many presidents have employed is to wait to issue controversial pardons until late in their term or after an election, at which point voters can no longer register their disapproval at the polls. For example, many of Bill Clinton's most controversial pardons were issued on his last day in office; he issued 140 pardons and 36 commutations in the last few hours of his presidency. As the journalist Carol Williams observed, "Clemency grants at the end of a governor's or president's term have become a routine departure ritual."[17] And the political scientist P. S. Ruckman Jr. argues that the phenomenon of "last-minute" pardons is "a great American tradition—a tradition that began with the administration of George Washington and has been, more often than not, adhered to by subsequent presidents."[18]

The main alternative to using timing to mute the force of political blowback for a pardon is to avoid it or minimize it by convincing people that the pardon is justified. Insofar as a pardon is a departure from what justice normally dictates, it is incumbent upon the person who grants the pardon to justify it. That is why strategic presidential rhetoric can be so important for pardons. As the political communication scholars Craig Smith and Kathy Smith note, "It is the pardon document that excuses the accused from punishment but the pardon rhetoric that protects the president from public disfavor."[19] That conception of the defensive and justificatory aspects of pardons will be seen in many of the mass pardons examined in the following chapters. As we will see, presidents have carefully employed rhetoric to try to convince both the recipients of a pardon and the broader public that the pardon and the broader purposes it serves are appropriate.

ACADEMIC LITERATURE

The long history, nuanced jurisprudence, and complicated politics of pardons are central to the analysis of this book, and those issues are examined at length in chapter 1. But the book is also informed by and seeks to engage with several strands of academic scholarship on other topics. Specifically, it connects with scholarship about domestic rebellions, the use of unilateral presidential directives in general, presidential pardons in particular, other governmental actions for political community and reconciliation, and presidential rhetoric. A thorough review of these five different academic literatures would be quite lengthy, but a brief summary may be instructive here.

AMERICAN REBELLIONS

Although this book explores how presidents have used mass pardons after rebellions, the rebellions are also important. Most political science literature about domestic rebellions comes from the comparative politics subfield and is often concerned with questions of state consolidation as well as regime strength and change.[20] In the U.S. context, there are numerous historical accounts of particular episodes of rebellion—more than 70,000 books have been published about the Civil War alone—and this study draws on some of them. Beyond treatments of various particular rebellions in the United States, there is only a small scholarly literature on the occurrence of domestic American rebellions generally and their significance.[21]

The small literature on American rebellions includes a book coedited by the Pulitzer Prize–winning historians Richard Hofstadter and Michael Wallace, which chronicles more than one hundred instances of significant collective violence in the United States. In a similar book written more than three decades later, the historians Christopher Waldrep and Michael Bellesiles describe dozens of such episodes. They contend that the United States has a significant tradition of organized domestic violence and that "violence forms a background for all American history."[22] Although both of these books construe the topic somewhat more broadly than just insurrections and rebellions per se, they underscore the point that such episodes are not altogether uncommon in the United States. As the eminent sociologist Charles Tilly suggested in 1969, when it comes to rebellions, American history is not as exceptional or unusual as some might think.[23]

The small academic literature on American rebellions tends to state that the topic has been neglected by scholars. For example, Waldrep

and Bellesiles complain that it "has attracted relatively little attention."[24] But this literature tends to locate the fault for this neglect not
just with academics but also with Americans in general. For example,
Hofstadter argues that Americans wrongly believe that American history has little of the political violence that many other countries have
experienced.[25]

Americans' ignorance of their history of rebellion is striking, in part
because the American Founders were openly concerned about rebellion. For example, the authors of *The Federalist Papers* discussed how
the new regime would deal with the recurring problem of rebellion:
Federalist Nos. 9 and 10 were entitled "The Union as a Safeguard
Against Domestic Faction and Insurrection." In number 9, Alexander
Hamilton argued, contrary to some interpretations of Montesquieu,
that the large size of the new constitutional regime would protect it
against "the tempestuous waves of sedition." For Hamilton, a proper
understanding of Montesquieu's points helps "illustrate the tendency of
the Union to repress domestic faction and insurrection." And in number 10, James Madison recognized the danger of political faction but
thought that the new constitutional system could contain it: "The influence of factious leaders may kindle a flame within their particular
States, but will be unable to spread a general conflagration through the
other States."[26]

Other Founders seemed less concerned about avoiding rebellions. As
Thomas Jefferson wrote in a letter to James Madison in early 1787, "I hold
it that a little rebellion now and then is a good thing." Indeed, Jefferson
believed that rebellions in some regimes were both natural and good.
They were natural, he argued, because periodic political turbulence is an
inevitable product of liberty, hence "as necessary in the political world as
storms in the physical."[27] For Jefferson, the only way to eliminate rebellion was through an oppressive government forcibly controlling the people, which he regarded as a cursed form of existence, saying, "It is a
government of wolves over sheep." Furthermore, Jefferson thought that
under the right conditions rebellions are not just natural but also
therapeutic or desirable. In his letter to Madison, he wrote: "This evil
[i.e., rebellion] is productive of good. It prevents the degeneracy of

government, and nourishes a general attention to the public affairs." In other words, Jefferson argued, the periodic existence of rebellion can safeguard good governance and encourage an attentive public.[28]

Insofar as the Founders were apparently quite aware of the possibility of future rebellions, why are so many Americans today apparently unaware of the rebellions that the United States has experienced? There are various possible explanations. Perhaps it is merely one instance of the broader phenomenon of Americans' considerable historical ignorance. According to Hofstadter, "We have a remarkable lack of memory." He even says that Americans have a great propensity for historical denial.[29] Similarly, the historian Simon Schama has suggested that the typical American is in some respects a "history-free citizen," willfully ignorant of all sorts of important historical information. Alternatively, Americans' historical ignorance might derive from a pragmatic desire to escape the encumbrances of the past. According to Schama, Americans are by nature disinclined to dwell on problems and instead prefer to invoke "the great American mantra of 'move on.'"[30]

Americans' limited awareness of their history of rebellions might also be attributable to their faith in the ultimate stability and durability of their government. In other words, Americans might downplay their history of rebellion because their confidence in the strength of the federal government causes them to downplay the threat posed by those rebellions. As Hofstadter explains this connection, "The old American tolerance for the violent act" was "certainly based upon an uncommon confidence in the stability and security of the country, the confidence that almost any kind of mess could be brought under control quickly enough."[31]

There is likely some truth to each of these explanations for why Americans are largely unaware of the significant history of rebellion in the United States. But Jefferson's letter to Madison in 1787 also alludes to another explanation that is equally plausible and more relevant for the analysis here. Specifically, the way that the federal government responded to rebellions might go a long way to explaining why those rebellions so little troubled later Americans. Jefferson argued that the government's response to rebellions ought to be limited: "Unsuccessful rebellions indeed generally establish the incroachments [*sic*] on the rights of the people which have produced them. An observation of this truth should render honest republican governors so mild in their punishment of rebellions, as not to discourage them too much."[32]

As we will see, even though Hamilton proved to be far less tolerant of rebellion than Jefferson, he initially also indicated that leniency could be a good way for government to respond to rebellion, at least in some circumstances. In Federalist no. 74, he suggests that although government should sometimes meet treason or sedition with "the terror of an example," in other circumstances "mercy" or "impunity" or "a policy of forbearance and clemency" might be appropriate. Hamilton recognized that there might be a "golden opportunity," when "well-timed offer of pardon to the insurgents or rebels may restore the tranquility of the commonwealth."[33]

The idea that mild punishment or even a pardon could be a good response to rebellion took hold and arguably characterized how presidents dealt with those who had engaged in rebellion. As Hofstadter notes, "From the beginning there was a benign and wise disposition to let bygones be bygones, where uprisings, even those with insurrectionary overtones, were involved: there were easy pardons and no official vindictiveness after the Shays' Rebellion, the Whiskey Rebellion, the Fries Rebellion."[34] The salient point here is that maybe Americans tend to forget their history of rebellion because the governmental responses to those rebellions were "so mild" or forgiving that the rebellions were effectively resolved with relatively little lasting animosity or alienation. In short, reconciliation after rebellion might have dulled Americans' memory of disharmony.

UNILATERAL PRESIDENTIAL DIRECTIVES

Although incidents of rebellion are the preconditions of the actions analyzed here, the book's main focus is on presidential responses to rebellion, most of which were enacted via unilateral presidential directives such as proclamations and executive orders. These tools can enable the president to control unilaterally the actions of much of the federal government with a mere "stroke of the pen."[35] They are not explicitly mentioned in the Constitution, and their regular use may be in tension with aspects of it. For example, they violate a strict separation of powers by allowing the chief executive to make binding policy unilaterally, without Congress. And their regular use for significant issues has abetted the historical rise of the executive branch at the expense of the legislative branch, disrupting the interbranch balance of power. Regardless, the judiciary has upheld the propriety of such presidential directives as long as they do not clearly violate a law or the Constitution. Every president has used unilateral directives, and they can be a convenient means to a variety of ends.

Until the early twenty-first century, political scientists had largely neglected the presidential use of unilateral directives. However, after a number of controversial last-minute directives that Bill Clinton issued, several controversial directives that George W. Bush promulgated for the "war on terror," Barack Obama's use of them to overturn many of his predecessor's policies, and Donald Trump's efforts to do likewise, the topic attracted both public and scholarly attention, and there is now a large and growing scholarly literature on it.[36] Today scholars of the presidency are well aware of this crucial aspect of presidential power, whereby a president can unilaterally enact significant, legally binding policy changes even in the face of significant congressional or political opposition.

This book is informed by that literature and seeks to contribute to it in at least two respects. First, although there have been studies of how presidents have used unilateral directives for various policy areas such as the environment or regulatory review or civil rights, their use of such directives for responding to rebellions has not attracted much scholarly attention.[37] This book seeks in part to end that neglect by examining in depth how presidents have used unilateral devices such as proclamations to respond to domestic rebellions.

Second, there is the question of whether unilateral presidential directives really afford presidents the power to do things without having to persuade others to go along. For many scholars, unilateral presidential directives call into question the accuracy of the conception of the presidency that Richard Neustadt articulated in his classic book *Presidential Power* (1960). Neustadt said that the Constitution gives presidents very few direct means of getting what they want, and, as a result, presidents generally cannot simply issue orders. Presidential power therefore consists largely of presidents' ability to persuade other political actors to do as they wish. Thus, for Neustadt, "the power of the presidency is the power to persuade."[38] However, cognizant of the power of unilateral presidential directives, some political scientists now claim that although presidential persuasion might be necessary for enacting policies via traditional legislation, unilateral directives enable presidents to make policy independently, without having to convince others. In the words of William Howell, unilateral presidential directives constitute "power without persuasion."[39]

This book challenges that assessment in part by examining one particular policy area in which unilateral presidential directives have incorporated and been accompanied by persuasive presidential rhetoric. Specifically, as we will see, presidential proclamations of mass pardon and amnesty tend to include significant rhetorical elements. Presidents placed importance on the rhetoric that was in and about these orders, as if the directives would be less effective without it. In other words, the words matter. The ways in which a mass pardon is presented, promoted, and defended matter, and they might even be as important as the legal change conferred by the pardon.

This view builds on some existing scholarship. Among presidency scholars, several have noted that unilateralism and rhetorical persuasion are not always at odds. For example, Matthew Dickinson has argued that Neustadt's "bargaining" paradigm remains highly relevant even as the field is more aware of the power of unilateral action.[40] Andrew Rudalevige has shown that executive orders are not always self-executing because actors within the executive bureaucracy must sometimes be persuaded to go along if the orders are to be effective.[41] Matthew Dickinson and Jesse Grub have demonstrated that executive orders can be used as the first step in a broader effort to persuade Congress to enact policies legislatively.[42] Christopher Kelley, Bryan W. Marshall, and Deanna J.

Watts have documented a wide range of rhetoric in presidential signing statements.[43] Karlyn Kohrs Campbell and Kathleen Hall Jamieson have argued that proclamations of pardon have an important rhetorical component.[44] This book seeks to build on those insights, demonstrate a robust rhetorical element in certain historic proclamations, and thus enhance our understanding of just how interactive and multilateral some putatively unilateral presidential directives really are.

PARDONS

Among the many powers that U.S. presidents have at their disposal, the power to issue or proclaim pardons is one of the best known and arguably also one of the most important. Pardons and similar actions are obviously important for those who receive them as well as for those who give them, but they also have a broader significance. As the political scientist Marie Gottschalk suggests, "Executive clemency is an important vehicle with which to make a statement about the criminal justice system and, more broadly, about what kind of society we want. As such, it shapes the wider political environment in which issues of crime and punishment are debated, and criminal justice is forged."[45] Indeed, this book demonstrates that pardons can be central to determining the nature of society and community, especially when they are mass pardons granted by the chief executive in response to rebellions.

Pardons are also important in terms of their place in the constitutional order. As we will see, the president's pardon power is essentially plenary, with very few strict limits. The pardon power is "the only constitutional power of the presidency that cannot be checked by Congress or the Supreme Court."[46] And as a conservative commentator observed, "Unchecked powers are rare in American law."[47] In short, the unusual constitutional status of the president's pardon power suggests that it is a topic deserving of some attention.

However, despite the importance of presidential pardons, the academic literature on them is not as extensive as one might think. There are several dozen law review articles on the topic, many of which were published shortly after Gerald Ford's pardon of Richard Nixon sparked interest in the topic of pardons. The law review articles tend to address specific pardons or specific legal cases, implications for criminal law, and particular constitutional issues. Writing in 1989, the law professor Alan Dershowitz noted, "Although the pardon is an integral part of our criminal justice mechanism and of our constitutional system of checks and balances, it is one of the most neglected subjects of analysis."[48]

Scholarly work on presidential pardons by political scientists and historians is also rather limited.[49] A "bibliographic essay" published by the political scientist Mark Rozell in 1989 listed thirty-three academic articles and research notes, seventeen books that "discuss this topic either centrally or occasionally," and two government documents. Rozell lamented, "There is not yet a complete, up-to-date book-length analysis of the President's power to pardon."[50] Twenty years later, Jeffrey Crouch's book *The Presidential Pardon Power* (2009) became the first book-length treatment of presidential pardons in decades. It combined historical, legal, and political analysis; served to significantly update older scholarship; and remains a valuable resource for scholars working on the topic. More recently, Andrew Novak's book *Comparative Executive Clemency* (2015) offers a comparative analysis of the clemency power, covering the United States, the United Kingdom, and the British Commonwealth countries.[51]

Although the general topic of presidential pardons is now somewhat less neglected than it once was, there is little scholarship that addresses—let alone focuses on—the presidential use of mass pardons or amnesties in the United States. This book seeks to remedy that shortcoming in part by examining a major type of mass pardon—namely, the pardon issued to foster reconciliation after rebellion.

POLITICAL RECONCILIATION

Construed broadly, mass pardons and amnesties are just one of many ways in which government can try to ameliorate political divisions, make up with alienated groups, and advance political reconciliation.

There is a large multidisciplinary literature on governmental actions for political reconciliation, such as official apologies issued by political leaders and countries to acknowledge and atone for various wrongs, both recent and ancient, domestic and international.[52] Some of this literature examines specific instances of such apologies and related acts of forgiveness and reconciliation, their use in circumstances of transitional justice, as well as the legal, psychological, rhetorical, and political aspects of such actions. In various ways, this literature explores the idea that state apologies and similar actions can help to reconcile with aggrieved groups, heal political divides, and move beyond a problematic past to a more inclusive and united future.

Mass pardons or amnesties are arguably one type of these actions, and they can help to achieve political reconciliation by getting beyond a troubled past and officially affirming the acceptance of the wayward group. Moreover, the acceptance of some conditional pardons may constitute a sort of apology because the wrongdoers may have to acknowledge the error of their ways or somehow make amends in order to be pardoned. This book proceeds from the idea that mass pardons are a main way in which the U.S. federal government can promote political reconciliation, and it presupposes that an awareness of how mass pardons may relate to the broader topic of governmental actions for political reconciliation can enhance our understanding of those pardons.

RHETORIC

The study of rhetoric dates to antiquity; there are numerous scholarly analyses of American political rhetoric; and U.S. presidential rhetoric is the subject of a large and growing field of academic inquiry.[53] This book seeks to engage mainly with two particular parts of the vast literature on presidential rhetoric, which address whether such rhetoric is uniform or effective.

Scholars of rhetoric have occasionally studied presidential pardons. The principal works in this vein are *Deeds Done in Words* by Karlyn Kohrs Campbell and Kathleen Hall Jamieson (1990) and their follow-up book *Presidents Creating the Presidency* (2008). Their main assumption is that "pardoning is a rhetorical act, an act capable of being performed more or less effectively."[54] In other words, they maintain that pardoning is not necessarily a simple, instantly effective act, as some unilateral presidential directives arguably are. By viewing pardons as rhetorical acts, Campbell and Jamieson are making a claim about the sort of politics that governs pardons, essentially claiming that the particular words as well as the act matter. That conception is the starting point for much of the analysis in this book.

However, Campbell and Jamieson also claim that the range of rhetorical possibilities of presidential pardons is quite narrow. They argue that "the presidential pardoning power, while highly discretionary, needs to follow traditional form, to be linked to conventional justifications, to be grounded in the constitutional power of the president, and be performed at an appropriate moment." Campbell and Jamieson say that because of those requirements, presidential pardons are a rhetorical genre in which "the impersonal tone, the archaic language, reliance on legalistic terminology, and the formality of the document overpower individual style and give these documents a quaint sameness." They also claim that "as they recur through time, these forms of rhetorical action become ritualistic," and individual style is suppressed.[55] Thus, they suggest that although the rhetoric of pardons matters, it is of a limited or narrow nature. This book comes to a different conclusion, however, and provides substantial evidence of robust variation in the rhetoric of mass pardons.

Apart from the question of the variability of presidential rhetoric, there is the question of its efficacy. Students of the presidency are perhaps naturally inclined to think that what the president says matters or that presidential words are almost necessarily consequential. After all, the U.S. president is arguably the most powerful person on the planet, such that great attention naturally follows that person's every word and act. But that is perhaps not always the case. Some scholarship on presidential rhetoric calls into question the ability of presidential words to have an impact. In his book *On Deaf Ears* (2003) and in later work, the political scientist George Edwards has argued that presidential rhetoric is almost always ineffective or even counterproductive in terms of moving public opinion toward the president's favored position.[56]

Edwards's point is perhaps counterintuitive, but it is underscored by occasions in which public figures cast doubt on the allegedly transformative power of political rhetoric. For example, during the lengthy contest for the presidential nomination of the Democratic Party in 2008, Senator Hillary Clinton sarcastically mocked Senator Barack Obama's vaunted rhetorical appeals: "Now I could stand up here and say: 'Let's get everybody together, let's get unified!' The sky will open, the light will come down, celestial choirs will be singing, and everyone will know we should do the right thing, and the world will be perfect. . . . But I have no illusions about how hard this is going to be."[57] Similarly, the journalist Adam Clymer wrote in the *Washington Post* in 2013: "These days it is hard to imagine a single presidential speech changing history."[58]

The idea that presidential rhetoric is ineffective is provocative, and this book seeks to engage with it. Ultimately, the examination of mass pardons contained here suggests that presidential rhetoric *can* be effective and even essential, at least in regard to the use of mass pardons for political reconciliation.

THIS STUDY

The areas of scholarship discussed earlier in this introduction are not entirely separate or distinct, but they are seldom combined.[59] Nevertheless, this book endeavors to engage with all of them in some fashion in order to better understand how presidents have responded to rebellions by using mass pardons and rhetoric for political reconciliation. The analysis here will demonstrate that presidents have at times been faced with domestic rebellions, to which they have responded forcefully but also with proclamations of mass pardon and varied rhetorical appeals that have resulted in significant political reconciliation.

The book proceeds in four basic parts. First, this introduction has provided a basic overview of the topic, discussed the definition of pardons, explored their purpose and pitfalls, and briefly noted several relevant strands of academic literature. Chapter 1 provides further background by examining the history, jurisprudence, and political aspects of presidential pardons. The third part is the heart of the book, and it consists of four chapters that analyze the major instances of mass pardons or amnesties in the United States in chronological order and in some detail. In the fourth and final part, the conclusion discusses some implications of the analysis presented here for broader debates in political science and public policy, and the epilogue takes a brief look at recent events.

Again, the book's primary goal is to carefully examine instances in which the U.S. president has used mass pardons to respond to rebellion and achieve political reconciliation. Accordingly, it devotes a chapter to each of the four main cases of such pardons throughout U.S. political history: George Washington's and John Adams's pardoning of participants in armed insurrections in Pennsylvania in the 1790s (chapter 2); James Buchanan's, Benjamin Harrison's, and Grover Cleveland's pardons of Mormon insurrectionists and polygamists over several decades in the nineteenth century (chapter 3); multiple pardons by Abraham Lincoln and Andrew Johnson for Confederates both during and after the U.S. Civil War (chapter 4); and Gerald Ford's clemency and Jimmy Carter's amnesty of Vietnam War draft evaders and military deserters (chapter 5). These cases arguably constitute the complete set of the main instances of presidents using mass pardons in response to rebellion.

The four cases are complex. Each concerns organized and at times violent resistance to federal authority that eventually led to reconciliatory action by two to three presidents. In some cases, the presidents in question issued multiple mass pardons. Each case essentially follows a similar, alliterative trajectory: resistance or rebellion, followed by governmental repression, then rhetoric and pardon, resulting (more or less) in reconciliation. The cases range across much of U.S. political history, address different types of intranational conflict, and contain significant variation in their institutional and political contexts. Moreover, the rhetoric used in promulgating each of these pardons varies considerably in its intent, approach, and efficacy.

To be clear, much of what follows is contested and open to different interpretations in several respects. First, some might argue that the case selection is biased or fails to include other relevant mass pardons. Indeed, the United States has had other instances of mass pardons (see the appendix for other examples). Nevertheless, the four cases highlighted in the book are the major ones in which a president has issued a mass pardon for domestic rebellion. Other examples of mass pardons may be distinguished on various grounds, but in many instances they did not address sustained, principled resistance to the government (i.e., rebellions) but rather concerned various narrower actions.

In contrast to the criticism that this book's case selection is too limited, an alternative criticism is that it is too expansive. In other words, some might claim that some of the episodes discussed here were not true rebellions or did not constitute sustained, principled challenges to the regime or its policies. Some of the conflicts were even at the time seen as somewhat overblown. For example, some contemporaries dismissed the Pennsylvania insurrections of the 1790s as minor affairs, and "Buchanan's War" against Mormons was also criticized by some at the time as much ado about nothing. But those criticisms are also likely overblown. Furthermore, the Civil War was inarguably a major rupture, and few would argue that the Vietnam War and its attendant controversies did not cause profound divisions. Indeed, the episodes examined here concerned not just minor political grievances or narrowly localized discontent. They involved principled resistance, sustained violations of significant federal policies, and, to varying degrees, violence. Moreover, they all led to authoritative and even military responses by the federal government and culminated in one or more mass pardons. Most severe political disputes of course do not rise to the level of rebellion, but the ones discussed here arguably did.

Even if one accepts the set of four cases included here as appropriate and neither too exclusive nor too expansive, one might well complain that they occurred in different settings, such that the institutional context is not constant across them. The president's pardon power was constant in the sense that the relevant parts of the constitutional text remained the same and were not formally amended during the periods in question, but jurisprudence on the pardon power developed, as did the deference of the judiciary. In addition, it is possible that the accretion of precedents mattered: with each new mass pardon, the practice might come to be seen as less radical.

This study is cognizant of the various changes in the presidency and its powers. Nevertheless, its focus on how different presidents used mass pardons to facilitate reconciliation need not suppose that each individual president operated in the exact same institutional setting, with identical resources, limitations, and motivations. What follows here is not a formal social scientific model in which this particular variable must be held strictly constant in order to observe variation in other variables and make attributions of cause and effect. The historical episodes examined are somewhat messier and more complicated than that. But as we will see, these cases strikingly have many of the same basic dynamics.

Then there is the question of how deserving of the pardons their recipients were. Each of the groups who were pardoned in this study had a mixed or controversial reputation: to their sympathizers, both historically and contemporarily, they were honorable and principled people who mostly meant well but who were met with enmity and ultimately with the awesome power of the federal government. Even today, scholars and others argue over the degree to which these groups deserve our sympathy and whether the federal government's responses were appropriate. Not surprisingly, because the target groups and the governmental actions are controversial, the terms of the pardons are also controversial.

This study examines four complex cases in which presidents responded to rebellions by using mass pardons to try to ameliorate the conflicts and to reconcile with the aggrieved groups. It is especially attentive to the proclamations of pardon, but it seeks to contextualize the pardon proclamations by considering the nature of the conflicts as well as what presidents and others did both before and after the pardons were issued. It draws on existing academic and journalistic treatments as well as legal and other governmental sources to analyze how presidents have used mass pardons and rhetoric to achieve political reconciliation after rebellions.

1

MASS PARDONS IN HISTORY, LAW, AND POLITICS

In seasons of insurrection or rebellion, there are often critical moments, when a well-timed offer of pardon to the insurgents or rebels may restore the tranquility of the commonwealth; and which, if suffered to pass unimproved, it may never be possible afterwards to recall.

—ALEXANDER HAMILTON, FEDERALIST NO. 74 (1788)

A pardon is an act of grace, proceeding from the power entrusted with the execution of the laws, which exempts the individual, on whom it is bestowed, from the punishment the law inflicts for a crime he has committed. It is the private, though official act of the executive magistrate.

—CHIEF JUSTICE JOHN MARSHALL, *U.S. V. WILSON* (1833)

B efore examining how presidents have used mass pardons and amnesties to respond to domestic unrest and to foster political reconciliation, it makes sense first to consider the nature of the president's pardon power. How did it come to be that the president possesses the power to grant pardons and amnesties, how extensive and variable is that power, how has it been used over the years, and how does it fit within the broader context of American politics and law? The power to issue pardons is one of the few powers that the Constitution gives explicitly to the president, so it might therefore seem fairly straightforward, at least compared to presidential powers that are shared, implied, or rooted in traditions or norms that have developed over decades or even centuries. However, the president's pardon power has a long and multifaceted history and jurisprudence as well as a complicated politics—considerations that this chapter explores.

HISTORY

BEFORE THE CONSTITUTION

The power of the U.S. president to issue pardons has a substantial pedigree. Long before the creation of the U.S. president's constitutional pardon power, pardons and similar acts were used and debated in ancient Greece and Rome as well as in the Bible (e.g., the Roman prefect Pontius Pilate's release of the prisoner Barabbas) and through the medieval era, as in Geoffrey Chaucer's *Canterbury Tales* (i.e., "The Pardoner's Tale"). In Tudor England, King Henry VIII ended a tradition of the monarchy sharing the pardon power with Parliament by arrogating it entirely to the Crown in 1535. The eminent English jurist Sir Edward Coke examined pardons in the early seventeenth century, asserting that "a pardon is a work of mercy" and trying to distinguish claims to the pardon power made by the monarch and Parliament. Thomas Hobbes wrote in *Leviathan* (1651): "A sixth Law of Nature, is this, That upon caution of the Future time, a man ought to pardon the offences past of them that repenting, desire it. For PARDON, is nothing but granting of Peace."[1] In 1701, England's Act of Settlement limited what had been the monarch's absolute pardon power by stating that a royal pardon cannot prevent an individual from being impeached by the House of Commons—"that no pardon under the Great Seal of England be pleadable to an impeachment by the Commons in Parliament."

In the mid–eighteenth century, the English jurist Sir William Black-stone wrote about pardons and clemency in his *Commentaries*, tracing them back to ancient Roman customs.[2] Blackstone claimed, "This is indeed one of the great advantages of monarchy in general, above any other form of government; that there is a magistrate, who has it in his power to extend mercy, wherever he thinks it is deserved: holding a court of equity in his own breast, to soften the rigour of the general law, in such criminal cases as merit an exemption from punishment." Black-stone also said that pardons could be problematic in democracies, "for there nothing higher is acknowledged than the magistrate who admin-isters the laws: and it would be impolitic for the power of judging and pardoning to center in one and the same person."[3]

In the colonial American context, many governors made use of par-dons. For example, Nathaniel Bacon's roughly 300-person rebellion in Jamestown in 1676 led to a pardon by Governor William Berkeley of Virginia. But not every colony gave the pardon power to its chief excecu-tive. For example, Connecticut and Rhode Island placed the pardon power with the legislature instead of the executive.[4] In Massachusetts, the governor could pardon convicts only with the advice of a council.[5]

During the Revolutionary War, British commissioners at the failed Staten Island peace conference in September 1776 offered to pardon rebellious Americans if they stopped resisting British authority. After the Revolutionary War, the question of a major mass pardon or amnesty came up in terms of how to deal with the 20 percent of Americans who had remained loyal to the British Crown. There were nearly a half-million "Loyalists," and many of them "suffered greatly for their devo-tion to the king."[6]

The Articles of Confederation (ratified in 1781) did not address par-dons, but there was at least one important development in terms of pardons during the eight years that the articles were in place: during Daniel Shays's rebellion in 1786–1787, the Massachusetts legislature offered to pardon the protesters if they would take an oath of alle-giance, sixteen rebels who had been sentenced to death were pardoned in 1787, and ultimately in 1788 Shays was pardoned even though he was never tried.[7]

THE CONSTITUTION

With this substantial tradition of pardons in mind, delegates at the Constitutional Convention in Philadelphia in 1787 debated what to do about the pardon power in the proposed new constitution. The New Jersey and Virginia plans did not address pardons, but Charles Pinckney advocated giving a robust pardon power to the president. However, Antifederalists noted instances in Europe in which leaders had abused the pardon power, and they expressed some concern that it could be similarly misused in the new American polity. For this reason, delegates debated a proposal requiring the Senate to consent to presidential pardons, but the measure was defeated by a vote of eight to one.

Debates about the pardon power continued after the convention. Alexander Hamilton described the need for establishing the pardon power in Federalist No. 74, which was published in March 1788. According to Hamilton, "The criminal code of every country partakes so much of necessary severity, that without an easy access to exceptions in favor of unfortunate guilt, justice would wear a countenance too sanguinary and cruel." Beyond suggesting that pardons were needed to ensure reasonableness in criminal justice, Hamilton also noted how large-scale pardons might be required to deal with rebellions: "In seasons of insurrection or rebellion, there are often critical moments, when a well-timed offer of pardon to the insurgents or rebels may restore the tranquility of the commonwealth; and which, if suffered to pass unimproved, it may never be possible afterwards to recall."[8] In Federalist No. 69, Hamilton repeated the possibility that the president could issue a pardon for rebellion, treason, or "conspiracies and plots against the government."[9]

Hamilton also argued against placing significant restrictions on the pardon power. In Federalist No. 74, he wrote, "Humanity and good policy conspire to dictate, that the benign prerogative of pardoning should be as little as possible fettered or embarrassed." In addition to arguing for a robust pardon power, Hamilton was also adamant about the merits of placing this robust power in the hands of just one person, the president. In Federalist No. 74, he stated,

As the sense of responsibility is always strongest, in proportion as it is undivided, it may be inferred that a single man would be most ready to attend to the force of those motives which might plead for a mitigation of the rigor of the law, and least apt to yield to considerations which were calculated to shelter a fit object of its vengeance. The reflection that the fate of a fellow-creature depended on his sole fiat, would naturally inspire scrupulousness and caution; the dread of being accused of weakness or connivance, would beget equal circumspection, though of a different kind. On the other hand, as men generally derive confidence from their numbers, they might often encourage each other in an act of obduracy, and might be less sensible to the apprehension of suspicion or censure for an injudicious or affected clemency. On these accounts, one man appears to be a more eligible dispenser of the mercy of government, than a body of men. . . . It is not to be doubted, that a single man of prudence and good sense is better fitted, in delicate conjunctures, to balance the motives which may plead for and against the remission of the punishment, than any numerous body.[10]

For Hamilton, an awareness of the possible use of mass pardons for rebellions provided yet another reason for the power to be given to just one person rather than a group. In Federalist No. 74, he explained this point with reference to Shays's Rebellion:

It deserves particular attention, that treason will often be connected with seditions which embrace a large proportion of the community; as lately happened in Massachusetts. In every such case, we might expect to see the representation of the people tainted with the same spirit which had given birth to the offense. And when parties were pretty equally matched, the secret sympathy of the friends and favorers of the condemned person, availing itself of the good-nature and weakness of others, might frequently bestow impunity where the terror of an example was necessary. On the other hand, when the sedition had proceeded from causes which had inflamed the resentments of the major party, they might often be found obstinate and inexorable, when policy demanded a conduct of forbearance and clemency.[11]

Thus, Hamilton suggested that in such cases it would be easier for a single individual to judge the merits of a possible pardon. In addition, given the need for timeliness in issuing pardons for rebellions, Hamilton argued that a single individual could act more quickly and thus be counted on to grant a pardon at the best moment, whereas the comparativeness slowness of a group's deliberations might result in missing an opportunity for an expeditious pardon.

On June 18, 1788, at the Virginia ratifying convention, George Mason argued against the proposed constitution's treatment of the pardon power. Mason, who was one of three delegates at the convention who refused to sign on to the proposed new constitution, said that the president "ought not to have the power of pardoning, because he may frequently pardon crimes which were advised by himself. It may happen, at some future day, that he will establish a monarchy, and destroy the republic. If he has the power of granting pardons before indictment, or conviction, may he not stop inquiry and prevent detection? The case of treason ought, at least, to be excepted. This is a weighty objection with me."[12] In response to Mason's objection, James Madison cautioned against placing the pardon power in Congress because the legislature would be more likely to be influenced by political passions and thus might push for vengeance and neglect humanity. In addition, Madison noted that if the president were to abuse the pardon power, he could be impeached and removed from office.

At the North Carolina ratifying convention on July 28, 1788, the Federalist leader James Iredell argued in favor of the proposed constitution's treatment of the pardon power in terms that echoed points that Hamilton had made four months earlier in Federalist No. 74:

I think there is a propriety in leaving this power to the general discretion of the executive magistrate, rather than to fetter it.... It may happen that many men, upon plausible pretences, may be seduced into very dangerous measures against their country. They may aim, by an insurrection, to redress imaginary grievances, at the same time believing, upon false suggestions, that their exertions are necessary to save their country from destruction. Upon cool reflection, however, they possibly are convinced of their error, and clearly see through the treachery and villainy of their leaders. In this situation, if the President possessed the power of pardoning, they probably would throw themselves on the equity of the government, and the whole body be peaceably broken up. Thus, at a critical moment, the President might, perhaps, prevent a civil war. But if there was no authority to pardon, in that delicate exigency, what would be the consequence? The principle of self-preservation would prevent their parting. Would it not be natural for them to say, "We shall be punished if we disband. Were we sure of mercy, we would peaceably part. But we know not that there is any chance of this. We may as well meet one kind of death as another. We may as well die in the field as at the gallows." I therefore submit to the committee if this power be not highly necessary for such a purpose.[13]

Regardless of how persuasive one finds arguments for a robust pardon power being given exclusively to the president, this view prevailed, and the Constitution was ratified, empowering the president to issue pardons unilaterally and without constraint other than that the scope of this power would not extend to impeachment or civil or state-level offenses.[14]

Although the focus of this study is the president's pardon power, it should be noted that the constitutional system of the United States also provides for other types of pardons. For example, Congress cannot directly interfere with the president's pardon power, but it has some de facto pardon power of its own. Per its power to tax and the "necessary and proper" clause of Article I of the Constitution, Congress can pass an amnesty law to remit penalties incurred under a national statute, and it can repeal a law that had imposed criminal liability. For example, in 1872 Congress passed the General Amnesty Act, which eliminated most of the political disabilities that the Fourteenth Amendment had imposed on some classes of former Confederates (which the amendment had provided that Congress could do via a two-thirds vote). However, because the act left in place limits on the political rights of a few hundred Confederates, Deputy Assistant Attorney General

Leon Ulman could testify before a House subcommittee in 1974 that "Congress has never enacted in our long history a general amnesty law purporting to confer clemency by its own actions." Moreover, Ulman told Congress that although "the subject of amnesty is one in which legal views are not entirely in agreement . . . my conclusion is that it is quite difficult to say that Congress has the constitutional power to legislate amnesty."[15]

Nevertheless, as a general rule it seems that Congress can pass a law to provide an amnesty if it wishes. Indeed, in *Brown v. Walker* (161 U.S. 591 [1896]), the Supreme Court indicated that the authority to grant pardons and amnesty is not the president's alone and that the Constitution's provision for presidential pardons does not preclude Congress from passing acts of amnesty.[16] In 1974, the American Bar Association affirmed the power of Congress "to enact broad amnesty legislation" as well as "to legislate immunity from prosecution" and "to modify the terms and conditions of judicial sanctions."[17] In 1975, the House Subcommittee on Courts, Civil Liberties, and the Administration of Justice said that "the power to grant amnesties is not exclusive to the President," drawing on the Supreme Court's opinion in *Burdick v. United States* (236 U.S. 79 [1915]), which this chapter discusses later.[18] Congress passed an amnesty for illegal immigrants in 1929; over the next half century, it passed more than twenty similar measures to legalize unlawful immigrants; and in 1986 it acted to offer amnesty to some three million illegal immigrants.

Apart from the possibility of enacting its own amnesties, Congress has also passed laws authorizing the president to issue certain pardons, though the president also has that power via the Constitution, independent of any congressional authorization.

STATES

In addition, the U.S. system of federalism also allows for pardons and related actions at the state level, though only for state-level crimes. In forty-one states, the governor has the pardon power, and nine states entrust this power to a pardon board. State-level pardons do not often rise to the level of prominence that presidential pardons do, but they can still be important. For example, there are several instances of governors pardoning or otherwise freeing inmates facing the death penalty. As Marie Gottschalk notes, "Governors Lee Cruce of Oklahoma (1911–1915), Winthrop Rockefeller of Arkansas (1967–1971), and Toney Anaya of New Mexico (1983–1987) issued mass commutations to empty their death rows. They justified their actions with calls for mercy for the condemned."[19] In early 2003, just two days before leaving office, Governor George Ryan of Illinois commuted the sentences of all inmates on death row in the state (167 people) to life sentences because of concerns about the fairness of capital punishment, and he pardoned four other inmates who were facing the death penalty but who had allegedly been tortured to confess.[20] And in November 2019, Oklahoma released 462 inmates in the largest single-day commutation in U.S. history. The release collectively erased 1,931 years that remained in the former inmates' sentences, and it followed a ballot measure in 2016 and a vote by the state legislature about revising penalties for drug possession.[21]

Governors have also issued various posthumous pardons. Some of them were for individuals who had been executed, and the pardons were given either because the deceased recipients had been wrongly convicted or because their crimes later came to be seen in more sympathetic terms.[22] For example, in 1893 Governor John Altgeld of Illinois posthumously pardoned several anarchists who had been executed for engaging in the deadly Haymarket riot in 1866. And there have been symbolic state-level pardons for criminal offenses committed during the civil rights movement: in 2006 and 2007, the states of Alabama, Louisiana, and Tennessee passed laws to facilitate pardons or expunge convictions that had been based on actions undertaken in protesting racial segregation.[23]

In terms of the distinction between individual and group pardons at the state level, Virginia's recent experience is notable. In April 2016, Governor Terry McAuliffe issued an executive order to restore voting rights to more than 200,000 former felons who were disenfranchised because of their criminal records per the state's constitution. Three months later, however, the Virginia Supreme Court in a four–three decision said that the governor could restore voting rights only on a case-by-case basis, not by one big general directive. The decision was based in part on the state constitution's requirement that the governor inform the legislature of the "particulars of every case" and state reasons for each pardon. The court said, "This requirement implies a specificity and particularity wholly lacking in a blanket, group pardon." (The court noted the different treatment of such directives under the U.S. Constitution.)[24] Undaunted, McAuliffe then began the laborious process of signing tens of thousands of individual restoration orders.

JURISPRUDENCE

Beyond the nature of the pardon power in the Constitution, the history of the U.S. judiciary's treatment of pardons is crucial because the practice of judicial review essentially renders the Supreme Court's understanding of constitutional matters authoritative and determinative. What is in the Constitution of course matters, but what really matters, practically speaking, is what the courts say the constitutional text means.

In 1950, the Supreme Court said, "Seldom, if ever, has this power of executive clemency been subjected to review by the courts."[25] Although there is some truth to that assertion, there is a long history of court cases that have clarified much about the pardon power and its place in the constitutional order. This section briefly reviews eleven cases that fleshed out the nature of the president's pardon power.[26] As we will see, the judiciary has found that the president's pardon power is essentially plenary and not subject to congressional approval or limitation; pardons can be conditional; they may cover a group rather than an individual; they may be issued without any prior consultation or formal process; and the legal effect of a pardon is immediate.

The first main legal case to concern presidential pardons was *U.S. v. Wilson* (32 U.S. [7 Pet.] 150 [1833]). In *Wilson*, Chief Justice John Marshall addressed the providence and promise of pardons:

> The constitution [*sic*] gives to the president, in general terms, "the power to grant reprieves and pardons for offences against the United States." As this power had been exercised from time immemorial by the executive of that nation whose language is our language, and to whose judicial institutions ours bear a close resemblance; we adopt their principles respecting the operation and effect of a pardon, and look into their books for the rules prescribing the manner in which it is to be used by the person who would avail himself of it. A pardon is an act of grace, proceeding from the power entrusted with the execution of the laws, which exempts the individual, on whom it is bestowed, from the punishment the law inflicts for a crime he has committed. It is the private, though official act of the executive magistrate, delivered to the individual for whose benefit it is intended, and not communicated officially to the court.

In short, Marshall treated Great Britain's experience with pardons as determinative for the United States, and he viewed the power as a personal prerogative of the president to which judges must defer entirely.

The *Wilson* case also addressed the question of whether pardons can be conditional and can be refused. The case concerned a pardon Andrew Jackson gave to George Wilson, who had been convicted of robbery and several other crimes and sentenced to death. Jackson pardoned Wilson for the crime for which he had been sentenced to death, but Wilson refused to accept the pardon, which ultimately led to his being hanged.[27] In *U.S. v. Wilson*, U.S. attorney general Roger Taney argued that Wilson was free to refuse the pardon: "The court cannot give the prisoner the benefit of the pardon, unless he claims the benefit of it. . . . It is a grant to him: it is his property; and he may accept it or not as he pleases." The Court agreed and determined that such a refusal was possible: "A pardon is a deed, to the validity of which delivery is essential, and delivery is not complete without acceptance. It may then be rejected by the person to whom it is tendered; and if it is rejected, we have discovered no power in this court to force it upon him. . . . A pardon may be conditional; and the condition may be more objectionable than the punishment inflicted by the judgment." The question of whether a pardon could be refused would come up again in later cases.

The next major case to consider the president's pardon power occurred more than three decades after *Wilson*: *Ex parte Garland* (71 U.S. [4 Wall.] 333 [1866]). *Garland* concerned congressional attempts to bar former Confederates from government employment even if they had received a presidential pardon. The Supreme Court said that the president's pardon power "is not subject to legislative control. Congress can neither limit the effect of his pardon, nor exclude from its exercise any class of offenders. The benign prerogative of mercy reposed in him cannot be fettered by any legislative restrictions"[28] The Court thus rejected Congress's attempt to nullify the effect of an individual pardon: "It is not within the constitutional power of Congress thus to inflict punishment beyond the reach of executive clemency."[29] Also in *Garland*, the Court said that the pardoning power "extends to every offense known to the law, and may be exercised at any time after its commission, either before legal proceedings are taken or during their pendency, or after conviction and judgment."[30] Moreover, it said, the president's pardon power is "unlimited" and that "Congress can neither limit the effect of his pardon, nor exclude from its exercise any class of offenders."[31] Thus, *Garland* affirmed the relatively unlimited nature of the president's pardon power.

Justice Stephen Field's opinion in *Garland* also addressed "the effect and operation of a pardon":

> A pardon reaches both the punishment prescribed for the offence and the guilt of the offender; and when the pardon is full, it releases the punishment and blots out of existence the guilt, so that in the eye of the law the offender is as innocent as if he had never committed the offence. If granted before conviction, it prevents any of the penalties and disabilities consequent upon conviction from attaching; if granted after conviction, it removes the penalties and disabilities, and restores

him to all his civil rights; it makes him, as it were, a new man, and gives him a new credit and capacity.... A pardon reaches both the punishment prescribed for the offence and the guilt of the offender ... so that in the eye of the law the offender is as innocent as if he had never committed the offence.

After *Garland*, the next case in which the Supreme Court addressed the pardon power in a significant manner was *U.S. v. Klein* (13 Wall. [80 U.S. 20] 128 [1871]). In *Klein*, the Court touched on several important points regarding pardons. First, it effectively found there to be no difference between pardon and amnesty and thereby recognized the propriety of mass pardons; as Chief Justice Field's majority opinion stated, "pardon includes amnesty." Thus, the Court said that mass pardons fall within the Constitution's provision of pardons. Second, the Court commented on the impact of a pardon: "It blots out the offence pardoned, and removes all its penal consequences." In other words, a pardon erases the judicial determination that a wrong was committed, as if the act had never occurred. Third, the Court declared that a pardon "may be granted on conditions."

Fourth, the Court also held that Congress had acted unconstitutionally in encroaching upon the president's power.[32] After Abraham Lincoln pardoned Confederates in December 1863, contingent upon their taking a loyalty oath, Congress passed a law in 1870 to prohibit such people from receiving compensation for confiscated property on the grounds that acceptance of such a pardon was evidence that the person who was pardoned had provided support to the Confederacy and was ineligible to recover sale proceeds. The Court in *Klein*, however, ruled that Congress had impermissibly infringed on the power of the executive branch by seeking to limit the effect of a presidential pardon, if not to override it altogether: "To the executive alone is entrusted the power of pardon; and it is granted without limit[;] ... the legislature cannot change the effect of ... a pardon any more than the executive can change a law."

Also in 1871, the Court considered Andrew Johnson's amnesty of Confederates in December 1868 in *Armstrong v. United States* (80 U.S.

154). At issue was whether someone who had been pardoned could recover the proceeds of property taken by the military per the Captured and Abandoned Property Acts of 1863 and 1864 without having to satisfy the act's requirement that the claimant had not aided the rebellion. In a very brief decision, the Court found that the president's pardon proclamation effectively overrode the act's requirement about evidence of having aided the rebellion. The Court said the president's proclamation of pardon was "a public act of which all courts of the United States are bound to take notice, and to which all courts are bound to give effect."[33] In other words, pardons—like congressional statutes, executive orders, treaties, and court decisions—are legally binding.

In *Knote v. United States* (95 U.S. 149 [1877]), the Court again considered Johnson's amnesty of December 1868 and indicated its views about several important issues relating to pardons. For example, the Court said, "As to offences against the United States, the pardoning power of the President is unlimited, except in cases of impeachment." Justice Field's opinion for the Court also noted the lack of a real distinction between pardons and amnesties:

Some distinction has been made, or attempted to be made, between pardon and amnesty. It is sometimes said that the latter operates as an extinction of the offence of which it is the object, causing it to be forgotten, so far as the public interests are concerned, whilst the former only operates to remove the penalties of the offence. This distinction is not, however, recognized in our law. The Constitution does not use the word "amnesty"; and, except that the term is generally employed where pardon is extended to whole classes or communities, instead of individuals, the distinction between them is one rather of philological interest than of legal importance. At all events, nothing can be gained in the consideration of the question before us by showing that there is any difference in their operation. All the benefits which can result to the claimant from both pardon and amnesty would equally have accrued to him if the term "pardon" alone had been used in the proclamation of the President. In Klein's case, this court said that pardon included amnesty.

The Court in *Knote* also indicated that although a pardon has the effect of removing the offense, it cannot undo everything or make thorough amends for what has occurred:

> A pardon is an act of grace by which an offender is released from the consequences of his offense, so far as such release is practicable and within control of the pardoning power, or of officers under its direction. It releases the offender from all disabilities imposed by the offense, and restores to him all his civil rights. In contemplation of law, it so far blots out the offense, that afterwards it cannot be imputed to him to prevent the assertion of his legal rights. It gives to him a new credit and capacity, and rehabilitates him to that extent in his former position. But it does not make amends for the past. It affords no relief for what has been suffered by the offender in his person by imprisonment, forced labor, or otherwise; it does not give compensation for what has been done or suffered, nor does it impose upon the government any obligation to give it. The offense being established by judicial proceedings, that which has been done or suffered while they were in force is presumed to have been rightfully done and justly suffered, and no satisfaction for it can be required. Neither does the pardon affect any rights which have vested in others directly by the execution of the judgment for the offense, or which have been acquired by others whilst that judgment was in force.

For some, the idea that a pardon cannot altogether undo what was done or make full amends for the past might call into question the ability of a pardon to achieve political reconciliation.[34]

Fifteen years later the Court again addressed the power of pardons to remake the past in *Boyd v. United States* (142 U.S. 450 [1892]). The case concerned a pardon that Benjamin Harrison granted at the request of a district attorney for a man convicted of larceny in order to restore his ability to testify as a competent witness at a criminal case. The Court noted that even though the pardon was issued just for this instrumental purpose, the impact of the "full and unconditional" pardon nevertheless erased the witness's conviction and thus rendered him admissible as a witness. Thus, the pardon "obliterated" the effect of the conviction.

The case of *Burdick v. United States* (236 U.S. 79 [1915]) concerned a newspaper editor's refusal to testify about the source of a story, supposedly because by doing so he might incriminate himself. President Woodrow Wilson offered to pardon him for whatever offenses he might have committed and thus remove his reason for refusing to testify, but the editor refused to accept such a pardon. The Court said that such a refusal was permissible (much as it had in *U.S. v. Wilson*):

> The grace of a pardon, though good its intention, may be only in pretense or seeming; in pretense, as having purpose not moving from the individual to whom it is offered; in seeming, as involving consequences of even greater disgrace than those from which it purports to relieve. Circumstances may be made to bring innocence under the penalties of the law. If so brought, escape by confession of guilt implied in the acceptance of a pardon may be rejected, preferring to be the victim of the law rather than its acknowledged transgressor, preferring death even to such certain infamy. This, at least theoretically, is a right, and a right is often best tested in its extreme.

The Court in *Burdick* also noted in passing the possibility of amnesty being conferred by legislation or statute as well as by executive action. And it made a distinction between a pardon, which could be refused, and a grant of immunity, which could not be refused: "This brings us to the differences between legislative immunity and a pardon. They are substantial. The latter carries an imputation of guilt; acceptance a confession of it. The former has no such imputation or confession. It is tantamount to the silence of the witness. It is noncommittal. It is the unobtrusive act of the law given protection against a sinister use of his testimony, not like a pardon, requiring him to confess his guilt in order to avoid a conviction of it."[35] Six decades after *Burdick*, Gerald Ford carried a copy of the Court's decision in his pocket and occasionally showed people this quoted passage to justify his pardon of Richard Nixon on the grounds that the pardon did not erase the guilt.[36]

Burdick is also notable in that it considered the difference between pardon and amnesty:

> It is of little service to assert or deny an analogy between amnesty and pardon. Mr. Justice Field, in *Knote v. United States*, 95 U.S. 149, 95 U.S. 153, said that "the distinction between them is one rather of philological interest than of legal importance." This is so as to their ultimate effect, but there are incidental differences of importance. They are of different character and have different purposes. The one overlooks offense; the other remits punishment. The first is usually addressed to crimes against the sovereignty of the state, to political offenses, forgiveness being deemed more expedient for the public welfare than prosecution and punishment. The second condones infractions of the peace of the state. Amnesty is usually general, addressed to classes or even communities—a legislative act, or under legislation, constitutional or statutory—the act of the supreme magistrate. There may or may not be distinct acts of acceptance. If other rights are dependent upon it and are asserted, there is affirmative evidence of acceptance. . . . If there be no other rights, its only purpose is to stay the movement of the law. Its function is exercised when it overlooks the offense and the offender, leaving both in oblivion.

The Court next considered pardons in *Ex parte Grossman* (267 U.S. 87 [1925]). The case concerned a pardon by Calvin Coolidge that commuted the sentence of Philip Grossman, whose violation of Prohibition had led to a conviction for contempt of court. The Court unanimously upheld Coolidge's action, affirming that a pardon can address a criminal contempt of court. Chief Justice William Howard Taft's opinion drew upon English monarchical precedents to argue that the pardon power extended to criminal contempt of court, and he indicated that this expansive view of the pardon power was not worrisome:

> Executive clemency exists to afford relief from undue harshness or evident mistake in the operation or enforcement of the criminal law. The administration of justice by the courts is not necessarily always

wise or certainly considerate of circumstances which may properly
mitigate guilt. To afford a remedy, it has always been thought essential
in popular governments, as well as in monarchies, to vest in some
other authority than the courts power to ameliorate or avoid particular criminal judgments. It is a check entrusted to the executive for special cases. To exercise it to the extent of destroying the deterrent effect
of judicial punishment would be to pervert it; but whoever is to make
it useful must have full discretion to exercise it. Our Constitution con-
fers this discretion on the highest officer in the nation in confidence
that he will not abuse it. An abuse in pardoning contempts would certainly embarrass courts, but it is questionable how much more it
would lessen their effectiveness than a wholesale pardon of other
offenses. If we could conjure up in our minds a President willing to
paralyze courts by pardoning all criminal contempts, why not a President ordering a general jail delivery?

Two years later in *Biddle v. Perovich* (274 U.S. 480, 486 [1927]), the
Supreme Court considered President Taft's commutation of a convicted
murderer's death sentence to life imprisonment, a move that the inmate
challenged. Solicitor General William Mitchell argued that the president's ability to confer a commutation or pardon should not depend on
the recipient's consent, notwithstanding what the Court had said in
Wilson and *Burdick*. In *Biddle*, Mitchell said of *Wilson*, "That case
merely followed the English rule that an executive pardon is a private
act of which the courts can not take notice unless pleaded and proved.
It is not authority for the proposition that a pardon may be rejected and
execution of his sentence insisted on by the convict." And he said of
Burdick, "The rule that a convict has the right to insist on execution
of his sentence overlooks the paramount public interest and places too
much emphasis on the preferences of the convict. It is not well supported by reason." Those arguments evidently persuaded Justice Oliver
Wendell Holmes, who in his opinion for the Court said that the reasoning from *Burdick* should not obtain in *Biddle*. Holmes wrote, "The
opposite answer would permit the President to decide that justice
requires the diminution of a term or a fine without consulting the

convict, but would deprive him of the power in the most important cases and require him to permit an execution which he had decided ought not to take place unless the change is agreed to by one who on no sound principle ought to have any voice in what the law should do for the welfare of the whole." Thus, the Court indicated that an individual could not reject a pardon.[37]

In *Biddle*, Holmes also countered some of Marshall's view from *Wilson* about whether a pardon is a public or private act: "A pardon in our days is not a private act of grace from an individual happening to possess power. It is a part of the constitutional scheme. When granted it is the determination of the ultimate authority that the public welfare will be better served by inflicting less than what the judgment fixed." Thus, for Holmes, a pardon enables the president to advance the public good as the president sees it.[38]

Nearly a half century after *Biddle*, the Court articulated several significant points about pardons in the case of *Schick v. Reid* (419 U.S. 256 [1974]). First, the Court upheld the president's ability to issue a conditional pardon, ruling that the president could condition commutation of a death sentence on the prisoner's acceptance of a life term of imprisonment without the possibility of parole. It furthermore indicated that any such condition need not be authorized by statute.[39] Second, the Court in *Schick* articulated a broad range for commutation: "The executive pardoning power under the Constitution, which has consistently adhered to the English common law practice, historically included the power to commute sentences on conditions not specifically authorized by statute."

Third, echoing *Klein*, the Court in Schick determined that Congress cannot interfere with the pardon power: "A fair reading of the history of the English pardoning power, from which our Art. II, 2, cl. 1, [of the Constitution] derives, of the language of that clause itself, and of the unbroken practice since 1790 compels the conclusion that the power flows from the Constitution alone, not from any legislative enactments, and that it cannot be modified, abridged, or diminished by the Congress."

Fourth, Chief Justice Warren Burger's majority opinion in *Schick* seemed to carve out a limitation in the judicial deference to pardons to "conditions which do not in themselves offend the Constitution." Thus, Burger appeared to say that some pardons might possibly be unconstitutional (contra *Garland*) if they dramatically upset the constitutional order.[40] This provocative possibility notwithstanding, the other cases noted here indicate that the judiciary has largely endorsed the president's pardon power as plenary and not open to limits or restrictions by Congress.[41]

After *Schick*, the judiciary affirmed the plenary nature of the president's pardon power. For example, in *Public Citizen v. Department of Justice* (491 U.S. 440 [1989]), Justice Anthony Kennedy wrote a concurring opinion that affirmed the view of *Klein* and *Schick* and various other cases that Congress cannot interfere with the pardon power: "In a line of cases . . . where the Constitution by explicit text commits the power at issue to the exclusive control of the President, we have refused to tolerate any intrusion by the Legislative Branch," and Kennedy's first example of such a power was the pardon power.

LINGERING AMBIGUITIES

Altogether, the eleven court cases discussed in the previous section clarified many of the constitutional ambiguities of the president's pardon power. Nevertheless, some questions remain about certain aspects of it. There is currently some debate about just how much of a criminal past a pardon can erase, the possibility of a withdrawn pardon, a pardon for civil rather than criminal offenses, a self-pardon, an unconstitutional pardon, and the ability of Congress to rein in presidential pardons.

There is some controversy about whether a pardon actually erases all vestiges of past wrongdoing. In *Garland*, Justice Field said a pardon "blots out of existence the guilt, so that in the eye of the law the offender is as innocent as if he had never committed the offence." But the reality might be more complicated than that pronouncement indicates. The case of Arizona county sheriff Joe Arpaio is relevant to this question. In

2017, Arpaio was convicted of criminal contempt of court for repeatedly ignoring an injunction issued in 2011 against detaining people whom he suspected of being undocumented immigrants. Before Arpaio was sentenced, however, he was pardoned by President Donald Trump. Arpaio then asked a U.S. District Court judge to throw out the ruling that had detailed his conviction to ensure that the information could not be used in future civil lawsuits against him. The judge declined and left Arpaio's conviction record on the books because, she argued, the pardon did not "revise the historical facts."[42]

Arpaio subsequently appealed to the Ninth Circuit Court of Appeals, which in February 2020 ruled that the guilty verdict could not be officially vacated because it had no legal significance after the pardon. This ruling suggests that a presidential pardon does not actually clear every aspect of a past offense.

Another point of confusion is whether a pardon can be reversed. The line of court decisions discussed earlier indicates that Congress cannot undo a pardon. Nor can a pardon be overturned by a future president. For example, during his ceremonial pardon of two turkeys before Thanksgiving Day in 2017, Donald Trump joked that his pardon was similar to one that President Obama had made the year before for two turkeys named Tater and Tot: "As many of you know, I have been very active in overturning a number of executive actions by my predecessor. However, I have been informed by the White House Counsel's Office that Tater and Tot's pardons cannot, under any circumstances, be revoked."[43]

Nevertheless, in certain circumstances it appears that a president may effectively undo a pardon. For example, on his third day in office in 1869, Ulysses Grant rescinded two pardons that had been granted by his predecessor, Andrew Johnson, but that had not quite been delivered to their recipients and hence had not really been issued (much like the delayed delivery that led to the case of *Marbury v. Madison* [5 U.S. 137 (1803)]).[44] Similarly, in December 2008 George W. Bush pardoned Isaac Toussie, who had been convicted of mortgage fraud, but one day later Bush rescinded the pardon after learning that Toussie's father had recently donated more than $30,000 to Republicans. Bush directed the pardon attorney at the Department of Justice not to deliver to Toussie the decision that the president had made the day before. A journalistic account explained that even though such a reversal was highly unusual, "the Justice Department said it believed that the original pardon announcement was not binding and could be revoked because Mr. Toussie had not received formal notification of the president's action."[45] The Grant and Bush reversals were possible because the final steps in the process of issuing the pardons had not been completed. But once a pardon is actually granted, it cannot be undone.

Apart from the issue of possibly undoing a pardon, there is also the issue of possibly redoing a pardon. In July 2019, Donald Trump pardoned Michael Tedesco, who had been convicted in 1990 of drug trafficking and fraud. Barack Obama had pardoned Tedesco in 2017, but due to a clerical error Tedesco's conviction for fraud remained on his record. According to a statement from the Trump White House, "By granting a full and unconditional pardon, President Trump has corrected this error, and Mr. Tedecso will now be eligible for state licenses he needs to expand his car warranty business."[46]

Another constitutionally ambiguous aspect of pardons is the scope of wrongs to which they may be applied. As discussed earlier, presidential pardons cover only federal offenses (except impeachment), not state offenses. However, there is some dispute as to whether pardons might address civil as well as criminal wrongs. The distinction between criminal and civil law is not always clear, and indeed one act might be a violation of both criminal and civil laws. Nevertheless, roughly, criminal law concerns public wrongs, whereas civil law concerns private wrongs; criminal law deals with actions against the government or society, whereas civil law concerns actions against individuals or private entities.[47] Article II of the Constitution limits the scope of the president's pardon power to "offenses against the United States," which arguably encompass only public or criminal actions and preclude civil offenses. In *Ex parte Grossman* (1925), Chief Justice Taft noted the distinction between criminal and civil offenses in his decision that the president's pardon power extended to contempt of court, but the Supreme Court has never clearly ruled on whether a presidential pardon might address a civil matter, and legal scholars are divided on the question.[48]

Another area in which some ambiguity persists is whether presidents may pardon themselves. This question came up during the Nixon and Clinton presidencies, and in June 2018 Donald Trump tweeted, "As has been stated by numerous legal scholars, I have the absolute right to PARDON myself."[49] Trump's boast notwithstanding, it is by no means clear that presidents can pardon themselves. The Constitution explicitly precludes that possibility for impeachment. And as the law scholar Frank Bowman III notes, the idea of a self-pardon contradicts "the basic common law principle that a person may not be a judge in his or her own case."[50] An opinion from the U.S. Office of Legal Counsel in 1974 invoked that same rationale and concluded that presidents cannot pardon themselves.[51]

Then there is the issue of whether a pardon might be unconstitutional. Again, Justice Burger suggested in *Klein* that if a pardon were to "offend the Constitution," it might be illegitimate. Similarly, Bowman contends that even if the president's pardon power is absolute, that "does not mean that any use of it is permissible."[52] How might a pardon be beyond the pale? Some scholars have suggested that a pardon that somehow violates constitutional principles such as due process or the separation of powers might be unconstitutional. Or as Donald Trump pondered proactive pardons for some of his family members in the summer of 2017, scholars argued that a pardon cannot be issued as part of a bribe or a similar illegitimate bargain.[53] Nor can a pardon be used to cover up a crime or to impede a federal investigation because that would amount to obstruction of justice.

Apart from the question of how a pardon might be inappropriate, there is also the question of what a response to such a pardon might be. According to Daniel Hemel and Eric Posner, "The broad and unreviewable nature of the pardon power does not shield the president from criminal liability for abusing it." And even if a sitting president cannot be indicted, per an Office of Legal Counsel internal memo in 1973, that president could still face prosecution after leaving office.[54]

Congress might also seek to respond to an illegitimate pardon in several ways. For example, the legislative branch could attempt to prompt the judicial branch. In September 2017 and again in March 2019, members of the U.S. House of Representatives filed an amicus brief urging a federal judge to reject Donald Trump's pardon of Sheriff Joe Arpaio for a contempt-of-court charge on the grounds that the pardon undermined the ability of the judiciary to ensure its orders were respected and thus encroached upon the independence of the judiciary by making the judicial branch reliant upon the executive.[55]

Within its own purview, Congress might enact requirements governing aspects of the pardon process. For example, in 2018 Representative Adam Schiff (D–CA) introduced the Abuse of the Pardon Prevention Act, which would require the Department of Justice to give Congress information about any presidential pardons for family members. And in July 2020, the House Judiciary Committee approved a bill that would forbid self-pardons and would criminalize quid-pro-quo pardons.[56] The *New York Times* said that this bill "amounts . . . to the most substantial attempt by Congress in recent history to put guardrails around one of the most powerful authorities granted to a president."[57] If such a measure became law, the president might decide to resist or not comply with it, and it is not clear how courts might rule on the matter.

Congress could also try to modify the president's pardon power by initiating the procedure for a formal constitutional amendment. For example, in 1974 Senator Walter Mondale (D–MN) proposed a constitutional amendment to permit Congress to overturn a pardon by a two-thirds vote. Senator Arlen Specter (R–PA) proposed a similar amendment in 2001. And in 2019, Representative Steve Cohen (D–TN) proposed an amendment to prohibit presidents from pardoning themselves or members of their family, administration, or campaign staff.

Ultimately, Congress might censure or even impeach and remove the president for abuse of the pardon power. At the Virginia ratifying convention in 1788, both James Madison and George Nichols noted that a president could be impeached for misuse or abuse of the pardon power. And among the various wrongs alleged in the articles of impeachment that the House Judiciary Committee passed for Richard

Nixon in 1974, one was that he had wrongly promised to pardon or give "favoured treatment and consideration" for top aides in return "for their silence or false testimony" in the investigations of the president.[58]

In short, Congress is not powerless to respond to the president's pardon power. And by some accounts, some sort of response would be appropriate. In May 2019, the *New York Times* opined, "It is past time for Congress to display a more robust appetite for exploring this president's [i.e., Trump's] use of the pardon power—if only to assure the public that he is pursuing his constitutional duties rather than his political interests."[59]

Altogether, these considerations indicate that despite the Constitution's clear provision of the president's right to grant pardons and the long history of legal cases about it, some legal questions still remain about the use and impact of the pardon power.

POLITICS

The preceding sections have covered the history and jurisprudence of the president's pardon power in some detail. Again, they indicate that the president's pardon power has a long pedigree and is robust and little constrained. But ultimately pardons are political. As the *New York Times* said in 2017, "Pardons are by definition political decisions."[60] They are rooted in the Constitution and broader historical traditions, and they confer a legal change, but their use is profoundly political. A host of political considerations influences what sorts of people and actions might receive a pardon, whether and when a president might grant a pardon, what sort of pardon (or clemency) might be conferred (i.e., if it is conditional in some fashion or limited in scope), and how the president might explain, promote, or defend a pardon. Obviously, key factors include the nature or severity of the wrongdoing, how generous or demanding the pardon is, and the attitudes of Congress and the public.

As discussed in the introduction, a pardon makes an exception to the rule. Via a pardon, the president is making a determination that in the given case justice or the broader interests of the country require that an exception be made to normal legal practices. Such a determination is necessarily political. And if the pardon is not well considered, or if the public is not persuaded by its merits, then it can damage the public's confidence in the president and even the public's faith in the legal system. The president must ensure that people agree that, on balance, the exception that a pardon makes is appropriate. But that can be easier said than done, especially when the pardon addresses rebellions and national unity. In short, even though the president's pardon power has a solid historical and constitutional foundation, the politics of any particular pardon are open to contestation.

Having now discussed the history, constitutionality, and politics of the president's pardon power, the book explores in the next four chapters how presidents have employed mass pardons to deal with rebellions and domestic unrest.

2

PENNSYLVANIA INSURRECTIONS IN THE LATE EIGHTEENTH CENTURY

George Washington and John Adams

Though I shall always think it a sacred duty to exercise with firmness and energy the constitutional powers with which I am vested, yet it appears to me no less consistent with the public good than it is with my own feelings to mingle in the operations of Government every degree of moderation and tenderness which the national justice and safety may permit.

—GEORGE WASHINGTON, 1795

It is become unnecessary for the public good that any future prosecutions should be commenced or carried on against any person or persons by reason of their being concerned in the said insurrection.

—JOHN ADAMS, 1800

The issue of presidential mass pardons for significant domestic resistance in the United States first arose during the first two presidencies, in both cases concerning insurrections in the commonwealth of Pennsylvania. George Washington issued a plural pardon for the Whiskey Rebellion in 1795, and John Adams issued one for Fries's Rebellion in 1800. Although these two instances of rebellions and pardons are distinct, they are considered in tandem here because of their close timing, the striking similarities of the political ruptures to which they responded, and the fact that some of the same people were involved in both cases.[1]

GEORGE WASHINGTON

Among the many important precedents established during George Washington's presidency, few were so dramatic as the federal government's response to the rebellion in western Pennsylvania in 1795. Popularly known as the Whiskey Rebellion, it was a serious domestic insurrection that threatened the new constitutional regime. Just two decades after the start of the American Revolution and seven years after the ratification of the Constitution, a segment of the population was once again protesting—at times violently—against a tax and arguably by extension also against the legitimacy of the government that imposed the tax.

TAX PROTEST

The traditional account of what is generally called the Whiskey Rebellion focuses on resistance to a tax on distilled spirits. When Alexander Hamilton wrote Federalist No. 12 in 1787, he noted, "The genius of the people will ill brook the inquisitive and peremptory spirit of excise laws."[2] Yet Hamilton adopted a different view about such taxes after he became the nation's first secretary of the Treasury. In September 1789, the U.S. House of Representatives commissioned a report on public credit, and in January 1790 Hamilton issued his report, which recommended an excise tax on domestic whiskey as a way for the federal government to pay for assuming tens of millions of dollars of preexisting state debts.[3] Congress then enacted the Excise Whiskey Tax in early 1791. It was the country's first national internal revenue tax and its first "sin tax."[4]

The tax was based on the capacity of stills and had to be paid in cash. It was very unpopular. For many, the tax on whiskey amounted to roughly 25 percent of the net value of their product.[5] For some, it constituted a direct threat to their livelihood because whiskey was a popular medium of exchange.[6] It was less perishable and less bulky than the grain from which it was distilled, so it was easier to get to market and hence was favored by many farmers along the nation's western frontier.[7] For others, the tax was objectionable because it appeared to benefit bigger producers and perhaps speculators. According to one historian, "Disdaining internal taxes, which they associated with British rule, country people wanted the government exclusively to rely on import duties collected at the seaports. Common farmers resented paying taxes to provide windfall profits to wealthy speculators in the public debt."[8] The U.S. National Park Service explains the opposition to the tax:

> Acceptance of the excise tax varied with the scale of the production; large producers, who produced alcohol as a business venture, were more willing to accept the new tax. They could make an annual tax payment of six cents per gallon. A smaller producer, who only made whiskey occasionally, had to make payments throughout the year at a rate of about nine cents per gallon. Large producers could reduce the cost of the excise tax if they produced even larger quantities. Thus, the new tax gave the large producers a competitive advantage over small producers. The smaller producers, who were generally in the western counties, had a very different perspective of the tax. To them the tax was abhorrent. The frontier farmers detested the excise because it was only payable in cash, something rare on the western frontier. Due to the great effort required to transport any product over the mountains back to the markets of the East, farmers felt it made much more sense to transport the distilled spirits of their grain rather than the raw grain itself.[9]

Drawing on these and other resentments, people in western Pennsylvania and elsewhere who opposed the tax began to voice their displeasure. As the Pulitzer Prize–winning historian Alan Taylor explains, "Settlers felt as justified in resisting the Federalist excise tax as they had in opposing Parliament's taxes. Claiming to defend the revolution, they erected liberty poles inscribed with slogans and topped with flags."[10] Resistance to the tax grew through the early 1790s in western Pennsylvania and elsewhere, eventually leading to what one historian describes as "the single largest armed confrontation among American citizens between the Revolution and the Civil War."[11]

A BROADER REBELLION?

In contrast to the traditional explanation of the Whiskey Rebellion just described, some scholars discern different, deeper reasons for the conflict. Indeed, the conflict's name itself is a matter of some dispute. As Taylor notes, "To denigrate their opponents, Federalists called the resistance 'the Whiskey Rebellion,' an insult that has stuck in histories."[12] And as Terry Bouton points out, Hamilton created the name "Whiskey Rebellion" to belittle the dissent to the tax: "The term implicitly ridicules the protest, much as Hamilton intended it. By adopting that label, historians have, intentionally or not, perpetuated the derision, ensuring that the first image that pops into the heads of schoolchildren in a history lesson on the subject is drunken, gun-wielding hillbillies, frightening but too comical to be taken seriously."[13]

Apart from the name of the rebellion, some scholars see it not as an instance of local, self-interested resistance but rather as part of a broader revolutionary tradition. For example, in his book *American Revolutions* (2016), Taylor argues that the American Revolution was part of a broader revolutionary era because it had much in common with actions elsewhere in the Western Hemisphere, and its true timing stretched to before the beginning and after the end normally attributed to it. The latter point is especially relevant here; Taylor contends that America's revolutionary era went beyond the Treaty of Paris of 1783 and even into the nineteenth century, such that the Pennsylvania insurrections of the 1790s were part of this broader revolutionary history, not just minor events or vestiges of an old revolutionary spirit.[14] Moreover, Taylor argues that for people in the western frontier regions, resistance to government was a long-standing phenomenon, and they felt little loyalty to the state.[15] Thus, the Whiskey Rebellion was arguably part of this broader phenomenon, not an aberration or a minor flare-up.

Similarly, Bouton contends that most historians have misunderstood the Whiskey Rebellion: "This insurgency has generally been seen as the product of a federal excise tax, problems specific to the frontier, or some kind of generic fear of centralized government. Historians have portrayed the protesters as acting out of base self-interest, ignorance, an intense commitment to 'localism,' or paranoia." Like Taylor, Bouton instead considers it a part of a long tradition of protest. He contends that it should "be seen as part of the broader effort by ordinary farmers in the political mainstream of Pennsylvania (and, indeed, the mainstream across the new nation) to defend their vision of the Revolution." For Bouton, "this protest was about popular beliefs that the state and national governments were undermining equality and democracy to enrich and empower a handful of moneyed men." The rebels were trying to ensure that their government acted "on behalf of the ordinary many rather than the wealthy few," and they "were following a well-worn path." Bouton notes similar uprisings in North Carolina in the 1760s and 1770s and in Massachusetts in the 1780s and claims that "the 1790s uprisings in Pennsylvania fit seamlessly into this pattern."[16]

In addition to Taylor and Bouton, various other authors share this basic view of the Whiskey Rebellion as part of a broader political phenomenon.[17] Some authors also refer to the whiskey rebels' actions as "regulations," a term used to describe the broader phenomenon of Americans seeking to alter the policies of their government. Bouton even claims that the "Whiskey Rebellion" should instead be called the "Pennsylvania Regulations."[18]

However, in contrast to the sympathetic interpretation by Taylor and Bouton and others, Forrest McDonald describes the residents of western Pennsylvania in less-flattering terms: "In mythology the people of that area were sturdy yeomen farmers, working hard to carve a decent living out of the wilderness for themselves and their families but neglected when not oppressed by a plutocratic government on the seaboard. In reality most of them were—as the Frenchman [J. Hector St. John de] Crevecoeur described them—uncouth, drunken, lazy, brutal, wasteful, and contentious, 'no better than carnivorous animals of a superior rank.' Law was a stranger among them; clan and kin were all. They rarely worked, hard or otherwise." According to McDonald, "Far from being oppressed by government, they ignored it; they rarely paid taxes or paid for the land they inhabited; any official who attempted to enforce the law among them did so at his mortal peril."[19] In short, the nature of the "Whiskey Rebellion" is a matter of some dispute.

RESISTANCE

Regardless of the reason(s) people had for opposing the tax on distilled spirits in 1791 and the degree to which the Whiskey Rebellion was similar to other conflicts, opposition to the tax became widespread and strong, especially in four counties near the frontier of western Pennsylvania.[20] According to the biographer Ron Chernow, "As soon as the tax took effect in July 1791, locals began to shun or even threaten inspectors" in western Pennsylvania.[21] Organized resistance began shortly after a meeting at Redstone Old Fort in southwestern Pennsylvania in July, and the resisters were supported by local organizations called associations or societies, which also coordinated their efforts.[22] On August 23, 1791, opponents of the tax in Washington County, Pennsylvania, passed a resolution declaring that tax collectors would be defied:

> That whereas men may be found amongst us so far lost to every sense of virtue and feelings for the distress of the country as to accept the office for the collector of the duty, resolved therefore, that in the future we will consider such persons as unworthy of our friendship, have no intercourse or dealings with them, withdraw from them every assistance, and withhold all the comforts of life, which depend upon those

duties that as men and fellow citizens we owe to each other, and upon all occasions, treat them with that contempt they deserve; and that it be, and it is hereby earnestly recommended to the people at large, to follow the same line of conduct towards them.[23]

Although most of the resistance to the tax initially took the form of demonstrations and petitions, it soon came to have more violent manifestations.[24] Under the unofficial leadership of attorney David Bradford, antitax gangs of rebels called "Tom the Tinker's Men" painted their faces black and coerced others to support them and not pay the tax. When federal agents sought to act against dozens of distillers in western Pennsylvania who had not paid the tax, the rebels forced the agents to flee for their lives.[25] In September 1791, a group of men in Pigeon Creek, Pennsylvania, accosted the revenue collector Robert Johnson, cut his hair, tarred and feathered him, and stole his horse. In October 1791, when John Connor attempted to serve warrants on those who had assaulted Johnson, he was whipped, robbed, and tarred and feathered by a mob, which left him tied to a tree.[26] By 1792, resistance to the excise tax had spread from Pennsylvania to Kentucky, Virginia, Georgia, and the Carolinas.[27]

On May 8, 1792, Congress passed a law that lowered some of the duties on whiskey. But opponents of the tax were not mollified. According to Chernow, "That summer, the newspaper editor and author Philip Freneau printed inflammatory letters that likened Hamilton's tax to those imposed arbitrarily under British rule" before independence.[28] A political cartoon from August 1792 entitled "An Exciseman" gives a sense of the hostility directed at collection of the tax, its accompanying poem depicting the killing of a tax assessor:

> Beneath this tar and feathers,
> lies as great a knave
> As e'er the infernal legions did receive
> A bum exciseman despicable name
> Fierce as ten thousand furies to these ports he came
> To make the farmers pay for drinking their own grog

But thank the fates that left him in the bog.
For his bad genius coaxed him to a tree
Where he was hanged and burned, just as you see.
Launched off quick to gauge the River Styx
Where he'll get Sulphur all his drink to mix.
Ah! Farmers come and drop the tear of woe
'Cause Pluto did get him long ago.
Just where he hung the people meet,
To see him swing was music sweet.
A Barrel of whiskey at his feet.
 Without the head.
They brought him for a winding sheet,
 When he was dead.
They clap'd a match unto the same
It flew about him in a flame,
Like shrouding for to hide his shame
 Both face and head.
The whiskey now will bear the blame;
 It burn'd him dead.[29]

Also in August 1792, tax protesters terrorized Captain William Faulkner for renting his house to the tax inspector Colonel John Neville and forced him to promise to evict Neville.[30]

Federalists were dismayed by these actions. According to Taylor, they "felt threatened by a revival of the regulator tradition in the backcountry from Pennsylvania south to Georgia as farmers resisted Hamilton's excise tax. . . . Federalists regarded the regulation as a rebellion that threatened the new constitutional order."[31] Hamilton wrote to George Washington on September 1, 1792, calling for "vigorous and decisive measures on the part of the Government." He also told Washington it might be necessary "to exert the full force of the law against the offenders."[32]

On September 15, 1792, Washington responded by issuing a proclamation on the rebellion. Prior to this proclamation, there had been just half-a-dozen presidential proclamations ever issued under the

Constitution, and they had addressed signing treaties with American Indian nations, fixing the borders of the new District of Columbia, and establishing a national day of thanksgiving. Beyond old colonial precedents, there was no template for an official presidential proclamation about domestic unrest. Thus, in this as in many other things, Washington's action set a precedent. Washington's proclamation noted the "moderation" that the government had thus far exhibited in the face of "violent and unsuitable proceedings" related to liquor laws. It cited the president's constitutional authority "to take care that the laws be faithfully executed." And it called on tax resisters to desist, threatened prosecution, and charged legal officials to ensure the laws were not obstructed.[33]

Tensions decreased somewhat after Washington's proclamation, but resistance soon reappeared.[34] In 1793, rebels harassed tax collectors Benjamin Wells in April and John Lynn in June. The resistance increased in the spring of 1794, when federal officials decided to prosecute thirty-seven delinquent distillers in federal district court in Philadelphia rather than in closer and more sympathetic state courts.[35] According to McDonald, "That was a dangerously provocative move." The law had been changed in June to permit proceedings in local state courts in response to local complaints about the burdens of having to travel across the state, so the imposition of this old, onerous requirement "evoked widespread anger."[36]

Anger against the tax and its enforcement spread. According to John Miller, "Revenue officers were terrorized—sometimes at gun point—into resigning their offices; United States marshals were forcibly prevented from serving processes upon rioters; and the United States mail was seized by armed bands."[37] In June 1794, there were more violent conflicts and one death.[38] As in 1792, the rebellion began to spread from western Pennsylvania into parts of Maryland, Virginia, and Kentucky.

On July 16, 1794, rebels shot at federal marshal David Lenox and tax collector General John Neville at Neville's home at Bower Hill in Allegheny County. The rebels despised Neville, who was in charge of tax collection in western Pennsylvania and was also a large-scale whiskey producer of the sort that the tax benefited. Neville's guards shot and killed one rebel, Oliver Miller. The next day, the size of the opposing group grew, and roughly five hundred tax resisters returned to Neville's home, which was then defended by ten soldiers. A gun battle ensued, resulting in deaths on both sides before the soldiers surrendered. The insurgents burned the house to the ground and captured Lenox, but Neville fled.[39] Major General John Gibson sent a report to George Washington regarding the attack on Neville's house: "I am sorry to have to inform your Excellency that a civil War has taken place in this Country."[40]

PITTSBURGH

As James Rogers Sharp explains, shortly after the attack on Neville, "more ambitious plans were laid by the rebels including the interception of the federal mails and an attack upon Pittsburgh to seize the garrison's military equipment and ammunition."[41] In early August 1794, the Whiskey Rebellion truly became a major threat as thousands of protestors gathered at Braddock's Field and began to march on Pittsburgh, eight miles away. Accounts of the numbers of marchers vary from 5,000 to 9,000.[42] According to Joseph Ellis, the protestors gathered outside Pittsburgh, "imbibed freely of their favorite liquid, then defied the federal government to come after them."[43] After citizens expelled prominent Federalists, the rebels decided against burning the city. But they terrorized tax collectors and their sympathizers, "and a general reign of lawlessness prevailed for about two weeks."[44] The rebels also threatened the Fort Pitt arsenal.

Unrest soon spread west to Kentucky and south to Georgia. In western Maryland, ninety rebels tried to seize the Fredericktown armory in September 1794 but were repelled by seven hundred troops sent in by the governor.[45] As Jonathan Keane notes, "The resistance in the west now had its own red-and-white striped flag."[46] Some rebels even spoke of seceding from the United States.[47]

WASHINGTON RESPONDS

Federalists were enraged by the rebellion. They often referred to the insurgents as "White Indians" because they "[deemed] the poor frontier settlers . . . to be savages and little different from the Indians."[48] Beyond that racial deprecation, however, according to Bouton, "Hamilton and his Federalist associates perceived the movement in Pennsylvania for what it was: a serious, if embryonic, political threat."[49] Indeed, the Whiskey Rebellion was a significant threat to the new nation. After all, the problematic governmental response to Daniel Shays's 4,000-person rebellion in western Massachusetts just seven years earlier was one of the chief catalysts for changing the young country's constitutional structure from the relatively weak Articles of Confederation to the U.S. Constitution and its stronger federal government and chief executive. Another armed insurrection was therefore a great concern for the new country. And just as an offer of pardon was part of the governmental response to Shays's Rebellion, pardon would ultimately be part of the reaction to the Whiskey Rebellion, though at the federal level.[50]

Washington met with his cabinet on August 2, 1794, to discuss whether the federal government might have to respond with force. His cabinet was split about whether to send in troops. Hamilton and Secretary of War Henry Knox supported the speedy use of a large force, but Secretary of State Edmund Randolph and Attorney General William Bradford argued for negotiations.[51] As William Hogeland explains, at the Constitutional Convention Randolph had argued "strenuously for creating a national power to put down insurgencies," but he now counseled Washington to delay military action and instead to negotiate with the rebels to try to achieve peace and reconciliation, saying that the new country's strength lay not in its coercive powers but rather in the people's affection for it.[52] In contrast, Hamilton pushed for an immediate military response by an overwhelmingly large force; he wanted at least 12,000 men.[53]

Washington was persuaded that a strong federal response was required, but the reality was that any force would take a while to mobilize because much of the regular army was engaged in General Anthony

Wayne's campaign against Native Americans along Ohio's western frontier.[54] Article II of the Constitution provided an alternative means of assembling troops, stating that the president would be commander in chief not only of the army and navy but also of "the Militia of the several States, when called into the actual Service of the United States." This was the avenue that Washington decided to pursue, but the Militia Act of 1792 required the president to get the assent of a federal judge before calling out the militia. Accordingly, Washington provided information to Supreme Court associate justice James Wilson, and on August 4 Wilson certified that local authorities were not sufficiently powerful to put down the insurrection.[55]

Even though the government was preparing for a forceful response, Hamilton continued to press the issue. On August 5, 1794, he wrote a lengthy letter to Washington about the rebellion, which he called a "disagreeable crisis" initiated by "Malcontents." Hamilton provided a detailed chronology of events from the passage of the tax to early August 1794, and he said that the dissatisfaction with the tax had taken an improper and unlawful turn, that its intention was "to embarrass the Government" and "to compel a repeal" of the excise law, so it would have to be dealt with strongly.[56]

Washington then issued a proclamation on August 7 ordering the insurgents in western Pennsylvania to disperse. Washington's proclamation described the insurrection in some detail and characterized it as "subversive" and "criminal." It also recounted the rebels' actions against Neville and Lenox and said that they "amount to treason." It invoked the Militia Act and noted Wilson's opinion that local authorities were not capable of putting down the unrest. It also said that Washington, although "feeling the deepest regret for the occasion," had nevertheless decided that it was necessary to call forth the militia because "the very existence of Government and the fundamental principles of social order are materially involved in the issue." The proclamation then directed the insurgents to disperse:

> I, George Washington, President of the United States, do hereby command all persons, being insurgents, as aforesaid, and all others whom

it may concern, on or before the 1st day of September next to disperse and retire peaceably to their respective abodes. And I do moreover warn all persons whomsoever against aiding, abetting, or comforting the perpetrators of the aforesaid treasonable acts; and do require all officers and other citizens, according to their respective duties and the laws of the land, to exert their utmost endeavors to prevent and suppress such dangerous proceedings.[57]

Secretary Knox then contacted the governors of Maryland, Pennsylvania, New Jersey, and Virginia to assemble a militia.[58]

COMMISSIONERS

On the same day that Washington issued his stern proclamation and that the militia began to assemble, he also sought to reach a peaceful resolution to the conflict. Against Hamilton's advice, Washington sent three peace commissioners, including Attorney General Bradford, to try to persuade the rebels to desist. By one account, "the purpose of the peace commission was merely 'political cover' for the military operation."[59]

Washington's commissioners met with the rebels' representatives in late August and told them the troops would invade unless the rebels agreed to submit to the federal government, in which case they would be given amnesty.[60] The representatives claimed that they had no authority to make decisions that would bind the rebels, but they arranged for a popular referendum to be held September 11, in which people would vote for or against a statement of submission to federal laws.[61] Those who voted for it would then sign a declaration: "I do solemnly promise henceforth to submit to the laws of the United States, that I will not, directly or indirectly, oppose the execution of the acts for raising a revenue on distilled spirits and stills; and that I will support, as far as the law requires, the civil authority in affording the protection due to all officers and other citizens."[62]

As Hogeland explains, many "people signed in fear of federal troops."[63] According to H. G. Cutler, "Those who had been most deeply engaged in the excesses generally signed," including David Bradford.[64] But as Leland Baldwin notes, "It would be difficult indeed to prove that the signing of the oath on September 11 and a law-abiding life after that date earned the promised amnesty in every case."[65]

Although some rebels submitted, many others did not. On September 24, 1794, the commissioners gave Washington a detailed report on their meetings with the remaining rebels and on these rebels' subsequent deliberations about whether they would submit. The commissioners said, "In some townships, the majority, and in one of them, the whole of the persons assembled, publicly declared themselves for resistance." Therefore, the commissioners advised Washington "that there is no probability that the act for raising a revenue on distilled spirits and stills can at present be enforced by the usual course of civil authority; and that some more competent force is necessary to cause the laws to be duly executed." They concluded that it was "absolutely necessary that the civil authority should be aided by a military force in order to secure a due execution of the laws."[66]

TULLY

In late August and early September 1794, while Washington's commissioners were trying to secure agreements of loyalty, Hamilton wrote four public letters under a pseudonym in which he equated the rebellion with anarchy. He used the name "Tully" to invoke Marcus Tullius Cicero's famous denunciation of Cataline's conspiracy against the Roman Republic in 63 BCE, as if the whiskey rebels' threat to the American republic were of the same magnitude.[67]

On August 28, 1794, Tully published a letter in the *American Daily Advertiser* in which he obliquely discussed the threat constituted by the Whiskey Rebellion and how to respond to it. He argued that in resisting the nation's legitimate laws, the rebels were also undermining its constitutional system and threatening citizens' enjoyment of liberty, so that a strong governmental response was necessary.

> Such a resistance is treason against society, against liberty, against everything that ought to be dear to a free, enlightened, and prudent people. To tolerate were to abandon your most precious interests. Not to subdue it, were to tolerate it. Those who openly or covertly dissuade you from exertions adequate to the occasion are your worst enemies. They treat you either as fools or cowards, too weak to perceive your interest and duty, or too dastardly to pursue them. They therefore merit, and will no doubt meet your contempt. To the plausible but hollow harangues of such conspirators, ye cannot fail to reply, How long, ye Catalines, will you abuse our patience?[68]

On September 2, 1794, Tully wrote another public letter on the rebellion and the need to respond forcibly to it. The letter argued that respect for law is a sacred duty and a source of security and that those who would undermine it would lead the people into slavery. Tully further contended that such people cannot be long tolerated but rather must be forcibly subdued. He decried the "dark conspiracy" that sought to dissuade good citizens from confronting lawlessness: "Fellow Citizens— You are told, that it will be intemperate to urge the execution of the laws which are resisted—what? will it be indeed intemperate in your Chief Magistrate, sworn to maintain the Constitution, charged faithfully to execute the Laws, and authorized to employ for that purpose force when the ordinary means fail—will it be intemperate in him to exert that force, when the constitution and the laws are opposed by force? Can he answer it to his conscience, to you not to exert it?"[69] Again, the clear message was that Washington would have to respond militarily.

MILITARY ACTION

Ultimately, Washington was persuaded that he would have to use force. On September 25, 1794, just one day after he received his commissioners' report, he issued a proclamation saying that he was prepared to crush the insurrection militarily. This was his third proclamation about the Whiskey Rebellion (following those of September 1792 and August 1794), and it authorized military intervention. The proclamation began:

> Whereas from a hope that the combinations against the Constitution and laws of the United States in certain of the western counties of Pennsylvania would yield to time and reflection I thought it sufficient in the first instance rather to take measures for calling forth the militia than immediately to embody them, but the moment is now come when the overtures of forgiveness, with no other condition than a submission to law, have been only partially accepted; when every form of conciliation not inconsistent with the being of Government has been adopted without effect; when the well-disposed in those counties are unable by their influence and example to reclaim the wicked from their fury, and are compelled to associate in their own defense; when the proffered lenity has been perversely misinterpreted into an apprehension that the citizens will march with reluctance; when the opportunity of examining the serious consequences of a treasonable opposition has been employed in propagating principles of anarchy, endeavoring through emissaries to alienate the friends of order from its support, and inviting its enemies to perpetrate similar acts of insurrection; when it is manifest that violence would continue to be exercised upon every attempt to enforce the laws; when, therefore, Government is set at defiance, the contest being whether a small portion of the United States shall dictate to the whole Union, and, at the expense of those who desire peace indulge a desperate ambition.

Washington's proclamation further indicated

> that a force which, according to every reasonable expectation, is adequate to the exigency is already in motion to the scene of disaffection; that those who have confided or shall confide in the protection of Government shall meet full succor under the standard and from the arms of the United States; that those who, having offended against the laws,

have since entitled themselves to indemnity will be treated with the most liberal good faith if they shall not have forfeited their claim by any subsequent conduct, and that instructions are given accordingly.

And I do moreover exhort all individuals, officers, and bodies of men to contemplate with abhorrence the measures leading directly or indirectly to those crimes which produce this resort to military coercion; to check in their respective spheres the efforts of misguided or designing men to substitute their misrepresentation in the place of truth and their discontents in the place of stable government, and to call to mind that, as the people of the United States have been permitted, under the Divine favor, in perfect freedom, after solemn deliberation, and in an enlightened age, to elect their own government, so will their gratitude for this inestimable blessing be best distinguished by firm exertions to maintain the Constitution and the laws.[70]

The militias were assembled, and Washington left Philadelphia with Hamilton on September 30, took personal charge of the troops, and marched west toward Pittsburgh. This was the first and only time a sitting president commanded forces in the field of battle.[71] Washington called the 15,000 troops "the Army of the Constitution," but they were poorly provisioned and took to raiding nearby crops and gardens, earning the nickname the "Watermelon Army."[72] The president went as far as Carlisle, then left the troops under the command of Hamilton and Governor Henry Lee of Virginia and returned to Philadelphia.[73]

On October 20, 1794, as Washington prepared to leave the troops, he gave instructions to Governor Lee about how to proceed. He directed Lee to suppress the rebellion and to cause the laws to be executed. More interesting, he also told Lee, "But before you withdraw the army you shall promise on behalf of the president a general pardon to all such as shall not have been arrested, with such exceptions as you shall deem proper."[74]

As the troops approached Pittsburgh in early November, thousands of rebels fled, and the resistance collapsed.[75] Hamilton wanted to capture some of the rebels, and he sent out search parties. More than 150 men were detained, and Hamilton even personally questioned some suspects.[76] Some 1,500 troops would remain in the rebellious areas to maintain order.

PARDON AND TRIAL

With the rebellion effectively over, Lee issued a pardon on November 29, 1794, pursuant to Washington's instructions from the previous month. Lee's pardon proclamation said:

> By the virtue of the powers and authority in me vested by the president of the United States, and in obedience to his benign intentions, therewith communicated, I do by this, my proclamation, declare and make known to all concerned, that a full, free, and entire pardon (excepting and providing as hereinafter mentioned) is hereby granted to all persons residing within the counties of Washington, Allegheny, Westmoreland and Fayette, in a state of Pennsylvania, and in the County of Ohio in the state of Virginia, guilty of treason or misprison [sic] of treason against the United States, or otherwise directly or indirectly engaging in the wicked and unhappy tumults and disturbances lately existing in these counties, excepting nevertheless from the benefit and effect of this pardon all persons charged with the commission of offenses against the United States, and now actually in the custody or held by recognizance to appear and answer for all such offenses at any judiciary court or courts, excepting all persons avoiding fair trial by abandoning their homes, and excepting, moreover, the following persons, the atrocity of whose conduct renders it proper to mark them by named for the purpose of subjecting them with all possible certainty to the regular course of judicial proceedings and whom all officers, civil in military, are required to endeavor to apprehend, or cause to be apprehended and brought to justice, to wit.

The proclamation then named thirty-three people who were excluded from the pardon (twenty-eight from Pennsylvania and five from Virginia), many of whom would soon stand trial.[77]

Roughly one dozen prisoners were taken to Philadelphia to be tried in federal courts rather than in more sympathetic state courts on charges that ranged from rioting and assault to treason.[78] As Hogeland reports, "On Christmas morning, 1794, twenty thousand Philadelphians mobbed the broad, cobbled streets of their city to see the defeated whiskey rebels brought in from the west."[79] According to Keane, the judicial proceedings were highly biased in that "none of the prisoners were informed of the charges against them before trial." But "despite judges instructing the juries to convict the prisoners, only two were found guilty," John Mitchell and Philip Weigel.[80] These two decisions were the country's first federal convictions for treason, and the men were sentenced to hang.

WASHINGTON ON THE CAUSE OF THE REBELLION

While the captured rebels awaited legal proceedings, Washington provided more information about how he perceived the rebellion. On November 19, 1794, in his Sixth Annual Message to Congress, he discussed the rebellion at length. His message said, "With the deepest regret do I announce to you, that during your recess, some of the citizens of the United States have been found capable of an insurrection."[81]

Washington said the opposition to the whiskey tax was contrary to "reason and patriotism" and had led to "riot and violence." He described his proclamation of August 7, 1794, which had sent commissioners to western Pennsylvania, and his proclamation of September 25, 1794, which had admonished the insurgents. He said of those involved in the rebellion that "some have not embraced the proffered terms of amnesty" and that "their malevolence was not pointed merely to a particular law" but "to all order."

In his message, Washington blamed the rebellion on "certain self-created societies," which had supposedly fanned the flames of discontent.[82] He was referring to Democratic-Republican societies that were sympathetic to leftist Republicans and to the criticisms of essayist Philip

Freneau and publisher Benjamin Franklin Bache.[83] According to Sharp, "By linking the societies with the insurrection and equating peaceful opposition to governmental policy with armed rebellion, Washington extended and deepened the political dimensions of the rebellion."[84] Washington's criticism of the societies for allegedly fomenting the unrest exacerbated the nation's growing political divide. For example, both James Madison and Thomas Jefferson were dismayed by Washington's denunciation of the Democratic-Republican societies, which Madison regarded as "the greatest error" of Washington's public service.[85] And insofar as Washington's criticism elided political dissent with treason, it perhaps foreshadowed the Alien and Sedition Acts of 1798.

In his Sixth Annual Message, Washington also claimed that the rebellion and the government's response to it had a positive side: "While there is cause to lament that occurrences of this nature should have disgraced the name or interrupted the tranquility of any part of our community, or should have diverted to a new application any portion of the public resources, there are not wanting real and substantial consolations for the misfortune." For Washington, these consolations were the demonstration of the quality and strength of the nation, its institutions, and its people.

WASHINGTON'S PARDON

Through the fall of 1794, amnesty for the rebels was actively sought and widely expected. For example, prominent publisher and state assemblyman Hugh H. Breckenridge advocated sending a group to Philadelphia to plead with the president for amnesty.[86] And in July 1795 hundreds of citizens signed petitions asking Washington to spare the condemned men. On multiple occasions during the Revolutionary War, Washington had offered pardon to deserters who returned to duty, so there was reason to think that he might be amenable to pardons for the convicted whiskey rebels, too. He had previously directed Lee to pardon some of the rebels, and on two occasions he had issued stays of execution for those who had been sentenced to die.

On July 10, 1795—nine months after Lee's pardon proclamation and after three presidential proclamations of warning—Washington issued his fourth and final proclamation on the rebellion. This was the first ever direct use of the presidential pardon power and thus another area in which Washington's action created a precedent. Like many of the pardons that subsequent presidents would issue, Washington's pardon started with an invocation of the context. It noted that the commissioners had promised that if rebels submitted to the federal government, a general pardon would be forthcoming:

> Whereas the commissioners appointed by the President of the United States to confer with the citizens in the western counties of Pennsylvania during the late insurrection which prevailed therein, by their act and agreement bearing date the 2d day of September last, in pursuance of the powers in them vested, did promise and engage that, if assurances of submission to the laws of the United States should be bona fide given by the citizens resident in the fourth survey of Pennsylvania, in the manner and within the time in the said act and agreement specified, a general pardon should be granted on the 10th day of July then next ensuing of all treasons and other indictable offenses against the United States committed within the said survey before the 22d day of August last, excluding therefrom, nevertheless, every person who should refuse or neglect to subscribe such assurance and engagement in manner afore said, or who should after such subscription violate the same, or willfully obstruct or attempt to obstruct the execution of the acts for raising a revenue on distilled spirits and stills, or be aiding or abetting therein.

Washington's proclamation then stated that he was extending Lee's pardon: "I have since thought proper to extend the said pardon to all persons guilty of the said treasons, misprisions of treasons, or otherwise concerned in the late insurrection within the survey aforesaid who have not since been indicted or convicted thereof, or of any other offense against the United States."[87]

Beyond the brief justification for the military action in the text of the pardon proclamation, five months later in his Seventh Annual Message on December 8, 1795, Washington elaborated on his view of the rebellion and his actions in response to it:

> It is a valuable ingredient in the general estimate of our welfare, that the part of our country, which was lately the scene of disorder and insurrections, now enjoys the blessings of quiet and order. The misled have abandoned their errors, and pay the respect to our Constitution and laws which is due from good citizens, to the public authorities of the society. These circumstances, have induced me to pardon, generally, the offenders here referred to; and to extend forgiveness to those who had been adjudged to capital punishment. For though I shall always think it a sacred duty to exercise with firmness and energy the constitutional powers with which I am vested, yet it appears to me no less consistent with the public good than it is with my own feelings to mingle in the operations of Government every degree of moderation and tenderness which the national justice and safety may permit.[88]

IMPACT

The pardon saved Weigel and Mitchell and seemed to bring the rebellion to an amicable conclusion. By one account, "order was restored, but the rebels and their supporters were not permanently alienated from the national consensus, which would have been the bitter price of pure justice."[89] According to McDonald, "The combination of strength and clemency had a salutary effect throughout the land: a wave of enthusiasm for the administration swept the country."[90]

However, not all rebels were placated by Washington's pardon. As Thomas Slaughter explains, "In the aftermath of the Whiskey Rebellion over 2,000 of the most disaffected frontiersmen migrated farther into the continent's interior, thereby ensuring for themselves at least a temporary escape from the ever-lengthening arm and increasingly strong grip of the central government."[91] In particular, states John Alden, "David Bradford, who had been made an exception in Washington's offer of amnesty, found safety in Spanish Louisiana," where he would remain for several years.[92] As documented in subsequent chapters, other aggrieved groups similarly were not altogether assuaged by pardons and instead sought to move beyond the reach of the federal government.

Washington issued four proclamations altogether about the Whiskey Rebellion over three years, the last of which contained his pardon. Washington's response to the rebellion established a number of precedents, including that the federal government could and would put down armed insurrection and make the rebels face justice yet that it would also be prepared to demonstrate mercy and leniency toward the conquered wrongdoers. In addition, Taylor maintains, "with a show of force, Federalists had discredited regulation as an alternative to institutional politics."[93]

Even though Hamilton despised the rebels, he did not publicly disapprove of Washington's pardon. Indeed, he had helped Washington write the address in which Washington explained the pardon to Congress. As Hamilton later explained Washington's rationale for pardoning the Whiskey rebels,

By the early submission of most of the leaders, upon an invitation of the government, few offenders of any consequence remained subject to prosecution. Of these, either from the humanity of the juries or some deficiency in the evidence, not one was capitally convicted. Two poor wretches only were sentenced to die, one of them little short of an idiot, the other a miserable follower in the hindmost train of the rebellion, both being so insignificant in all respects, that after the lenity shown to the chiefs, justice would have worn the mien of ferocity, if she had raised her arm against them. The sentiment that their punishment ought to be remitted was universal; and the President, yielding to the special considerations, granted them pardons.[94]

However, Chernow claims that despite Hamilton's public acceptance of the pardon, he "feared that this clemency would only encourage lawless elements."[95] As we will see, this fear was arguably borne out just three years later.

JOHN ADAMS

The second president followed the first president's use of unilateral directives to manage domestic disturbances over taxes in Pennsylvania, though for John Adams they occurred in the eastern part of the state. As Washington's vice president for eight years, Adams had seen how the president had dealt with a rebellion. Even though Adams had opposed Hamilton's excise tax in 1791, he disdained the whiskey rebels, whom he said had engaged in terrorism and treason.[96] Despite his experience in Washington's administration, Adams was a different president and governed in a different way.[97] He could be emotionally volatile, and he had little tolerance for dissent, yet he was somewhat constrained by the commitments of his popular predecessor and also by the growing power of High Federalists such as Hamilton.[98]

TAX RESISTANCE

The proximate cause of the rebellion that Adams faced in 1799 was once again dissatisfaction with a federal tax. The first year of Adams's presidency saw tensions between the United States and France increase, and as the "Quasi War" threatened to heat up, Federalists sought to build up America's military. The United States added vessels to its navy and enhanced the army, and in 1798 it brought back both George Washington and Alexander Hamilton to lead the army. To fund the increase, the federal government turned to a tax. In July 1798, it enacted the Direct House Tax, which levied a tax on private property, including land, houses, and slaves. The tax was intended to raise $2 million, of which some $237,000 would come from Pennsylvania alone.

For most people, the tax amounted to a single payment of less than one dollar. Nevertheless, many people disliked the tax. Some thought that it was unconstitutional, that along with the Alien and Sedition Acts it was part of a broader Federalist threat to freedom, or that it hurt farmers while helping speculators. Others thought its application was overly intrusive because some tax assessors determined the value of a house by counting the number and size of its windows, and they often had to trespass on private property to ascertain this information.

The tax was especially unpopular in Pennsylvania's Lehigh Valley area and the counties of Bucks, Northampton, and Montgomery, all of which had large populations of German immigrants.[99] Resistance to the tax began in August 1798 and grew through the fall. People erected liberty poles and threatened tax assessors. The tax resisters were informally led by John Fries. He was an auctioneer who had served as the commander of a company of troops that was sent to quell the Whiskey Rebellion, but by 1798 Fries had become the leader of an armed group that physically threatened and even imprisoned tax assessors.

A SMALLER OR BIGGER REBELLION?

As with respect to the Whiskey Rebellion, scholars disagree about the nature and severity of Fries's Rebellion. On one view, the resistance to the tax hardly amounted to a real rebellion, in part because tax resisters arguably did not see themselves as rebels; they simply sought to oppose legislation with which they disagreed, generally via nonviolent means.[100] Some historians have argued that the opposition was a simple misunderstanding that resulted from a language barrier, with German speakers mistakenly thinking that the tax was more onerous than it actually was. Others claim that the rebellion was driven by parochialism in that some residents resented the federal government intruding in their insular community. Some commentators trivialize the rebellion by calling it "the hot water war" in reference to how one tax opponent poured boiling water on the head of a revenue agent.[101] On yet another interpretation, the rebellion was the result of cynical manipulations by Hamilton to artificially create something to further Federalist ends; some scholars allege that Hamilton pushed the tax and its stiff penalties and their enforcement in order to gin up resistance that the federal government would then have to forcibly put down.[102]

In contrast, some historians contend that Fries's Rebellion was indeed a genuine and serious threat but that it was the result of deeper causes than the standard version admits. Bouton is one of the main adherents of this view, arguing that the uprising of 1799 "was in many respects a replay of what happened in 1794." Bouton says Fries's Rebellion, like the Whiskey Rebellion, was another instance of a long-standing tradition of principled resistance to perceived government wrongdoing, so we should see the two rebellions as connected to each other and indeed as part of a broader pattern:

> For the last 200 years, this uprising has been seen as being entirely distinct from the one in 1794: historians tell us that 1799 was caused by conditions unique to the German population in the eastern counties and involved issues separate from those that had inspired westerners. To be sure, there were differences between the two. But those disparities have been exaggerated to the point where they mask the stunning similarities. In both regions, people rose up for fundamentally the same reason: because they believed that their governments were undermining equality through policies that favored land and war debt speculators and because they opposed how the governments were attempting to stifle democratic self-expression.[103]

Similarly, Paul Douglas Newman argues that Fries's Rebellion was not just the result of religious or ethnic tensions or the product of opposition to the Alien and Sedition Acts or of political conflicts between Federalists and Republicans; it was instead, he contends, an attempt to expand the role of the people in the country's governance.[104]

RESISTANCE

Regardless of the causes of the antipathy toward the tax, it soon resulted in acts of resistance. In the fall of 1798, people denounced the tax, raised liberty polls, and threatened to harm tax assessors. In early 1799, the antitax resistance appeared to be spreading. In February, Fries led a group of armed men that forced tax assessors to flee the town of Milford. When tax assessor James Chapman told Fries that the government might employ force to ensure compliance with the law, Fries reportedly replied, "Huzza! Then it shall be as it is in France!"[105] On March 5, Fries and about one hundred rebels briefly imprisoned three tax assessors in a tavern in Quakertown. The assessors were released later that day, but only after the rebels took their papers and threatened to kill them if they returned.

The federal government had issued arrest warrants in January for rebels who obstructed tax assessments, and several weeks later U.S. marshal William Nichols began to serve the warrants and to arrest people, who would soon face trial in Philadelphia. In early March, Nichols placed more than a dozen tax resisters in a temporary jail at the Sun Inn in Bethlehem. On March 7, Fries brought a group of 150 men to Bethlehem and compelled Nichols to free the resisters.[106]

Federalists saw Fries's Rebellion as the second armed insurrection in just five years. According to Newman, "Many Federalists suspected that it was the lack of capital punishment in the first case [i.e., the Whiskey Rebellion] that precipitated the second [i.e., Fries's Rebellion]. Worse still, some suspected that the French and their American sympathizers, the Republican Party, had orchestrated the entire affair."[107]

Adams was incensed at the rebellion. And although Washington had been reluctant to respond forcefully to the tax protest that he faced, Adams was not. According to John Miller, "Fears that the government would not act decisively against the rioters were quickly set at rest. President Adams was of Hamilton's opinion that the occasion called for a display of overwhelming force."[108]

On March 12, 1799, Adams issued a proclamation stating that people had engaged in "subversive" actions "to defeat the execution of the laws." These actions "amount to treason, being overt acts of levying war against the United States." The proclamation noted in particular the actions against William Nichols. It further stated that efforts at conciliation had failed, and so Adams had called forth military forces and commanded the insurgents "to disperse and retire to their respective abodes" within six days.[109]

Adams also ordered that some 1,200 troops be sent to quell the insurrection and to restore order, much as they had been for the Whiskey Rebellion four years earlier. On April 4, the troops left the capitol of Philadelphia with Hamilton essentially in command and marched north to put down the rebellion. As with the Whiskey Rebellion, the force that went with Hamilton was far larger than necessary.[110] And, once again, the rebellion largely dissipated before the troops actually arrived in eastern Pennsylvania. Thus, the rebellion's end "was as anticlimactic as [the end of] the one in 1794."[111]

CAPTURE AND TRIAL

Adams ordered the militia to capture Fries. They eventually found him hiding in the woods when they tracked his pet dog, whose name was "Whiskey."[112] Fries and the other captured rebels were brought to Philadelphia to be tried for treason and other crimes. Sources disagree as to the total number of rebels arrested and charged but variously claim between twenty-nine and sixty.[113]

In May 1799, Fries was tried for treason, convicted under the Sedition Act, and sentenced to death.[114] Two of Fries's companions were sentenced to hang alongside him: John Gettman and Frederick Hainey. Thirty-two other rebels were convicted of crimes calling for less than two years in jail and fines up to $1,000.[115] Fries was granted a second trial on a technicality, and while waiting for this trial, he and two other condemned men appealed to the president for pardons.[116] Other rebels who were given stiff sentences also made pleas for clemency.[117] However, on the advice of Attorney General Charles Lee, Adams did not grant a pardon at that time.[118]

Supreme Court justice Samuel Chase served as a trial judge in circuit court and presided over Fries's second trial for treason. Before the trial began and without any input from Fries's lawyers, the committed Federalist Chase issued a controversial definition of the crime of treason. He determined that "any insurrection . . . for the purpose of resisting or preventing by force . . . the execution of any statute of the United States . . . is levying war against the United States." Thus, Chase said that any resistance to a law was treason, even though the Sedition Act had defined such resistance only as a misdemeanor.[119] Fries's lawyers protested by resigning from the case, leaving Fries without legal representation. (Several years later, Chase's action in the trial was part of the basis of his impeachment by the U.S. House.) On April 25, 1800, Fries was once again found guilty of treason and sentenced to hang a month later.[120] As he had done after his first trial, he again sought clemency from the president.

FEDERALISTS PLEASED

Some Federalists had feared that Adams was beginning to deviate from Federalist orthodoxy, but they were encouraged by the government's prosecution of the rebels.[121] According to Newman, "Now Hamiltonians were smugly confident that at long last the government would defend its shores, uphold its honor, and preserve the public order necessary for liberty to survive in their republican society by executing John Fries and his two neighbors and making an example of them and the rest of the convicts."[122] As Secretary of State Timothy Pickering wrote to Adams on May 10, 1799,

> This conviction is of the highest importance, to vindicate the violated laws & support the Government. It was therefore anxiously expected by the real friends to the order & tranquillity of the country, and to the stability of its government. Among such men I have heard of but one opinion—That an *example* or *examples* of *conviction* and *punishment* of such high-handed offenders were *essential, to ensure future*

obedience to the laws, or the exertions of our best citizens to suppress future insurrections. The examples appear singularly important in Pennsylvania, where treason and rebellion have so repeatedly reared their heads. And painful as is the idea of taking the life of a man, I feel a calm and solid satisfaction that an opportunity is now presented, in executing the just sentence of the law, to crush that spirit which if not overthrown and destroyed, may proceed in its career, and overturn the Government.[123]

Hamilton later (in October 1800) articulated much the same view:

The general opinion of the friends of the government demanded an example, as indispensable to its security. The opinion was well founded. Two insurrections in the same State, one upon the heels of the other, demonstrated a spirit of insubordination or disaffection which required a strong corrective. It is a disagreeable fact, forming a weighty argument in the question, that a large part of the population of Pennsylvania is of a composition which peculiarly fits it for the intrigues of factious men, who may desire to disturb or overthrow the Government. And it is an equally disagreeable fact, that disaffection to the national Government is in no other State more general, more deeply rooted, or more envenomed. . . . It ought to be added, that the impunity, so often experienced, had made it an article in the creed of those who were actuated by the insurgent spirit, that neither the General nor the State Government dared to inflict capital punishment. To destroy this persuasion, to repress this dangerous spirit, it was essential that a salutary rigor should have been exerted, and that those who were under the influence of the one and the other should be taught that they were the dupes of a fatal illusion.[124]

PARDON

Notwithstanding the Federalists' glee with the convictions, other voices called for forgiveness, and Adams seemed open to the possibility of a pardon. In terms of Adams's general attitude toward pardons and for-giveness, several of his experiences before Fries's Rebellion suggest that he was amenable to forgiving rather than forever condemning his opponents. In his autobiography, Adams said of his service in the American Revolution:

> Nothing could be more false and injurious to me, than the imputation of any sanguinary Zeal against the Tories [i.e., Loyalists], for I can truly declare that through the whole Revolution and from that time to this I never committed one Act of Severity against the Tories. On the contrary I was a constant Advocate for all the Mercy and Indulgence consistent with our Safety. Some Acts of Treachery as well as Hostility, were combined together in so atrocious a manner that Pardon could not be indulged. But, as it happened, in none of these had I any particular concern.[125]

Indeed, in the debate about a possible amnesty for Loyalists after the American Revolution, Adams had been sympathetic to the idea of con-ciliation and compensation for, as he calls them in his autobiography, "the wretches how little soever they deserve it, nay, how much soever they deserve the contrary."[126] Adams's disinclination to hold a grudge is notable in that he later learned that he was one of a few American revo-lutionaries who were specifically but secretly excluded from those who could be offered a pardon by the British brothers Admiral Richard Howe and General William Howe in 1776 if they would cease treason-able actions against the king.[127]

In addition, on March 9, 1799—just three days before his proclama-tion commanding Fries's rebels to disperse—Adams pardoned the fugi-tive David Bradford for his actions in the Whiskey Rebellion. Adams's pardon noted that Bradford had submitted a petition declaring his "contrition, and sincere repentance of all his errors and misdeeds," that he had spent several years in exile in Spanish territory away from his family, and that the restoration of peace and submission to the law in western Pennsylvania rendered it "less necessary to make examples of those who may have been criminal."[128] These experiences no doubt informed and reflected Adams's general views about pardons for political resistance.

Although Adams had initially been angry about Fries's Rebellion and had seen fit to respond militarily, he decided to proceed cautiously with the condemned men's requests for pardons.[129] According to Ralph Brown, Adams "asked for all possible information about Fries, and the president undertook to read whatever the common law said about treason and to study the precedents he could locate."[130] Adams wrote, "The issue of this investigation has opened a train of very serious contemplations to me, which will require the closest attention of my best understanding, and will prove a severe trial to my heart."[131] As he weighed his options, he was determined that "neither humanity be unnecessarily afflicted, nor public justice essentially violated, nor the public safety endangered."[132] Adams continued to think into May 1800 about what to do. He may have hoped that the second trial would produce more lenient punishments and thus obviate the demand for a pardon.[133]

Adams asked his cabinet for advice on the matter. On May 20, 1800, he gave the cabinet a list of thirteen questions about a possible pardon, one of which was "Is there not great danger in establishing such a construction of treason as may be applied to every sudden, ignorant, inconsiderable heat among a part of the people wrought up by political disputes, and personal or party animosities"?[134] The cabinet quickly and unanimously voted that Adams should not issue a pardon and should permit the executions to go ahead.[135]

On May 21, 1800, however, Adams wrote to Attorney General Lee to indicate that he was rejecting the advice he had received from the cabinet and would instead issue a pardon: "As I differ in opinion, I must take on myself alone the responsibility of one more appeal to the humane and generous natures of the American People." Adams's letter then said,

> I pray you therefore to prepare, for my Signature this morning a Pardon for each of the Criminals John Fries, Frederick Hainey and John Gettman. I pray you alsso [sic] to prepare the Form of a Proclamation of a General Pardon of all Treasons and Conspiracies to commit

Treasons heretofore committed in the three offending Counties in opposition to the Law laying Taxes on Houses &c that Tranquility may be restored to the Minds of those People if possible. I have one request more, that you would consult the Judge and the late and present Attorneys of this district concerning the Circumstances of Guilt and Punishment of those now Under sentence for fines and Imprisonment and report to me a List of the Names of Such, if there are any, as may be proper Object of the Clemency of government.[136]

Adams issued his pardon that same day. His pardon proclamation for Fries's rebellion began with the following explanation of its motives:

Whereas the late wicked and treasonable insurrection against the just authority of the United States of sundry persons in the counties of Northampton, Montgomery, and Bucks, in the State of Pennsylvania, in the year 1799, having been speedily suppressed without any of the calamities usually attending rebellion; whereupon peace, order, and submission to the laws of the United States were restored in the aforesaid counties, and the ignorant, misguided, and misinformed in the counties have returned to a proper sense of their duty, whereby it is become unnecessary for the public good that any future prosecutions should be commenced or carried on against any person or persons by reason of their being concerned in the said insurrection.[137]

Fifteen years later, in 1815, Adams explained his view thus in a letter: "My judgment was clear, that their crime did not amount to treason. They had been guilty of a high-handed riot and rescue, attended with circumstances hot, rash, violent, and dangerous, but all these did not amount to treason. And I thought the officers of the law had been injudicious in indicting them for any crime higher than riot, aggravated by rescue." As Adams further explained his thinking, "What good, what example would have been exhibited to the nation by the execution of three or four obscure, miserable Germans, as ignorant of our language as they were of our laws, and the nature and definition of treason?"[138]

Adams's decision to pardon the rebels was likely influenced by a number of political considerations. First, on some accounts Adams had decided to grant the pardon before asking for the advice of his cabinet but nevertheless asked them just to foster the appearance of deliberation and impartiality.[139] Second, Fries and the rebels remained very popular, especially in Pennsylvania, so Adams's pardon held out the promise of electoral gain among German voters in the coming presidential election.[140] Third, the timing of the pardon raised serious questions about the president's motives in that it was issued fewer than forty-eight hours before the three rebels were scheduled to be executed. Indeed, according to Newman, "many people likely heard of the reprieve on the day they had thought Fries would hang." "Adams had all his information and could have issued the pardon weeks before." Yet he procrastinated, waiting almost exactly a year to act, perhaps because he sought the "drama of drawing the thing out for effect."[141]

IMPACT

Although "most Americans approved the pardon and applauded the President for granting it," Federalists strongly disapproved.[142] Hamilton had argued for a broad and unrestrained pardon power in *The Federalist Papers*, and he had publicly assented to Washington's decision to issue a pardon for the Whiskey Rebellion, but he did not see these later rebels as appropriate recipients of governmental leniency. Hamilton believed that by not executing the men Adams had failed to uphold the High Federalist principle of ordered public liberty and therefore could not be trusted.[143] Hamilton had been increasingly at odds with the president, and Adams's pardon of Fries was the last straw. According to Newman, "From this point onward, Hamiltonians got to work against Adams's bid for reelection . . . [and] one by one withdrew their support from John Adams."[144]

In October 1800, Hamilton published a fifty-four-page pamphlet sharply criticizing Adams for pardoning Fries and other matters, *Letter*

Concerning the Public Conduct and Character of John Adams. It was Hamilton's first public criticism of Adams, and it was fierce. He derided Adams's character, egotism, animosity, temper, and self-command. According to David McCullough, "Nothing that Hamilton ever wrote about Jefferson was half so contemptuous."[145] The pamphlet's treatment of Fries's Rebellion included the following passage:

> Every thing loudly demanded that the Executive should have acted with exemplary vigor, and should have given a striking demonstration, that condign punishment would be the lot of the violent opposers of the laws. The contrary course, which was pursued, is the most inexplicable part of Mr. Adams's conduct. It shews him so much at variance with himself, as well as with sound policy, that we are driven to seek a solution for it in some system of concession to his political enemies; a system the most fatal for himself, and for the cause of public order, of any that he could possibly devise. It is by temporisings like these, that men at the head of affairs, lose the respect both of friends and foes: it is by temporisings like these, that in times of fermentation and commotion, Governments are prostrated, which might easily have been upheld by an erect and imposing attitude.[146]

There is some debate about the political impact of Hamilton's pamphlet. According to Newman, "Although the execution of John Fries might not have salvaged the election for the divided federalists [sic], it might have been just enough to quiet Hamiltonian critics about the president's overtures to France, prevent Hamilton's letter, and perhaps allow the Federalists to survive the election and reorganize under a conservative consensus. But that is all conjecture. Instead, Adams issued the pardons, and the Hamiltonians broke from the party in the summer of 1800."[147]

Thus, Adams's pardon succeeded in bringing the conquered rebels back into the national fold but at the considerable political cost of dividing his own governing regime. The split among Federalists benefited Thomas Jefferson, who defeated Adams in the presidential election in late 1800. In 1801, Jefferson repealed the Sedition Act and pardoned those convicted under it, and he repealed the excise tax on whiskey in 1802.

This chapter has examined the first two U.S. presidents' uses of plural pardons for domestic insurrection. As we have seen, the two instances of pardon discussed here are distinct but similar and in fact closely related. The Whiskey Rebellion was larger and a more serious threat than Fries's Rebellion, but both were driven by resistance in Pennsylvania to a federal tax; both were arguably manifestations of the same political spirit or movement; and both culminated in the use of federal militias against the armed rebellions, which were easily put down, and ultimately in pardons to avoid capital punishment and to foster political reconciliation.

The first two presidents' actions regarding the insurrections in Pennsylvania created important precedents for later presidents. They established that the federal government would forcibly put down rebellions: the government would not long tolerate provocations or threats to its authority and would use military force to end any such uprisings. The two events also established that presidents could issue mass pardons to reconcile with domestic insurgents. These cases also indicate the variety of motives than can underlie such merciful actions as well as the varied outcomes that they can produce. As we will see, subsequent presidents' mass pardons for subsequent rebellions further developed these themes.

3

MORMON RESISTANCE IN
THE NINETEENTH CENTURY

James Buchanan, Benjamin Harrison, and Grover Cleveland

Being anxious to save the effusion of blood and to avoid the indiscriminate punishment of a whole people for crimes of which it is not probable that all are equally guilty, I offer now a free and full pardon to all who will submit themselves to the just authority of the Federal Government. If you refuse to accept it, let the consequences fall upon your own heads.

—JAMES BUCHANAN, 1858

The time has now arrived when the interests of public justice and morality will be promoted by the granting of amnesty and pardon.

—GROVER CLEVELAND, 1894

Several decades after the Pennsylvania rebellions of the 1790s but before the Civil War, the United States experienced another episode of domestic dissention and group animus that culminated in military intervention and mass pardons. In the nineteenth century, Mormons (members of the Church of Jesus Christ of Latter-day Saints, or LDS) were often at odds with the rest of American society. Those tensions led to significant legal and military conflicts with the U.S. federal government and eventually compelled three presidents over four decades to issue mass pardons in order to reconcile with Mormon dissenters and to affirm their status as law-abiding members of the national community.

The first episode in this decades-long conflict is variously called the Utah Expedition, the Utah War, the Mormon War, and Buchanan's Blunder. The historian Daniel Boorstein characterizes it as "the unsung and inglorious Civil War of 1857–58," and the historians David Bigler and Will Bagley term it "America's first civil war," invoking the image of a national civil war to underscore the significance of the conflict between Mormons and the federal government.[1] Yet despite the magnitude of the conflict, the episode is little known today, especially among non-Mormons. As Bigler and Bagley explain, "Today the Utah War of 1857–58 is largely forgotten and even less understood."[2] According to the historian John Eldredge, "It's absolutely fascinating—and almost nobody knows about it."[3] As a recent academic book review put it, "Massacre, martial law, and secession aren't terms we usually associate with Mormons."[4] Nevertheless, those elements were part of the conflict between Mormons and the federal government in the mid–nineteenth century.

Not only is the conflict that led to a mass pardon in 1858 little known, but some of its basic facts are disputed by the relatively few people who are familiar with it. Indeed, accounts of the nature of the conflict vary significantly, depending largely on how sympathetic or critical the teller is regarding the Mormon faith and its leaders in the nineteenth century. One version, which Bigler and Bagley unflatteringly character-ize as the "heroic" Mormon characterization promoted by some Mormons today, may be stated as follows: "The United Sates in 1857 sent an army to persecute their long-suffering Mormon progenitors, based on nothing more than the malicious reports of corrupt carpetbaggers. Valiant forbears rallied under their inspired leader, Brigham Young, to defeat an invading army using guerilla tactics that shed not a drop of blood. This brought America to its senses, and the president sent commissioners to negotiate an end to what will be forever remembered as 'Buchanan's blunder.' "[5]

Bigler and Bagley disparage the accuracy of this characterization: "In this carefully constructed legend, a patriotic but misunderstood and abused religious minority defied the imperial ambitions of an unjust and unrighteous government and bloodlessly defended their religion and their families against unprovoked persecution and tyranny."[6] They claim that in reality the United States was forced to respond to a militant group that openly disdained and opposed the American government and sought to create an independent theocracy in the American West.[7] According to Bagley, even though some historians today use the term *alleged* in referring to the Mormon rebellion, there were in fact "plenty" of "repeated acts of provocation" as "angry Utahns had seized federal court records and chased every non-Mormon judge, surveyor and Indian agent out of the territory by the end of 1857."[8]

In addition to such provocations, the conflict of the late 1850s grew out of long-standing tensions and animosities. Scholars tend to explain anti-Mormon sentiment in the nineteenth century in terms of a broader climate of fear of internal subversion, Mormons' alleged theocracy or lack of a church–state distinction, or divergence from widely held Protestant norms.[9] From its founding in 1830 through much of the nineteenth century, Mormonism was often considered so different from other faiths as to be un-American. According to Marvin Hill and James Allen, "The Mormons attracted attention in the popular press . . . as a useful counterimage, a glaring example of what America was not and should not be. They were considered so different in their fundamental institutions—theocratic government, plural marriage, communitarianism—that joining them seemed to constitute an un-American activity. John Wesley Hill, a Methodist minister in Ogden Utah, put the matter succinctly in 1889. Mormonism, he said, "'is an enemy to this government, a traitor to the flag, and the foe of American civilization.'"[10] In their introduction to their collected volume on Mormons and American popular culture, Hill and Allen state that even today "Mormons are widely perceived to be unconventional" and have a sense of "outside-ness" vis-à-vis mainstream American culture.[11]

PERSECUTION AND FLIGHT

Regardless of the reasons for the widespread suspicion of and animosity toward their faith, Mormons often had difficult relations with other

Americans in the nineteenth century. Mormonism began in the early nineteenth century under Joseph Smith Jr. in western New York. Smith founded the Church of Jesus Christ of Latter-day Saints in 1830, and it grew rapidly in Ohio and Missouri, as did tensions with non-Mormon neighbors. In 1832, a mob in Hiram, Ohio, tarred and feathered Smith.[12] In 1833, hundreds of Mormons were forcibly driven out of Jackson County, Missouri. And on October 27, 1838, Governor Liburn Boggs of Missouri issued Executive Order 44, known as the "Extermination Order," which charged that Mormons held "the attitude of an open and avowed defiance of the laws, and of having made war upon the people of this state." Boggs's order declared, "The Mormons must be treated as enemies, and must be exterminated or driven from the state if necessary for the public peace—their outrages are beyond all description."[13] Three days later Missouri militiamen attacked a Mormon settlement at Haun's Mill, which resulted in eighteen deaths.

Thousands of Mormons were forced to flee Missouri and soon moved to Illinois, where they bought the small town of Commerce on the Mississippi River and renamed it Nauvoo in 1839. The town's population grew quickly, as did tensions with neighboring towns, once again leading to violence. In early 1844, Smith ran for U.S. president as an independent, largely in an effort to increase public sympathy regarding the mistreatment of Mormons.[14] Unrest broke out in Nauvoo, and in June 1844 Smith and his brother Hyrum were arrested and charged with treason and conspiracy. Three days later they were killed by an angry mob that attacked the jail where they were being held in Carthage, Illinois.[15]

Hostilities continued after the murders, and Governor Thomas Ford of Illinois advised Mormons to leave the area.[16] Some Mormons were prepared to move away from the unsympathetic authorities. In November 1845, the Mormon apostle Orson Pratt spoke to a meeting of Mormons in New York City, where he reminded them of their long persecution and called for them to flee the country, saying, "Brethren Awake! Be determined to get out of this evil nation by next spring. We do not want one Saint to be left in the United States by that time. Let every branch in the north, south, east, and west be determined to flee Babylon, either by land or by sea."[17]

In early 1846, hundreds of Mormons left Nauvoo. Led by Brigham Young, they headed more than a thousand miles west, past the western border of the United States to a vast area controlled by Mexico.[18] They arrived at the Great Salt Lake Valley in July 1847 and were soon joined by thousands of other Mormons. The Mormons hoped their new isolation would free them from persecution and other difficulties with non-Mormons, whom they called "gentiles." As a nonsympathetic late nineteenth-century author put it, the mid-1840s "found the so-called Latter Day Saints leaving our Republic, embittered against all things American, and determined to find, in the unexplored West, a haven where they would be free from interference."[19]

RENEWED TENSION

In February 1848, Mexico and the United States signed the Treaty of Guadalupe Hidalgo, which gave the United States more than half a million square miles of territory, including the land where the Mormons had just settled. Thus, barely "six months after arriving in their new Zion, the Mormons found themselves back under the authority of the United States."[20] However, as Thomas Stenhouse explains, "The United States government was slow in extending its political jurisdiction over the newly-acquired domain, and this furnished the apostles and prophets an opportunity of creating 'a provisional independent government' for themselves."[21] In March 1848, Mormons adopted a constitution to create their own independent government. It said that they "do ordain and establish a free and independent government by the name of the state of Deseret," which was a word from the Book of Mormon.[22]

In 1849, Mormon authorities submitted a formal petition to become the state of Deseret, which would be the thirty-first state in the union. A year later Congress denied the request for statehood, and the area instead officially became the Utah Territory. Some Mormons foresaw that territorial status would create problems for them with federal authorities, whereas statehood would have facilitated self-government without undo federal interference.[23] According to James Allen and Glen Leonard in *The Story of the Latter-day Saints*, territorial status meant that Mormons "were unable to elect their governor, judges, or executive officials, for these officers were appointed in Washington. They could send a delegate to Congress who could lobby, debate, and participate in committee work, but not vote."[24]

Nevertheless, at first the federal government did little to assert control over the Utah Territory. Federal officials were eventually appointed to govern the territory, some of whom were Mormons. President Millard Fillmore appointed Brigham Young the governor of the new territory in January 1851. Serving as the leader of both the LDS Church and the Utah Territory, Young made no distinction between church and state. He indicated that he intended to remain governor for as long as he liked, and he boasted that "any President of the United States who lifts his finger against this people shall die an untimely death and go to hell!"[25] This tension grew over the next several years, yet Young was reappointed governor by President Franklin Pierce in 1854.

Other federal appointees were not Mormons. In 1851, four such federal officers who were appointed by Fillmore—Perry Brocchus, Lemuel Brandenbury, Broughton Harris, and Henry Day—arrived in Utah and were promptly met with defiance. Young and other Mormons openly despised the non-Mormon officials. For example, Young refused to meet with Brandenbury on the grounds that he was not a Mormon. The other federal officials encountered utter contempt for the federal government.[26] After a few months of this treatment, all four officials fled back to Washington, leaving their posts vacant and earning the nickname the "runaway officials." Subsequent federal officials encountered similar treatment. Indeed, "a succession of federal officers—judges, Indian agents, surveyors—came to the territory only to find that the governor would circumvent or reverse their decisions. . . . Through the mid-1850s, federal appointees returned East frustrated or intimidated or both."[27]

In 1855, President Pierce appointed several federal judges in Utah who were critical of Mormons. They included William W. Drummond, who was appointed to the Supreme Court of the Territory of Utah and encountered trouble shortly after his arrival in Salt Lake in July 1855. Drummond sparred with Mormons over the jurisdiction of Utah's local probate courts and complained that religious leaders were thwarting his authority. He wrote to the U.S. attorney general, "We cannot enforce the U.S. Laws" because of the "iron rule of a Religious Priest or Church Desperado" bent on "slaughter & violence."[28] Drummond also claimed that Mormons had poisoned his predecessor and had directed Indians to kill federal surveyors. Young, in turn, called Drummond "a rotten-hearted loathsome reptile," "proud as a peacock and ignorant as a jackass."[29]

According to Ronald Walker, "The drama being acted out between the Mormons and Drummond was only one part in a broader play. By the middle of 1856, tensions between the settlers and the Washington-appointed officers also included other appointees—including government surveyors, U.S. postal contractors, and Indian agents."[30] For example, in December 1856 Mormons vandalized the offices of Judge George Stiles, an excommunicated Mormon. On March 20, 1857, Territorial Chief Justice John F. Kinney sent a report to Washington in which he alleged that Young had mistreated him and had systematically thwarted the territorial justice system.[31] In his letter of resignation of March 30, 1857, Drummond alleged that Mormons had destroyed federal court records, regularly harassed federal authorities, and even killed three federal officials.[32] Drummond, Stiles, and Kinney fled back to Washington with stories of alleged mistreatment by Mormons. "The judges claimed they had been prevented from exercising their duties, their official papers had been confiscated and burned, and they had been driven from the territory in fear of their lives."[33]

By April 1857, "almost every federal official had left Utah,"[34] and Utah's territorial legislature demanded greater say over the appointment of federal officials. In September 1857, Young called the federal officials whom the president had sent "damned rascals" and "poor, miserable blacklegs, brokendown political hacks, robbers, and whoremongers—men that are not fit for civilized society."[35] Relations between the federal government and Mormons were openly hostile.

ANTI-MORMON SENTIMENT

Beyond the chorus of complaints from federal officials, anti-Mormon sentiment was becoming increasingly widespread in the country. This attitude was evident in John Hyde's book *Mormonism: Its Leaders and Designs* (1857) and in lectures by Frederick Margetson.[36] Much of the popular antipathy related to polygamy. Joseph Smith came to support polygamy or plural marriage around 1831 and eventually had about fifty wives.[37] The practice grew in Nauvoo and elsewhere in the early 1840s, such that hundreds of Mormons practiced polygamy by the time they came to Salt Lake in 1847. In 1852, the Mormon Church publicly announced the doctrine of plural marriage, leading to criticisms of immorality and lawlessness.[38]

In the 1850s, many Americans were deeply suspicious of Mormons, whose "practices seemed to conflict with traditional American values."[39] Antipathy toward Mormons was one of the few things that united other Americans at the time because it was shared by many people across the political spectrum and bridged the country's growing sectional divide. Northerners and Southerners were united in their desire for federal action against the Mormons. In the spring of 1856, Senator Stephen Douglas (D–IL), who was once friendly toward Mormons, gave a speech in Springfield, Illinois, in which he criticized Mormonism as "the loathsome ulcer of the body politic."[40]

Mormonism and the governance of the Utah Territory were issues in the federal election of 1856. James Buchanan and the Democrats advocated "popular sovereignty," whereby western territories could make their own decisions about slavery and other matters, but members of the newly organized Republican Party charged that this policy of deference to local sensibilities might enable Utah to allow plural marriage. As Allen and Leonard explain, "When the opponents of slavery joined together in the Republican party [*sic*] with the goal of keeping slavery out of the territories, Mormonism was used as a bad example of what might happen under popular sovereignty. If popular sovereignty meant that the people of a territory could pass legislation protecting slavery, it also meant that the latter-day Saints [sic] could practice their peculiar marriage system without congressional interference."[41] In an effort to take votes from Buchanan, the Republican Party's platform that year included a resolution that said, "It is both the right and the imperative of Congress to prohibit in the Territories those twin relics of barbarism—Polygamy and Slavery."[42] Even though Buchanan won and enjoyed Democratic majorities in the House and Senate, the "twin relics" charge was politically effective, and Democrats were loath to appear sympathetic to Mormons.[43]

JAMES BUCHANAN

When James Buchanan became president in March 1857, the United States faced a number of serious problems, particularly concerning slavery and the growing tension between North and South. Both pro-slavery forces and abolitionists such as John Brown were engaging in violence. And just two days after Buchanan was sworn in, the Supreme Court handed down its decision in *Dred Scott v. Sandford* (60 U.S. 393 [1857]), denying the rights of African Americans, affirming the rights of slave owners, and thus pushing the country closer to civil war.

In addition to those problems, tensions between Mormons and the U.S. government were high. As the popular author John Krakauer writes, "In March 1857, shortly after James Buchanan was inaugurated as president, the Utah Territorial Legislature sent a truculent message to Washington announcing that the Saints would ignore any and all federal statutes they determined to be unjust and would expel from their midst any federal officers who didn't meet the rigorous moral standards of the Mormon Church."[44]

Robert Tyler, the son of former president John Tyler and a Democratic Party operative, urged Buchanan to focus on Utah rather than on slavery, to "supersede the negro-Mania with the almost universal excitements of an Anti-Mormon Crusade."[45] Buchanan was receptive to this plan. The new president decided to focus on, of all the nation's problems, difficulties with Mormons, perhaps because it was a problem that seemed easier to deal with than slavery. As Krakauer explains, "Utah Territory was an annoying problem for the new leader of the nation, but compared to other national problems then looming it was a relatively small one, which President Buchanan thought he could handle quickly and easily. And in the Mormon insurrection he saw a means to distract Americans from much larger, much less tractable issues—the increasingly divisive rancor over slavery, for instance, which was threatening to tear the country to tatters." According to Krakauer, "Because the Mormons were widely reviled on both sides of the Mason–Dixon line, Buchanan calculated that by coming down hard on pro-slavery Utah he could curry favor among Northern abolitionists without antagonizing voters in the South."[46]

MILITARY ENFORCEMENT

Soon after being sworn in, Buchanan resolved to deal with the Mormons forcibly. In May 1857, he decided to replace Young with a new, non-Mormon governor, Alfred Cumming. He also ordered that 2,500 troops (approximately one-third the size of the entire U.S. Army) be mobilized to escort Cumming and several other newly appointed federal officials all the way to Utah to restore the rule of law and subdue the Mormon resisters. As Krakauer puts it, "For all intents and purposes, the United States had declared war on the Mormons."[47]

Officials in Utah were initially unaware of Buchanan's decision. By one account, Buchanan did not notify Young that he was being replaced as governor.[48] Other sources say that Young did not receive the official message indicating that he was being replaced because the Pierce administration had canceled the Utah mail contract.[49] Regardless of the reason, Young learned two months later, on July 24, 1857, that an army was on its way to Utah—ten years to the day since he had arrived at Salt Lake—and he did not know why. According to Allen and Leonard, the Mormons believed "that once again hostile forces would attempt to drive them from their homes. Recalling the persecutions of earlier years, the settlers . . . feared the worst."[50] The Mormons braced themselves for war. On July 26, LDS apostle Heber Kimball boasted: "I will fight until there is not a drop of blood in my veins. Good God! I have wives enough to whip out the United States."[51]

On August 5, Young issued a proclamation that forbade entry to the federal troops, declared martial law, mustered the militia (known as the Nauvoo Legion), and ordered the people to help repel the coming attack.[52] Young's proclamation began with the statement, "We are invaded by hostile forces, who are evidently assailing us to accomplish our overthrow and destruction." It complained that Mormons had done nothing wrong and were being denied their constitutional rights "as American citizens," and it asserted their right of self-defense.[53] In September, Young issued a letter to the approaching federal troops, saying that he was still the rightful governor as well as the superintendent of Indian Affairs and commander in chief of the territorial militia.[54] As the troops marched west, Captain Stewart Van Vliet was sent ahead. He entered Salt Lake City on September 7, becoming the first official contact. When Young met with Van Vliet, he informed him that the people would resist. With the troops nearing Utah, war seemed inevitable.[55]

The looming military conflict and Mormons' suspicion of outsiders led to the Mountain Meadows massacre in southern Utah in September 1857. With the assistance of Paiute tribesmen, several dozen Mormon militiamen led by John D. Lee attacked and executed some 120 immigrants in a wagon train en route from Arkansas to California. Only seventeen young children were spared. (Two decades later Lee was tried for his role in the attack, convicted, and then executed on the site of the massacre.) According to Allen and Leonard, "Coming, as it did, while the Utah Expedition was marching toward the territory, the massacre added fuel to the already inflamed public opinion against the Saints."[56]

On September 25, Mormon forces tried to drive off the mules from the troops' infantry and artillery camps. Other harassments followed. According to David Roberts, "Over several weeks, militiamen raided the troops' supplies, burned the grass to deny forage to the soldiers' horses, cattle and mules, even burned Fort Bridger."[57] In October, Mormon forces destroyed three supply trains with seventy-four wagons of provisions for the troops. They also stampeded the troops' horses. The two sides had not fully engaged, but such hostilities appeared to anticipate large-scale military conflict in the near future. Yet with the arrival of winter, Colonel Albert Sidney Johnston decided to keep the troops in Wyoming and thus delay major military action until the spring of 1858.

In his First Annual Message to Congress on December 8, 1857, Buchanan described the tense situation in Utah and the need for forceful federal action: "All the officers of the United States, judicial and executive, with the single exception of two Indian agents, have found it necessary for their own personal safety to withdraw from the Territory, and there no longer remains any government in Utah but the despotism of Brigham Young."[58] In January 1858, Young remained defiant. Referring to the nearby troops, he vowed that if the "damned Scoundrels" tried to take him, he would "send them to Hell across Lots" and "make millions of them Bite the dust.'"[59] In a sermon in March, Young repeated his threat to "send them to hell across lots" and said, "If they kill me, it is alright."[60] By the end of the winter, the federal troops had grown to roughly 5,000 men.[61] As the troops prepared to enter Utah, violence appeared imminent.

Yet in early 1858 several crucial developments occurred, nearly on top of one another. First, Thomas L. Kane, who had long been friendly toward Mormons, persuaded Buchanan to let him serve as an unofficial mediator to try to negotiate a peaceful resolution. Kane arrived at Salt Lake in late February. After two weeks of negotiations, Kane managed to persuade Young to accept the appointment of Cumming as governor of Utah Territory and not to oppose the federal troops. According to some accounts, Kane mentioned the possibility of a presidential pardon as an inducement for Young to submit, though it is not clear if Buchanan had authorized Kane to offer a pardon.[62] Kane then met with Cumming and Colonel Johnston and persuaded Cumming to come to Salt Lake City without the troops, which he did in April.[63] Kane thus helped to avert armed conflict.

Second, in March 1858 Young decided it would be better to flee than to submit. On March 23, he declared that his people would undertake a "Move South," whereby all settlements in northern Utah would be abandoned and the community would move to a new area rather than submit to federal rule. Young vowed, "Rather than see my wives and daughters ravished and polluted, and the seeds of corruption sown in the hearts of my sons by a brutal soldiery, I would leave my home in ashes, my gardens and orchards a waste, and subsist upon roots and herbs, a wanderer through these mountains for the remainder of my natural life."[64]

Young personally led the procession south on April 1.[65] Some 30,000 people moved more than fifty miles away from Salt Lake City to Provo and other locations in central and southern Utah, an exodus that was larger than the previous Mormon migrations from Missouri and Illinois.[66] The city was rapidly emptying when Cumming arrived on April 12 and assumed the governorship. According to Allen and Leonard, "The sight of thirty thousand people moving south was awesome, and the amazed Governor Cumming did all he could to persuade them to return to their homes. Brigham Young replied that if the troops were withdrawn from the territory, the people would stop moving, but that 99 percent of the people would rather spend the rest of their lives in the mountains than endure governmental oppression."[67]

The third development in the spring of 1858 was political. By that time, the Utah War had become politically unpopular, and Buchanan sought to put the matter behind him and the country. With a new governor nearly in place in Utah, Buchanan sought to end the confrontation yet also to ensure that residents would submit to federal authority.

PRESIDENTIAL PROCLAMATION

On April 6, 1858—the twenty-eighth anniversary of the founding of the LDS Church—Buchanan issued a proclamation entitled "Proclamation on the Rebellion in the Territory of Utah."[68] In the proclamation,

Buchanan described the problems in Utah that had caused him to send troops:

> Whereas the Territory of Utah was settled by certain emigrants . . . who have for several years past manifested a spirit of insubordination to the Constitution and laws of the United States. The great mass of those settlers, acting under the influence of leaders to whom they seem to have surrendered their judgment, refuse to be controlled by any other authority. They have been often advised to obedience, and these friendly counsels have been answered with defiance. The officers of the Federal Government have been driven from the Territory for no offense but an effort to do their sworn duty; others have been prevented from going there by threats of assassination; judges have been violently interrupted in the performance of their functions, and the records of the courts have been seized and destroyed or concealed. Many other acts of unlawful violence have been perpetrated, and the right to repeat them has been openly claimed by the leading inhabitants, with at least the silent acquiescence of nearly all the others. Their hostility to the lawful government of the country has at length become so violent that no officer bearing a commission from the Chief Magistrate of the Union can enter the Territory or remain there with safety, and all those officers recently appointed have been unable to go to Salt Lake or anywhere else in Utah beyond the immediate power of the Army. Indeed, such is believed to be the condition to which a strange system of terrorism has brought the inhabitants of that region that no one among them could express an opinion favorable to this Government, or even propose to obey its laws, without exposing his life and property to peril.[69]

Buchanan's proclamation then noted that he had sent in troops and that their supplies had been attacked and destroyed by Mormon forces. The proclamation called Mormons "misguided" and decried their attitude of "unreserved enmity to the United States." Yet it also sought to engage and persuade its recipients: "Fellow-citizens of Utah, this is rebellion against the government to which you owe allegiance. It is levying war against the United States, and involves you in the guilt of treason." It told them not "to suppose that this Government will fail to put forth its strength and bring you to submission." "Do not deceive yourselves," it said, "nor try to mislead others by propagating the idea that this is a crusade against your religion."

After these justifications and entreaties, the proclamation announced a pardon: "Being anxious to save the effusion of blood and to avoid the indiscriminate punishment of a whole people for crimes of which it is not probable that all are equally guilty, I offer now a free and full pardon to all who will submit themselves to the just authority of the Federal Government. If you refuse to accept it, let the consequences fall upon your own heads."

The proclamation then indicated that the president was "offering to the inhabitants of Utah, who shall submit to the laws, a free pardon for the seditions and treasons heretofore by them committed." If the Mormons did not submit, then they should expect "no further lenity, but look to be rigorously dealt with according to their deserts." Buchanan's threat to use military force if the pardon's would-be recipients spurned it echoed George Washington's pardon offer for the Whiskey Rebellion sixty-four years earlier. And it noted that "the military forces then in Utah, and hereafter to be sent there, will not be withdrawn until the inhabitants of that Territory shall manifest a proper sense of the duty which they owe to this government." Thus, Buchanan's pardon was a political tool, employing both carrot and stick, to induce the Mormon rebels to submit to federal authority.

Pursuant to this proclamation, Buchanan sent peace commissioners to Utah in June. Commissioners Lazarus Powell and Benjamin McCulloch delivered an ultimatum to the Mormons: they could agree to obey the law and the federal government and receive a pardon, or they could refuse and face the forcible imposition of the law.[70] The Mormon leaders found the pardon offer objectionable. According to Bagley, the Mormons believed "they had done nothing to warrant a gratuitous presidential pardon for which they had not applied."[71] Young claimed that the pardon contained inaccurate accounts of Mormon actions. The apostle Wilford Woodruff complained that Buchanan's proclamation was "accusing us of treason and some fifty other crimes, all of which charges are false."[72] Similarly, prominent Mormon Gilbert Clements claimed that none of the forty to fifty charges of alleged Mormon misconduct contained in the pardon was substantiated and thus that accepting the pardon would amount to an inappropriate confession of guilt.[73]

Ultimately, on June 12, 1858, Brigham Young announced that he would accept Buchanan's pardon offer. He said, "I have no character—no pride to gratify—no vanity to please. If a man comes from the moon and says he will pardon me for kicking him in the moon yesterday, I don't care about it. I'll accept his pardon."[74] According to MacKinnon, "Young's comments were a rhetorical fig leaf designed to cover the humiliation of his acceptance."[75] Other Mormons who faced indictments likewise accepted the pardon, and the charges against them were dropped.

On June 14, Governor Cumming issued his own pardon proclamation, essentially to amplify Buchanan's pardon of two months earlier and to indicate that it was now in effect. Cumming's proclamation referenced the president's pardon and its acceptance by the citizens of Utah, and it extended Buchanan's pardon to criminal offenses: "All criminal offenses associated with or growing out of the overt acts of sedition and treason are merged in them, and are embraced in the 'free and full pardon' of the President."[76] Cumming's pardon also said, "I exhort all persons to persevere in a faithful submission to the laws and patriotic devotion to the Constitution and government of our common country." It declared, "Peace is restored in our Territory," and said, "Fellow citizens, I do offer you my congratulations for the peaceful and honorable adjustment of recent difficulties." It then invited people who had recently fled in the "Move South" to return: "Those citizens who have left their homes I invite to return as soon as they can do so with propriety and convenience."[77]

When the federal troops finally entered Salt Lake City in late June, the city was nearly deserted from the "Move South." The troops moved forty miles southwest of Salt Lake City to what would soon become Camp Floyd and agreed to stay there. (Thousands of troops remained there for three years, until the Civil War necessitated their return east.) Young then announced that he would go back to Salt Lake, and most of the Mormon refugees who had fled gradually returned home to live under the control of the federal government.[78]

As Richard Poll notes, "What seemed like an inevitable military confrontation was ultimately resolved peacefully."[79] Mormons submitted to federal authority and were pardoned, and the two groups settled into an awkward cohabitation. According to David Vaughn Mason, the federal troops and Young had arrived at a standoff that was mutually unsatisfactory: "The two populations of the Salt Lake Valley—the Mormon settlers and the military force—entered unceremoniously into a grim détente that stood for the defeat that both sides felt. Johnston had not been able to satisfy what he regarded as justice by conquering the rebel Mormons and executing Brigham as a traitor."[80]

In the end, Buchanan's proclamation of pardon succeeded in easing tensions, avoiding significant armed conflict, and formally if uneasily bringing Mormons into the national fold. As one mid-nineteenth-century journalist described the end of hostilities in Utah, "Thus was peace made—thus was ended the 'Mormon War,' which, miracle dictu, was much less sanguinary and direful than the 'Kansas War,' and may thus be summarily historicized: killed, none; wounded, none; fooled, everybody."[81] Similarly, a *New York Times* editorial at the time characterized the episode as "a mass of blunders from beginning to end."[82] Allen and Leonard conclude, "Thus 'Buchanan's blunder,' as people were beginning to call it, was effectively whitewashed by a pardon that did not need to be issued, carried by a peace commission that followed an army of occupation that never needed to be sent."[83]

Regardless of how one characterizes the peace of 1858, it marked the end of Mormon dreams of an independent theocratic state. As Allen and Leonard explain the situation, "Within ten short years of their exodus from the United States, the Saints once again realized that their place of refuge was not a place of isolation, and their efforts to build the Kingdom would have to be conducted in the presence of others, under the watchful eye of the nation."[84] According to Bigler and Bagley, Young's assent to federal authority marked "the beginning of the end of

Young's vision to establish the Kingdom of God as a sovereign state in the American West."[85]

BENJAMIN HARRISON

President James Buchanan's mass pardon and Brigham Young's acceptance of it greatly reduced but did not altogether eliminate tensions between Mormons and the federal government. For some, this was because Buchanan's decision to pardon rather than punish Mormons had the effect of encouraging further disrespect of the federal government among them. (This was the same dynamic that some Federalists had complained about after the Whiskey Rebellion sixty-three years earlier.) For example, in March 1860 Utah judge John Cradlebaugh called the pardon an "ill-advised act of grace" and an "ill-timed and ill-judged clemency." He said, "When treason is thus dealt with, traitors will be numerous. If they are thus rewarded for the first offence, what shall they not expect in the way of honor for the second? When this strange doctrine, first inaugurated by the present Administration, becomes better established, good citizens had better keep a sharp look out for traitors. . . . An unpunished insurrectionary movement which proceeds from general disaffection, and is only concealed or covered up by nations of temporary expediency, is never followed by good government."[86] Indeed, despite Young's putative acceptance of federal authority, it was likely the case that his submission was not made in good faith because Mormon leaders continuously endeavored to obstruct federal officials for the next three decades.[87] And they had something of an unlikely ally in their new governor. After Cumming assumed power, he proved sympathetic to Mormon concerns and generally helped Young. According to Poll, "Governor Cumming soon became more popular with the latter-day Saints [sic] than with the military."[88] In addition, some Mormons "reactivated the State of Deseret[,] which continued to function as a ghost government, apart from the territorial government."[89] As Bigler and Bagley explain, Young "was able to regain total control of Utah's judicial system and render the U.S. army as impotent as if it had never arrived in Utah."[90] This control blocked an investigation of the Mountain Meadows massacre for more than a decade.

Nevertheless, the federal government undertook various measures to try to control Mormons. Many of these actions involved Congress. For example, between 1861 and 1868 Congress repeatedly shrank the Utah Territory by giving parts of it to the new Territories of Colorado, Nevada, Nebraska, and Wyoming.[91] And four years after Buchanan's pardon, Abraham Lincoln signed into law the Morrill Anti-Bigamy Act of 1862, which made polygamy a federal offense, annulled Utah's legal incorporation of the LDS Church, and limited Mormon property holdings to just $50,000 for the entire territory.[92] Yet the Morrill Act was not strongly enforced, and polygamy continued to be common among Mormons. According to the historian Stephen Cresswell, "Twenty years after the passage of the Morrill Act U.S. attorneys had achieved only two convictions under this federal law."[93]

In 1870, the House of Representatives passed the Cullom bill, authorizing the president to send the army to Utah to enforce antipolygamy laws, although the measure died in the Senate.[94] In 1874, Congress passed the Poland Act to curtail the vast judicial powers of Mormon-controlled probate courts, which retained something of their origin as ecclesiastical courts and had authority over most civil and criminal matters. The Poland Act moved jurisdiction for all civil and criminal cases to federal district courts, which were less sympathetic to Mormons, in order to facilitate prosecutions for violations of the Morrill Act. The result was that crimes that had long gone unpunished were finally prosecuted, including the Mountain Meadows massacre.

Congressional antipathy toward Mormons was also evident with regard to who would represent Utah in Congress. In 1880, George Cannon, who had served four terms in Congress as the delegate from Utah Territory, won his race for reelection by a factor of ten to one. However, his opponents claimed that Congress should not seat him because his practice of polygamy violated federal law and his oath of office. After a lengthy dispute, Congress refused to seat him.[95] And in 1882, Congress passed a law to forbid seating a territorial delegate who was bigamous.[96]

Apart from congressional actions to confront Mormons, presidents also gave voice to anti-Mormon sentiment. Back in 1861, Abraham Lincoln had told a Mormon official, "Tell Brigham Young to let me alone and I will let him alone." But later presidential administrations were less accommodating. For example, in 1869 Ulysses Grant's vice president Schuyler Colfax asked "whether the authority of the nation or the authority of Brigham Young is supreme in Utah; whether the laws of the United States or the laws of the Mormon Church have precedence."[97]

In the early 1880s, three Republican presidents spoke out against Mormons in major addresses. In December 1880, Rutherford B. Hayes warned in his fourth and final Annual Message to Congress:

> The Mormon sectarian organization which upholds polygamy has the whole power of making and executing the local legislation of the Territory [of Utah]. By its control of the grand and petit juries it possesses large influence over the administration of justice. Exercising, as the heads of this sect do, the local political power of the Territory, they are able to make effective their hostility to the law of Congress on the subject of polygamy, and, in fact, do prevent its enforcement. Polygamy will not be abolished if the enforcement of the law depends on those who practice and uphold the crime. It can only be suppressed by taking away the political power of the sect which encourages and sustains it.

Hayes further said, "To reestablish the interests and principles which polygamy and Mormonism have imperiled, and to fully reopen to intelligent and virtuous immigrants of all creeds that part of our domain which has been in a great degree closed to general immigration by intolerant and immoral institutions, it is recommended that the government of the Territory of Utah be reorganized."[98]

In his Inaugural Address in March 1881, James Garfield said that religious organizations in the Utah Territory were blocking the authority of Congress and thwarting the constitutional guarantee of religious freedom. Garfield charged, "The Mormon Church not only offends the moral sense of manhood by sanctioning polygamy, but prevents the administration of justice through ordinary instrumentalities of law." He then said it was up to Congress to rein in the Mormons: "In my judgment it is the duty of Congress, while respecting to the uttermost the conscientious convictions and religious scruples of every citizen, to prohibit within its jurisdiction all criminal practices, especially of that class which destroy the family relations and endanger social order. Nor can any ecclesiastical organization be safely permitted to usurp in the smallest degree the functions and powers of the National Government."[99]

In December 1881, in his First Annual Message, Chester Arthur said the growth of Mormonism "imposes upon Congress and the Executive the duty of arraying against this barbarous system all the power which under the Constitution and the law they can wield for its destruction." Two years later, in his Third Annual Message, Arthur said, "I am convinced . . . that polygamy has become so strongly intrenched [sic] in the Territory of Utah that it is profitless to attack it with any but the stoutest weapons which constitutional legislation can fashion. I favor, therefore, the repeal of the act upon which the existing government depends, the assumption by the National Legislature of the entire political control of the Territory, and the establishment of a commission with such powers and duties as shall be delegated to it by law." In 1884, in his Fourth Annual Message, Arthur again called on Congress to resolve the problems with Mormons by assuming "absolute political control of the Territory of Utah" and ruling it via federally appointed commissioners.[100]

Following the critical remarks by Presidents Hayes, Garfield, and Arthur, Congress again acted to curtail Mormons. Two decades after the ineffective Morrill Act was passed, Congress enacted tougher anti-polygamy legislation via the Edmunds Act of 1882, which made polygamy a felony and stripped polygamists of the right to vote, made them ineligible to serve on juries, and prohibited them from holding political office. This law soon led to the disenfranchisement of some 12,000 people. The Edmunds Act also gave the president the power to issue an amnesty to polygamists who abandoned the practice, even though the president already had that power via Article II of the Constitution.

Section 6 of the Edmunds Act read: "That the President is hereby authorized to grant amnesty to such classes of offenders guilty of bigamy, polygamy, or unlawful cohabitation, before the passage of this act, on such conditions and under such limitations as he shall think proper; but no such amnesty shall have effect unless the conditions thereof shall be complied with."[101] President Arthur began to issue individual proclamations of amnesty for erstwhile polygamists in 1884.[102]

In March 1887, Congress passed the Edmunds-Tucker Act, which was "the harshest legislation yet directed at the Mormons."[103] The act provided for an oath for would-be voters in which they would promise to obey antipolygamy laws. It also disincorporated the LDS Church and forfeited to the federal government all church property worth more than the $50,000 limit imposed by the Morrill Act.[104]

As Krakauer explains, "With their feet held fast to the fire, the Saints ultimately had no choice but to renounce polygamy."[105] In September 1890, Wilford Woodruff, who had become the fourth president of the LDS Church in 1889, bowed to pressure from Washington and declared his intention to submit to federal laws and to forsake polygamy. Woodruff's manifesto of 1890 said in part: "Inasmuch as laws have been enacted by Congress forbidding plural marriages, which laws have been pronounced constitutional by the court of last resort, I hereby [sic] declare my intention to submit to those laws, to use my influence with the members of the Church over which I preside to have them do likewise." He concluded, "I now publicly declare that my advice to the Latter-day Saints is to refrain from contracting any marriage forbidden by the law of the land."[106] This concession greatly enhanced the chances for official reconciliation.

In his Second Annual Address to Congress in December 1890, Benjamin Harrison mentioned Woodruff's position on polygamy and said, "It is hoped that its influence will be highly beneficial in restraining infractions of the laws of the United States." However, Harrison cautioned that the Mormon rejection of polygamy was not complete: "But the fact should not be overlooked that the doctrine or belief of the church that polygamous marriages are rightful and supported by divine revelation remains unchanged. President Woodruff does not renounce the doctrine, but refrains from teaching it, and advises against the practice of it because the law is against it." Harrison then declared his determination to ensure "that those who believe polygamy to be rightful shall not have the power to make it lawful."[107]

In December 1891, more than thirty-three years after Buchanan's conditional pardon and following various individual pardons, Mormon leaders formally petitioned Harrison for a general amnesty. Harrison was somewhat reluctant, given political concerns with the approaching presidential election. (He had won the electoral vote in 1888 but had lost the popular vote to Grover Cleveland, and the contest in 1892 would be a rematch.) But public sentiment seemed to be in favor of an amnesty. In February 1892, the *Washington Post* endorsed a Mormon amnesty: "It is wholly contrary to the theory of our institutions to keep any class or body of the people under the ban of political disenfranchisement after they have once abandoned the offenses that provoked the curtailment of their rights. With the undoing of the causes should come a suspension of the consequences." The *Post* continued, "What is to be gained by perpetuating their disabilities?" It further said, "The Government has succeeded in all that it undertook to do, and having gained its points beyond the peradventure of a relapse or reaction, it can now afford to be magnanimous."[108] In September 1892, the federally appointed Utah Commission also endorsed the request for a general amnesty.

PARDON FOR POLYGAMY

On January 4, 1893, after Harrison had lost the election and was near the end of his term, he finally granted amnesty to Mormons who had complied with the law since 1890. In what had by then become the traditional practice, the preamble of Harrison's mass-pardon proclamation noted some of the relevant facts, including the passage of federal antipolygamy legislation in 1882, the Mormon renunciation of polygamy in 1890 (which the proclamation noted had been largely complied with since then), the petition for amnesty in 1891, the findings of the Utah Commission, and the large number of individual amnesty requests over the years, most of which were granted, but many of which were still pending. It then conferred pardon upon polygamists "who have since November 1, 1890, abstained from such unlawful cohabitation, but upon the express condition that they shall in the future faithfully obey the laws of the United States." It also warned that "those who shall fail to avail themselves of the clemency hereby offered will be vigorously prosecuted."[109]

Mormon leaders had hoped for a less-restrictive pardon, but they still welcomed Harrison's action. Newspapers in Utah hailed the proclamation, but they suggested it was late in coming for political reasons, as it recognized a state of affairs that had existed for some time. For example, the *Deseret News*, a Mormon publication, said, "We believe the proclamation will be received graciously by those for whom it is intended. Possibly it would have been more acceptable had it not been so long delayed." The *Deseret News* continued, "It will give no encouragement to promoters of strife, and may be regarded as a distinct rebuke to the narrow souled element that is bent on restoring and prolonging the season of discord and bitterness from which the Territory has happily been freed."[110] The Democratic *Salt Lake Herald* said,

> An apologetic air pervades the document, as though the author felt it necessary to remind the people of the United States of facts that are, or ought to be, well known, as an excuse for his action; or as if someone might think that this tardy recognition of notorious facts might injure him in the estimation of strangers. Outside of this feature, the proclamation is a very tame and inconsequential paper. It is principally useful as an official recognition and high statement of the "changed conditions" among the Mormon people, and as testifying to the President's belief in their good faith and honest purpose.[111]

Some newspapers on the East Coast characterized Harrison's pardon as sensible but unremarkable. For example, the Republican *New York Mail and Express* said the proclamation "was neither a sentimental nor a sensational action on the part of the retiring Executive, but a careful and judicious response to the earnest solicitations of the Utah

Commission, the Governor of the Territory and many prominent citizens through the country."[112] And the *Washington Star* said that in his proclamation Harrison "has done just what might have been expected of a broad-minded statesman."[113] The *Washington Post* offered more fulsome approval: "The strained relations that so long existed between Utah and the General Government no longer exist. Smiles have been substituted for frowns, amnesty for proscription, friendly recognition for statutory confiscation, and a resplendent future of liberty and progress is now assured to a Territory that was so long under a double ban of repression."[114]

GROVER CLEVELAND

Grover Cleveland occasionally dealt with Mormon issues during his first term as president (1885–1889), before Harrison issued his amnesty in 1893. As the first Democratic president in many years, Cleveland was sometimes perceived as friendly toward Mormons. Yet he railed against polygamy in his address to Congress in December 1885, and he let the Edmunds-Tucker Act become law (albeit without his signature) in March 1887. In December 1887, he pardoned the LDS Church apostle Rudger Clawson, who was the first person prosecuted for polygamy and unlawful cohabitation under the Edmunds Act, shortly before the end of Clawson's sentence.[115]

But Cleveland's main act to address Mormons occurred in his second term (1893–1897). Thirty-five years after Buchanan's pardon proclamation and twenty months after Harrison's pardon proclamation, Cleveland became the third president to issue a mass pardon for Mormons. By that time, Utah had drafted a constitution forbidding polygamy and containing strict provisions for separation of church and state. Mormon leaders had been working for decades to make Utah a state, and statehood advocates began to lobby federal officials for a broad pardon or amnesty as a means of clearing the way for statehood. Although some Mormons continued to practice polygamy and to defy federal authority, in July 1894 Congress passed an act to enable statehood for Utah.

It was in this context that on September 25, 1894, Cleveland issued a proclamation granting amnesty to persons convicted of polygamy under the Edmunds Act. Cleveland's proclamation began by noting the passage of the antipolygamy Edmunds Act in 1882. It then referenced the decision of the head of the Mormon Church to abandon polygamy: "Whereas, On or about the 6th day of October, 1890, the Church of the Latter Day Saints, commonly known as the Mormon Church, through its President, issued a manifesto proclaiming the purpose of said Church no longer to sanction the practice of polygamous marriages, and calling upon all members and adherents of said Church to obey the laws of the United States in reference to said subject matter." The proclamation then cited Harrison's proclamation: "Whereas, On the 4th day of January, 1893, Benjamin Harrison, then President of the United States, did declare and grant a full pardon to certain offenders, under condition of future obedience to their requirements."

Cleveland's amnesty proclamation then noted his assessment that "the members and adherents of said church generally abstain from plural marriages and polygamous cohabitation and are now living in obedience to the laws." And it invoked broader interests: "The time has now arrived when the interests of public justice and morality will be promoted by the granting of amnesty and pardon." The proclamation then declared and granted "a full amnesty and pardon to all persons who have in violation of said acts committed either of the offenses of polygamy, bigamy, adultery, or unlawful cohabitation under the color of polygamous or plural marriage, or who, having been convicted of violations of said acts, are now suffering deprivations of civil rights in consequence of the same, excepting all persons who have not complied with the conditions contained in said executive proclamation of January 4, 1893."[116]

Cleveland's action was thus both a pardon and an enfranchisement of all Utahns who had earlier been disqualified to vote because of their practice of polygamy. This was an extension of the initial amnesty and pardon offered by Harrison the previous year, but it was also an affirmation of an important ruling by the congressionally appointed Utah Commission in 1893 that amnestied polygamists should be allowed to vote.

Reaction to Cleveland's pardon was positive. In September 1894, the *Washington Post* claimed that "the interests of public justice and morality will be promoted by the granting of amnesty and pardon to all such offenders." The *Post* opined that "the day of polygamy is practically at an end. The [Mormon] church repudiates it. The law against it is loyally observed. The government's authority in the matter is supreme, and in the recent proclamations of amnesty for past offenses has been wisely exercised. Between the Federal and ecclesiastical authorities relations are no longer strained, and none of the Territories more cordially than Utah will be welcomed to the sisterhood of the States."[117] And in October 1894, Governor Caleb West of Utah reported to the U.S. secretary of the interior that the actions of Presidents Harrison and Cleveland in enacting amnesty had met with the approval "of all classes of people, and is especially appreciated by hundreds of our best citizens who were disenfranchised, and have, since the issuance of the amnesty, availed themselves of the very important duty of registering to vote at our approaching election."[118]

On January 4, 1896, one hundred days after issuing his pardon, Cleveland proclaimed Utah's admission to the union as the forty-fifth state, effectively cementing the rapprochement between Mormons and the federal government. Although Utah was one of the first places in the West to be extensively settled, it was one of the last to become a state.[119] With violence and widespread criminal prosecution in the past, the fact of statehood finally indicated a high degree of reconciliation between Mormons and the U.S. federal government.

This chapter has examined the use of mass pardons by three presidents across four decades to reconcile with Mormons. The first mass pardon resolved the threat of armed conflict, while the second and third mass pardons assuaged the legal inferiority that came from Mormons' religious practices, though full reintegration into the national community arguably did not occur until statehood. The three mass pardons discussed here varied considerably in their intent, rhetoric, and effect, but altogether they sought to place Mormons firmly within the national community and to ensure that they both adhered to the nation's laws and could fully participate in its political life. Even if America's conflicts with Mormons in the nineteenth century are little known by most people today, they nevertheless constitute a major and prolonged episode of a domestic group's political alienation, hostility, and eventual integration into the nation following multiple proclamations of mass pardon.

4

THE CIVIL WAR

Abraham Lincoln and Andrew Johnson

This proclamation is intended to present the people of the States wherein the national authority has been suspended and loyal State governments have been subverted a mode in and by which the national authority and loyal State governments may be reestablished.

—ABRAHAM LINCOLN, 1863

It is believed that amnesty and pardon will tend to secure a complete and universal establishment and prevalence of municipal law and order in conformity with the Constitution.

—ANDREW JOHNSON, 1868

The Civil War was the most significant political rupture in American history, and it led to some of the most important and well-known presidential efforts to achieve political reconciliation via mass pardons. Unlike in some of the other conflicts explored in this book, the major elements and themes of the Civil War are familiar to many Americans in part because of the magnitude of the conflict. Starting with South Carolina in December 1860, eleven of the thirty-four states, containing almost one-third of the country's population, formally seceded from the Union. In the four years between the Confederate attack on Fort Sumter in April 1861 and General Robert E. Lee's surrender at Appomattox in April 1865, some 620,000 soldiers and 50,000 civilians died because of the war, and half a million were wounded.[1] If ever there were a need for political reconciliation in the United States, this was it. The effort to reintegrate Confederates and to reunite the United States led to a total of six separate proclamations of mass pardon by two presidents over five years, both during and after the Civil War. As we will see, these pardons varied considerably in their intent, scope, conditions, rhetoric, and impact.

ABRAHAM LINCOLN

Abraham Lincoln is famous for his great rhetorical ability, and it is worth noting that he had decades of experience in persuading people before he became president. As the Lincoln scholar Douglas Wilson explains, "For over a quarter century, as both lawyer and politician, Lincoln had been in the persuading business."[2] According to Wilson, Lincoln's views about rhetorical persuasion can be found in his Temperance Address of 1842, in which Lincoln said that it is counterproductive to dictate or to try to force your opinion upon someone else because such a person "will retreat within himself, close all the avenues to his head and his heart; and tho' your cause be naked truth itself, transformed to the heaviest lance, harder than steel, and sharper than steel can be made, and tho' you throw it with more than Herculean force and precision, you shall no more be able to pierce him, than to penetrate the hard shell of a tortoise with a rye straw." Indeed, he said, "if you would win a man to your cause, first convince him that you are his sincere friend."[3]

As president, Lincoln was by most accounts temperamentally and politically inclined toward reconciliation.[4] As one scholar puts it, "Lincoln was in general lenient. . . . His adherence to a policy of nonvindictiveness toward the South extended to the end of his life."[5] This attitude was reflected in Lincoln's use of pardons. According to a contemporary author, "No president in the history of this nation has been so praised, or so criticized, for his use of the pardoning power."[6]

As we shall see, Lincoln's most famous proclamation for pardon and amnesty was issued in December 1863, but he also engaged in significant reconciliatory actions as president before then for both civil and military matters. By one count, "during his tenure, Lincoln reviewed 456 civil cases; 375 of them—over 82 percent—received pardons."[7] This generosity also applied to political prisoners. On February 14, 1862, Lincoln ordered political prisoners freed and pardoned. According to the historian Jonathan Truman Dorris, Lincoln's administration decided "a more lenient course should be pursued in dealing with the large number of persons detained as political prisoners. It was evident that there were those among them who were innocent of any offense against the government, and there were others who had repented of their imprudent acts and were ready to declare their loyalty to the Union, or at least agree not to render assistance to the Confederacy. . . . [T]he President believed it prudent to release a large number of prisoners forthwith."[8] Lincoln's pardon led to the release of scores of prisoners who took the following oath of allegiance: "I do solemnly swear (or affirm) that I will support, protect, and defend the Constitution of the United States against all enemies, whether domestic or foreign, and that I will bear true faith, allegiance and loyalty to the same, any ordinance, resolution or law of any State convention, or legislature to the contrary, notwithstanding; and further, that I do this with a full determination, pledge, and purpose, without any mental reservation or evasion whatsoever. So help me God."[9]

Lincoln was also generous with pardons for military infractions and failures. He considered hundreds of cases of individual soldiers who had been condemned to death, and in his own words the criterion that he invoked in deciding their fates was "whether this soldier can better serve the country dead than living."[10] As Lincoln said of a soldier whom he decided to pardon for desertion, "If a man had more than one life, I think a little hanging would not hurt this one; but after he is once dead we cannot bring him back, no matter how sorry we may be; so the boy shall be pardoned."[11] In March 1863, General Joseph Hooker "sent an envelope to the president containing the cases of 55 convicted and doomed deserters; Lincoln merely wrote 'Pardoned' on the envelope and returned it to Hooker."[12]

Not everyone approved of Lincoln's generosity with pardons. According to Doris Kearns Goodwin, "Lincoln acknowledged to General John Eaton that some of his officers believed he employed the pardoning power 'with so much freedom as to demoralize the army and destroy the discipline.' "[13] Indeed, some officials did not share Lincoln's inclination to grant pardons for military infractions. Two members of Lincoln's cabinet felt the president was often too generous with pardons:

> Gideon Welles, the secretary of the Navy, confided to his diary that the president "is always disposed to mitigate punishment, and to grant favors," adding that "sometimes this is a weakness." Edward Bates, Lincoln's first attorney general, defined the president as an ideal man, with but one failing: "I have sometimes told him," Bates recalled, that "he was unfit to be entrusted with the pardoning power. Why, if a man comes to him with a touching story his judgment is almost certain to be affected by it. Should the applicant be a woman—a wife, a mother or a sister—in 9 cases out of 10 her tears, if nothing else, are sure to prevail."[14]

These civil and military pardons foreshadowed Lincoln's larger-scale pardons of Confederates.[15] Early in the war, Congress passed the Confiscation Acts of August 1861 and July 1862 to govern the punishment of Confederate traitors. According to the mid-twentieth-century historian E. Merton Coulter, who was clearly sympathetic to the Confederacy, Lincoln had a "desire to ameliorate the harsh terms of the two Confiscation Acts."[16] Perhaps ironically, the acts contained the means by which Lincoln could alter these terms in that they authorized the president to issue proclamations of pardon and amnesty even though the president already possessed this authority via the Constitution.[17] Based on these dual sources of authority, Lincoln issued two mass pardons. The pardons followed his two most famous speeches—the Gettysburg Address and his Second Inaugural—by just three weeks each, and although neither pardon rose to the rhetorical heights of those famous speeches, both were nevertheless significant examples of a president using both words and deeds to try to foster unity and reconciliation.[18]

LINCOLN'S FIRST PARDON

When Lincoln issued his first mass pardon in late 1863, the Civil War was well into its third year, and starting with Union victories at Gettysburg and Vicksburg in early July that year, the end was arguably in sight. According to the historian Rick Beard, "By early November 1863, Abraham Lincoln found himself frustrated with the glacial pace of wartime reconstruction efforts" because he had a "sense of urgency" about Reconstruction.[19] That sense was one of several factors that influenced his mass-pardon policy. Other factors included Lincoln's inclination for compassion and leniency as well as his desire to hasten the end of the war, reestablish regular state governments in the South, entrench emancipation, and do it all quickly before Congress would reconvene and try to impose its own preferences.[20]

With all of these considerations in mind, Lincoln carefully drafted his pardon proclamation throughout the fall of 1863 with input from his cabinet, before issuing it on December 8 as part of his Annual Message to Congress. It was entitled "Proclamation of Amnesty and Reconstruction." It referenced the Constitution's provision of the president's power to grant pardons as well as congressional legislation authorizing the president to issue pardons concerning the rebellion. It also said that "it is now desired by some persons heretofore engaged in said rebellion to resume their allegiance to the United States, and to reinaugurate legal state governments."[21]

The pardon contained the following account of its motivations: "This proclamation is intended to present the people of the States wherein the national authority has been suspended and loyal State governments have been subverted a mode in and by which the national authority and loyal State governments may be reestablished." Thus, its ostensible aim was to return to regular governance.

Lincoln's pardon promised to restore citizenship and property (except slaves) to anyone who had fought for or supported the Confederacy. The pardon would be conditional on taking a lengthy oath of allegiance, which was contained in Lincoln's proclamation:

> I, ___, do solemnly swear, in presence of Almighty God, that I will henceforth faithfully support, protect, and defend the Constitution of the United States and the Union of the States thereunder; and that I will in like manner abide by and faithfully support all acts of Congress passed during the existing rebellion with reference to slaves, so long and so far as not repealed, modified, or held void by Congress or by decision of the Supreme Court: and that I will in like manner abide by and faithfully support all proclamations of the President made during the existing rebellion having reference to slaves, so long and so far as not modified or declared void by decision of the Supreme Court. So help me God.

Thus, the oath pertained to future loyalty, not to past allegiance.

Lincoln's pardon was not motivated solely by a sense of compassion or leniency because it was intended both to help win the war and to reintegrate the former rebels. According to Harold Hyman, Lincoln hoped "that the terms of his proclamation would attract rebel soldiers still fighting against the Union, and Southern civilians living where the Stars and Bars still flew, to desert the secession standard at the first opportunity. . . . His proclamation proved to be a powerful solvent to the dissolving bands of sectional allegiance which the contracting Confederacy could muster. As a forerunner of psychological warfare, the December 1863 proclamation deserves a high place."[22] Similarly, Goodwin notes that Lincoln "recognized that it would devastate Confederate morale to see Southern citizens declare their fealty to the Union and their support for emancipation."[23] And Joshua Zeitz claims that Lincoln wanted "to foster political dissent and chaos behind enemy lines."[24]

Beyond seeking to help the Union militarily, Lincoln's pardon of December 8, 1863, also sought to facilitate Reconstruction in that it set forth the conditions for states to be readmitted to the Union based on the numbers of people who took the oath:

> And I do further proclaim, declare, and make known that whenever, in any of the States of Arkansas, Texas, Louisiana, Mississippi, Tennessee, Alabama, Georgia, Florida, South Carolina, and North Carolina, a number of persons, not less than one tenth in number of the votes cast in such state at the presidential election of the year of our Lord one thousand eight hundred and sixty, each having taken the oath aforesaid, and not having since violated it, and being a qualified voter by the election law of the state existing immediately before the so-called act of secession, and excluding all others, shall re-establish a state government which shall be republican, and in nowise contravening said oath, such shall be recognized as the true government of the state, and the state shall receive thereunder the benefits of the constitutional provision which declares that "the United States shall guaranty to every state in this Union a republican form of government, and shall protect each of them against invasion; and on application of the legislature, or the executive (when the legislature cannot be convened), against domestic violence."

Thus, Lincoln's Ten Percent Plan tied the reestablishment of regular self-governance to taking the oath.

Lincoln's proclamation ended with a candid statement that although it was intended to present to the residents of rebellious states "a mode in and by which the national authority and loyal State governments may be reestablished . . . and while the mode presented is the best the Executive can suggest, with his present impressions, it must not be understood that no other possible mode would be acceptable." In other words, although Lincoln saw the pardon as a good means of returning to regular governance, he was clear that other means toward that end also existed.

The proclamation also stated that some groups would be ineligible for the pardon, including Confederate officials, those who had abandoned federal offices to participate in the rebellion, "and all who have engaged in any way in treating colored persons, or white persons in charge of such, otherwise than lawfully as prisoners of war, and which persons may have been found in the United States service as soldiers, seamen, or in any other capacity."

Lincoln was well known for his rhetorical skill, but his pardon proclamation was linguistically muddled. According to the historian David Donald, it "lacked his usual literary elegance" and clearly showed it "had been composed under difficulty." Several newspapers even remarked it was less "Lincolnian" than the president's other messages.[25] The proclamation's stylistic shortcomings were undoubtedly a product of its various political imperatives. It was almost defensive in tone as Lincoln carefully explained that his action was justified, legitimate, and appropriate. It sought to persuade rather than to coerce and seemed to want to avoid even the appearance of authoritarian dictation.[26] It was consciously flexible and presented itself as just one possible approach to reconciliation, and it reassured Congress and the states that they had important roles to play.

In striving to be inclusive, Lincoln's proclamation had elements to appeal to a variety of different interests. For example, despite the oath's oblique requirement to support the Emancipation Proclamation, the pardon arguably did little to discourage Southerners who hoped for a postwar system that might approximate slavery in that it promised a provisional arrangement in which states could largely determine their own policies for former slaves: "And I do further proclaim, declare, and make known that any provision which may be adopted by such state government in relation to the freed people of such state, which shall recognize and declare their permanent freedom, provide for their education, and which may yet be consistent as a temporary arrangement with their present condition as a laboring, landless, and homeless class, will not be objected to by the National Executive." According to the historian Bruce Levine, "The inclusion of that language was not accidental."[27]

Even if Lincoln's pardon was rhetorically awkward, it was politically successful. A week after the pardon was issued, the *Chicago Tribune* reported that "all shades of opinion among loyal men" supported it.[28] The uniformly positive reaction was, as the presidential aide John Hay reported, "something wonderful."[29] Even within the divided Republican Party, both the conservative and the radical wings endorsed it, leading the *New York Herald* to declare, "The art of riding two horses is not confined to the circus."[30] According to the historian John Rodrigue, conservatives liked how "the plan considered secession the work of individuals requiring pardons rather than of states," while radicals liked the roles that it acknowledged for military power and executive oversight as well as how pardons and state restoration required taking the oath and thus accepting emancipation.[31]

But not everyone liked the pardon or the broader program of Reconstruction of which it was a part. Critics such as Senator Lazarus Powell (D–KY), who several years earlier had urged Mormons to accept James Buchanan's pardon offer, charged that Lincoln's amnesty offer would influence coming elections and permitted the president to wrongly decide who could vote in a state.[32] And in January 1864, the Confederate president Jefferson Davis asked of Lincoln's December 1863 proclamation: "Have we not just been apprised by that despot that we can only expect his gracious pardon by emancipating all our slaves, swearing allegiance and obedience to him and his proclamations, and becoming in point of fact the slaves of our own negroes?"[33]

Yet the pardon was well received by some Southerners, and many Confederates were persuaded to take the oath. For example, less than six months after Union forces prevailed in New Orleans, some 60,000 city residents took the oath.[34] As Hyman explains, "The Presidential pardon and reconstruction proclamation penetrated deeply into the defiant South. . . . Thousands of captured Confederates and tens of thousands of Southern civilians living within the expanding lines of Union occupation petitioned to take advantage of Lincoln's clemency long before Lee surrendered and thus made turncoating respectable in the South."[35]

However, there was a sense that many of the Southerners who took the oath did so for instrumental reasons rather than because they earnestly wanted to submit to the federal government. According to Coulter, "Confederates did not judge all of them too severely, for there was a feeling that an expedient act did not change their fundamental attitude."[36] Thus, just as Lincoln's motive in issuing the pardon was in part instrumental, so were the motivations of many who took the loyalty oath and thereby were pardoned.

LINCOLN'S SECOND PARDON

On March 26, 1864, four months after his first pardon and three weeks after his Second Inaugural Address (in which the president declared "with malice toward none, with charity for all"), Lincoln issued a second proclamation of mass pardon. The motivation for the second proclamation was in part the same as for his first, but the new statement's main purpose was to address practical problems related to the first proclamation. Despite the care with which Lincoln crafted and promoted his initial mass pardon, problems had soon arisen. As Dorris explains,

> As months passed, a number of problems arose. . . . Who would administer the oath? How could abuses be avoided? Should loyal men, as well as those considered disloyal, be required to swear? Would loyalists refuse the oath on the ground that it was unfair and unnecessary for them?. . . What about prisoners of war, or those under sentence of military courts, or those under Federal indictment for some war-connected offense?. . . These and other problems show how difficult and elaborate the pardon program became, even though conceived on the simplest lines and announced in the most direct terms.[37]

The ambiguities of the December 1863 pardon may have resulted from Lincoln's flexibility in restoring national unity or from the multiple motives behind his pardon, but the practical problems that it presented prompted the president to clarify things with another pardon, which he issued on March 26, 1864, via the "Proclamation About Amnesty."

Lincoln's second mass pardon began with a justification rooted in these practical concerns: "Whereas it has become necessary to define the cases in which insurgent enemies are entitled to the benefits of the proclamation [of December 1863]." It then noted the purposes of the initial proclamation had been "to suppress the insurrection and to restore the authority of the United States," thereby associating the second proclamation with those same aims. It indicated that commissioned federal and state-authorized civil and military officers could administer the oath, which was the same as the oath in the first proclamation, and it gave directions concerning the transmittal of oath-related records. The proclamation specified that those individuals under civil or military custody or confinement (e.g., prisoners of war) were not eligible, yet it said that people who were excluded from the amnesty offer could nevertheless individually apply to the president for clemency, "and their applications will receive due consideration."[38]

According to P. S. Ruckman and David Kincaid, reaction to Lincoln's second pardon was mixed, and there are conflicting scholarly and contemporaneous reports on the manner in which it was received by public officials, in particular those in Congress. According to their summary, Mark E. Neely Jr. suggests that both radicals and conservatives viewed the proposal favorably, and Joseph H. Barrett echoes similar sentiments. Charles H. McCarthy, in contrast, notes that the proclamation was initially greeted with "universal favor" but was shortly followed by various congressional efforts to challenge or supplant it. Representative Isaac Arnold (R) of Illinois, an abolitionist and Lincoln loyalist, discerned "a wide difference of opinion among the friends of the President in regard to the Amnesty Proclamation" in that "many thought the terms much too favorable to the rebels."[39] Predictably, the reaction from the partisan press was likewise mixed, though less temperate. The Democratic *New York Daily News* lamented Lincoln's proclamation as "treachery" that stripped the people of their constitutional liberties, usurped legislative authority, and was dictatorial and arbitrary in its terms for restoration of Southern states to the Union. The

Daily News also said that Lincoln wished to see the seceded states returned to the Union fold with the hope of gaining their votes for his upcoming reelection bid.[40] The charge of election politics was also made by the weekly *Spirit of the Times*, which asserted Lincoln was "granting pardons to military rebels . . . in order that they may come within our lines and electioneer to carry out his personal purposes."[41] In contrast, the *New York Tribune* described the plan as eminently reasonable and wondered why anyone would doubt that its provisions were fair to the South: "How can any one who means to be loyal at all, object to these conditions?. . . We proffer them equality with ourselves. Should not that suffice and content them?"[42] Lincoln died on April 15, 1865, six days after Confederate general Robert E. Lee surrendered to Union general Ulysses S. Grant, a little more than a year after his second pardon, and one month after his pardon of Union deserters. His program of reconciliation and Reconstruction, like his presidency, was thus incomplete.[43]

ANDREW JOHNSON

Andrew Johnson had been Lincoln's vice president for just a little more than one month before he ascended to the presidency. Initially, there was reason to think that the new president would eschew reconciliation and instead deal harshly with former Confederates, given things he had said and done before becoming president. For example, as the military governor of Tennessee, Johnson had given a three-hour speech at a Union meeting in Indiana on March 2, 1863, in which he had declared, "Treason must be made odious, and traitors punished and impoverished." Furthermore, Johnson partially undercut Lincoln's initial pardon policy when on January 26, 1864, he issued a more stringent proclamation on the issue of restoring civil government in Tennessee.[44] According to the historian James Sefton, Johnson's proclamation generally employed "prose more ornate than Lincoln['s]."[45] For example, it noted the "disloyalty and hostility" of the many "enemies" in the state.

It also placed many restrictions and qualifications on those who could vote and required an oath of loyalty, which included the phrase "I ardently desire the suppression of the present insurrection and rebellion."[46] The oath was so strict that it became known as the "Damnesty Oath."[47] Lincoln nevertheless accepted Johnson's stricter policy in Tennessee as a matter of local decision making.[48]

Soon after Johnson became president, this general retributive attitude was apparently still in evidence. Just six days into his presidency, Johnson spoke at length to a delegation from Indiana about his attitude toward Confederates: "The time has arrived, my countrymen, when the American people should be educated and taught what is crime, and that treason is a crime, and the highest crime known to the law and the Constitution . . . and those engaged in it should suffer all its penalties."[49]

Momentarily stepping back from the sternness of those comments, Johnson then spoke of the possibility of mercy: "I know it is very easy to get up sympathy and sentiment where human blood is about to be shed, easy to acquire a reputation for leniency and kindness." That may well have been a reference to his predecessor, given Lincoln's reputation for being merciful. Johnson continued:

> But sometimes its effects and practical operations produce misery and woe to the mass of mankind. Sometimes an individual whom the law has overtaken, and on whom its penalties are about to be imposed, will appeal and plead with the Executive for the exercise of clemency. But before its exercise he ought to ascertain what is mercy and what is not mercy. It is a very important question, and one which deserves the consideration of those who moralize upon crime and the morals of a nation, whether in some cases action should not be suspended here and transferred to Him who controls all. There, if innocence has been invaded, if wrong has been done, the Controller and Giver of all good, one of whose attributes is mercy, will set it right.

Having broached the possibility of mercy, Johnson then returned in even stronger terms to his theme of punishment:

It is not promulgating anything that I have not heretofore said to say [*sic*] that traitors must be made odious, that treason must be made odious, that traitors must be punished and impoverished. They must not only be punished, but their social power must be destroyed. If not, they will still maintain an ascendancy, and may again become numerous and powerful; for in the words of a former senator of the United States, "when traitors become numerous enough, treason becomes respectable." And I say that, after making treason odious, every Union man and the Government should be remunerated out of the pockets of those who have inflicted this great suffering upon the country.

This obviously suggested that Johnson was not about to be lenient with Confederates. But in the next sentence Johnson articulated a more nuanced stance and suggested a more accommodating posture, at least toward the Confederate rank and file if not their leaders:

But do not understand me as saying this in a spirit of anger, for, if I understand my own heart, the reverse is the case; and while I say that the penalties of law, in a stern and inflexible manner, should be exercised upon the conscious, intelligent and influential traitors—the leaders, who have deceived thousands upon thousands of laboring men who have been drawn into this rebellion—and while I say, as to the leaders, punishment, I also say leniency; conciliation and amnesty to the thousands whom they have misled and deceived.

Ultimately, Johnson adopted the more forgiving stance that he hinted at in these remarks. Scholars differ as to whether the cause of Johnson's new magnanimity was the compliance of many erstwhile rebels or a wish to curry favor with white Southerners for political purposes, but for whatever reason Johnson came to embrace reconciliation.[50] Johnson issued a great number of unilateral directives to cease various restrictions that Lincoln had imposed on the South, especially for commercial trade. He also issued four separate proclamations of pardon and amnesty for erstwhile confederates between 1865 and 1868.

On April 21, 1865, not even a week after Lincoln's death, Johnson asked Attorney General James Speed to advise him about the power of the president to issue pardons. Johnson also asked about the "construction and effect" of Lincoln's proclamations of December 1863 and March 1864 and whether another amnesty should be offered.[51] Speed submitted a lengthy report on May 1, which stressed Lincoln's leniency and compassion and noted both the promise and the peril of forgiveness:

> The excellence of mercy and charity in a national trouble like ours ought not to be undervalued. Such feelings should be fondly cherished and studiously cultivated. When brought into action they should be generously but wisely indulged. Like all the great, necessary, and useful powers in nature or government, harm may come of their improvident use, and perils which seem past may be renewed, and other and new dangers be precipitated. But by a too extended, thoughtless, or unwise kindness the man of the government may warm into life an adder that will requite that kindness by a fatal sting from a poisonous fang.[52]

Speed also claimed that Lincoln's proclamations were intended to suppress the insurrection and to restore the authority of the federal government, so they were ineffective in the postwar period. Speed therefore advised Johnson to issue a new, wider amnesty proclamation.

JOHNSON'S FIRST PARDON

Like Lincoln, Johnson wanted to institute his pardon and Reconstruction policy unilaterally before Congress reconvened and sought to impose its own views, which would be far less lenient.[53] He carefully but quickly drafted a pardon proclamation and secured the unanimous approval of his cabinet.[54] On May 29, 1865, four weeks after receiving Speed's memo and just six weeks into his presidency, Johnson issued a proclamation of mass pardon.

Johnson's proclamation referenced both of Lincoln's mass-pardon proclamations, which it said were issued "with the object to suppress the existing rebellion, to induce all persons to return to their loyalty, and to restore the authority of the United States." After those references, Johnson's proclamation articulated the following rationales: "Whereas many persons who had so engaged in said rebellion have, since the issuance of said proclamations, failed or neglected to take the benefits offered thereby; and Whereas many persons who have been justly deprived of all claim to amnesty and pardon thereunder by reason of their participation, directly or by implication, in said rebellion and continued hostility to the Government of the United States since the date of said proclamations now desire to apply for and obtain amnesty and pardon." Johnson's pardon proclamation then cited the need to restore the authority of the United States and to establish "peace, order, and freedom."[55]

The amnesty would be granted to all who took the following oath: "I, _____, do solemnly swear or affirm, in presence of Almighty God, that I will henceforth faithfully support and defend the Constitution of the United States and the Union of the States thereunder. And that I will, in like manner, abide by and faithfully support all laws and proclamations which have been made during the existing rebellion with reference to the emancipation of slaves, so help me God." Johnson's proclamation explicitly "excepted" or excluded fourteen classes of people, which was more than Lincoln had excluded. The list of those ineligible for the pardon included people who had been high-ranking officials and agents "of the pretended Confederate government," who had left positions in the judiciary or Congress "to aid the rebellion," who had mistreated prisoners of war, and "who have been engaged in the destruction of the commerce of the United States." Johnson's pardon also excluded "all persons who, at the time when they seek to obtain the benefits hereof by taking the oath herein prescribed, are in military, naval, or civil confinement or custody, or under bonds of the civil, military, or naval authorities or agents of the United States as prisoners of war, or persons detained for offenses of any kind, either before or after conviction." It also exempted "all persons who have voluntarily participated in said rebellion and the estimated value of whose taxable property is over $20,000," thus targeting the Southern elite that Johnson so disliked. And it excluded "all persons who have taken the oath of amnesty as prescribed in the President's proclamation of December 8, A.D. 1863, or an oath of allegiance to the Government of the United States since the date of said proclamation and who have not thenceforward kept and maintained the same inviolate."

Johnson's proclamation of pardon said that people in the exempted classes could apply to the president for a pardon on an individual basis, "and such clemency will be liberally extended as may be consistent with the facts of the case and the peace and dignity of the United States." During the summer of 1865, many wealthy Southerners individually sought pardons from the president. By one count, Johnson pardoned Confederates at the rate of nearly 100 per day and by the fall of 1867 had issued more than 13,000 individual pardons.[56]

Robert E. Lee applied to Johnson for a pardon in June 1865 and signed a loyalty oath in October 1865, but he did not receive a pardon.[57] And Confederate general James Longstreet applied for a pardon in August 1865, but Johnson refused. In a personal discussion, Johnson told Longstreet, "There are three persons of the South who can never receive amnesty: Mr. Davis, General Lee, and yourself. You have given the Union cause too much trouble." Longstreet replied, "You know, Mr. President, that those who are forgiven most love the most." "Yes," said Johnson, "you have very high authority for that, but you can't have amnesty."[58] Johnson evidently changed his mind, though, because he pardoned Longstreet in 1867.

Many people were favorably impressed with Johnson's mass pardon. By one account, it "delighted Democrats, pleased Conservative Republicans, and relieved Southerners."[59] But it worried moderate Republicans and shocked the radicals, who thought that it was far too generous. As they saw it, Lincoln's pardons were intended largely to help win the war, but Johnson seemed more interested in using pardons to ease the federal government's postwar control of the South. Later in 1865, Congress sought to assert its own more demanding view of Reconstruction. Radical Republicans tried to curtail and undermine Johnson's amnesty policy via a series of laws that placed restrictions on pardoned Southerners. In *Ex parte Garland* (71 U.S. [4 Wall.] 333 [1866]), the Supreme Court struck down Congress's attempt to limit the impact of the president's pardon, but Congress and the president remained at odds over Reconstruction.

In September 1866, Johnson spoke to a crowd in St. Louis and defended his liberal pardon policy:

> I reckon I have pardoned more men, turned more loose and set them at liberty that were imprisoned, I imagine, than any other living man on God's habitable globe. Yes, I turned forty-seven thousand of our men who engaged in this struggle, with the arms we captured with them, and who were then in prison, I turned them loose. Large numbers of have applied for pardon, and I have granted them pardon. Yet there are some who condemn and hold me responsible for doing wrong. . . . There are some who can talk about blood, and vengeance, and crime, and everything to "make treason odious". . . . Yes, they can condemn others and recommend hanging and torture, and all that. If I have erred, I have erred on the side of mercy. . . . Think of it! To execute and hang, and put to death eight millions of people. It is an absurdity, and such a thing is impracticable even if it were right. But it is the violation of all law, human and divine.[60]

The question of how demanding Reconstruction should be was prominent in the midterm elections of 1866, which significantly strengthened Republicans. In the spring of 1867, radical Republicans seized control of Reconstruction and sought to use the military to force the South to accept black rights.

JOHNSON'S SECOND PARDON

More than two years after his first pardon, on September 7, 1867, Johnson issued another proclamation of amnesty in order to extend his pardon policy. It referenced Lincoln's two pardons and Johnson's first pardon as well as Congress's determination in 1861 that the Civil War was waged not for conquest but rather to preserve the Constitution and the Union, and it mentioned his proclamation of April 2, 1866—issued a year after his initial pardon proclamation—which declared that the insurrection had ended.

Johnson's new proclamation then stated that "there now exists no organized armed resistance of misguided citizens" and that "there no longer exists any reasonable ground to apprehend within the States which were involved in the late rebellion any renewal thereof." It explained, "Whereas large standing armies, military occupation, martial law, military tribunals, and the suspension of the privilege of the writ of *habeas corpus* and the right of trial by jury are in time of peace dangerous to public liberty, incompatible with the individual rights of the citizen, contrary to the genius and spirit of our free institutions, and exhaustive of the national resources, and ought not, therefore, to be sanctioned or allowed." And it noted that "a retaliatory or vindictive policy, attended by unnecessary disqualifications, pains, penalties, confiscations, and disfranchisements, now, as always, could only tend to hinder reconciliation among the people and national restoration, while it must seriously embarrass, obstruct, and repress popular energies and national industry and enterprise."[61]

After that lengthy preamble, the proclamation indicated that Johnson's first pardon would henceforth be extended to all people who had participated in the late rebellion, with the restoration of all privileges, immunities, and rights of property (except slaves), on the condition that such persons take an oath of allegiance contained in the proclamation, which was virtually identical to the one in his first mass pardon. The proclamation was sweeping and was intended to restore the vote to those who had been disenfranchised by congressional legislation.[62] However, some people were still exempted: "The chief or pretended chief executive officers of the late Confederacy, all heads of departments of the Confederate Government, all agents thereof in foreign States and countries, all having held military rank or title above the grade of Brigadier-General, or naval rank or title above that of Captain, all Governors of States, all persons having treated otherwise than as lawful prisoners of war persons in the military or naval service of the United States, and all persons, who were engaged, either directly or indirectly, in the assassination of the late President." By one account written at the time, Johnson's second pardon did not significantly extend the reach of his first pardon and perhaps really affected only a few hundred people.[63] Insofar as this claim is accurate, the second pardon may have been issued more for political effect than to advance a genuine process of reconciliation.

JOHNSON'S THIRD PARDON

Five months after his second proclamation, Johnson was impeached for his dismissal of Secretary of War Edwin Stanton and other matters. During his subsequent trial in the Senate, Johnson considered issuing a third, wider proclamation of amnesty. However, the initial House impeachment investigation included an allegation that "he has corruptly used the pardoning power," and the close Senate vote on removal from office—Johnson was acquitted by one vote in May 1868—might have temporarily dissuaded him from further antagonizing Congress with a universal amnesty.[64] Ultimately, however, on July 4, 1868, he did issue a third mass-pardon proclamation.

Johnson's Independence Day pardon proclamation contained several justifications. It referenced the four previous pardons pertaining to the Civil War (i.e., the two by Lincoln and the two by Johnson); noted that the "lamentable civil war has long since ceased"; expressed a desire to end military occupation and wartime legal restrictions on people and the press; and echoed his previous pardon's language that "such encroachments upon our free institutions in time of peace [are] dangerous to public liberty, incompatible with the individual rights of the citizen, contrary to the genius and spirit of our republican form of government, and exhaustive of national resources." The proclamation also contained the following statement of its goals: "Whereas it is believed that amnesty and pardon will tend to secure a complete and universal establishment and prevalence of municipal law and order in conformity with the Constitution of the United States, and to remove all appearances or presumptions of a retaliatory or vindictive policy on the part of the Government attended by unnecessary disqualifications, pains, penalties, confiscations, and disfranchisements, and, on the contrary, to promote and procure complete fraternal reconciliation among the whole people, with due submission to the Constitution and laws."[65]

Johnson's third pardon restored property rights and exempted only those who were under indictment for treason or other felonies, thereby excluding perhaps just three hundred people. Significantly, it did not require a loyalty oath, as had his first two pardons as well as Lincoln's two pardons. Therefore, Johnson did not need to convince the recipients of this pardon, who were covered and pardoned whether they liked it or not. But broader political considerations such as Johnson's political future and national reconciliation nevertheless required some rhetorical attention. Indeed, Johnson's third pardon may have been intended in part to appeal to Southern delegates at the Democratic National Convention, which started on the very day he issued the new proclamation, July 4.[66]

Presidential efforts at reconciliation via mass pardon soon had to contend with a major constitutional change, though: the Fourteenth Amendment, which was ratified in July 1868, two years after Congress had proposed it and very shortly after Johnson's third proclamation. The amendment is perhaps best known for seeking to secure the rights of newly freed slaves via its due process and equal protection clauses and its definition of citizenship, but it also addressed those who had engaged in rebellion against the United States. Sections 2–4 of the amendment made exemptions for erstwhile rebels for voting, holding high office, and debts, effectively disenfranchising many people who had received presidential pardons and thus significantly limiting the ability of presidential pardons to fully bring former rebels back into the national fold.[67]

JOHNSON'S FOURTH PARDON

Five months after his third pardon and less than three months before the end of his presidency, Johnson issued a fourth pardon on December 25,

1868. His Christmas proclamation was a universal amnesty that covered all who remained unpardoned for their role in supporting the rebellion, which meant that it covered those under indictment in federal court.[68] It was the shortest of Johnson's four mass-pardon proclamations and, like its predecessor, did not require an oath.[69] According to the historian Frank Klingberg, "Thereafter only the disabilities imposed under the Fourteenth Amendment remained to bar a group of high-ranking military and civil officers of the Confederacy, initially estimated at twenty thousand, from holding national office unless specifically relieved by Congress. Such relief was generally granted on application."[7]

Johnson's fourth proclamation briefly noted each of the five previous presidential mass pardons for Confederates and said there was no longer a need for their "reservations and exceptions," which "may now wisely and justly be relinquished." It also stated the belief that a universal amnesty "will tend to secure permanent peace, order, and prosperity throughout the land, and to renew and fully restore confidence and fraternal feeling among the whole people, and their respect for and attachment to the National Government, designed by its patriotic founders for the general good." The proclamation then declared "unconditionally and without reservation, to all and to every person who, directly or indirectly, participated in the late insurrection or rebellion a full pardon and amnesty for the offense of treason against the United States or of adhering to their enemies during the late civil war, with restoration of all rights."[71]

Although Johnson's final pardon was thus presented in general terms, it may well have been motivated by a desire to avoid drawn-out legal proceedings against former Confederate president Jefferson Davis, who had been imprisoned in May 1865. Davis was initially suspected of being part of a conspiracy to assassinate Lincoln, but in May 1866 he was indicted for treason. A year later he was released on bail (provided by Horace Greeley and others), but then he was indicted again in 1868, and his trial had just begun when Johnson issued his pardon.

Davis had wanted to defend secession as constitutionally permissible. He also objected to a portion of the oath in Johnson's first two proclamations: "To abide by and faithfully support all laws and proclamations which have been made during the existing rebellion with reference to the emancipation of slaves." This proviso was objectionable to Davis because he regarded the Emancipation Proclamation as illegitimate and unconstitutional, and he wanted to contest the point. He complained later in his history of the Confederate government that "the Confederate citizen was required to bind himself by an oath to abide by and faithfully support all these usurpations."[72] Johnson's fourth pardon ensured that Davis could not defend his views in court, nor could he become a martyr for the Confederate cause. The pardon also avoided an authoritative judicial decision about the constitutionality of secession.

AFTER AMNESTY

Johnson's amnesty was the sixth and final presidential mass pardon for Confederates, and it came more than five years after Lincoln conferred the first pardon. Altogether, these pardons gradually became broader in scope, less limited, and less demanding, moving from conditional pardon for some to blanket amnesty for all. They helped to end the war and to foster reconciliation.

But the effectiveness of the six mass pardons for the Civil War was limited by several factors. This constraint may be seen in in terms of the politics of Reconstruction, the actions of legislative and judicial branches, the limits of Johnson's amnesty for Jefferson Davis, the decision of some Confederates to leave the United States, and the general culture of postbellum America. Each of these five points merits some attention here.

RECONSTRUCTION

The contested politics of Reconstruction and its legacy offers evidence of the mixed efficacy of the Civil War pardons. Lincoln's first mass pardon sought to hasten the end of the war and to initiate the process whereby states could return to self-governance and the Union, which was a crucial part of Reconstruction, the process of reintegrating the South. Johnson, of course, had a different, more conciliatory view of Reconstruction, which informed his own pardons and led to major battles with congressional Republicans, who were intent on instituting their own more demanding version.[73] The variegated process of Reconstruction was effectively terminated by the Compromise of 1877, when Rutherford B. Hayes agreed to withdraw federal troops from the state capitol buildings of South Carolina and Louisiana, leading to the end of Republican state governance in the South and the rise of revanchist "Redeemer" regimes that quickly reestablished white supremacy. According to most contemporary historians, Reconstruction failed, and the South was not truly remade or reintegrated but rather persisted as a region apart.[74] The politics of Reconstruction have long been controversial, but for the analysis here the main point is that insofar as some of the six Civil War pardons were tied to one side or another of this controversial project that was never fully realized, they cannot all have been effective.

CONGRESS AND THE COURTS

The other two branches differed in their reactions to the presidential policy of reconciliation via mass pardons. Many Republican members of Congress were not sympathetic to some of the presidential pardons. As Klingberg explains, "Congressional reconstruction in fact involved the use of other weapons, including test and loyalty oaths and the reconstruction acts and amendment, to contest the presidential program."[75] Indeed, "presidential proclamations of pardon during the late 1860s had run almost directly counter to the ever-more-restrictive acts on Capitol Hill."[76] For example, the Senate required that its members take an "ironclad oath" that they had never aided the Confederacy, as if a presidential pardon did not exculpate them, and Congress "refused to seat representatives elected by persons amnestied by Presidents Lincoln and Johnson."[77] However, congressional hostility gradually eased. The oath requirement was repealed in 1884, and Congress acted in 1869, 1872, and 1898 to lift sanctions against former Confederates that had been imposed by the Fourteenth Amendment.[78]

In contrast to Congress's resistance, the judiciary generally acceded to the executive's pardons as a matter of legitimate presidential prerogative. As discussed in chapter 1, cases such as *Ex parte Garland* (1866), *U.S. v. Klein* (13 Wall. [80 U.S. 20] 128 [1871]), *Armstrong v. United States* (80 U.S. 154 [1871]), and *Knote v. United States* (95 U.S. 149 [1877]) upheld the president's right to grant pardons as he saw fit without legislative interference and upheld the exculpatory impact of the pardons. As Klingberg recounts, "Pardons were liberally interpreted by the courts as restoring discharge of guilt for complicity in the rebellion. Not a single life was taken, few were even indicted for treason or conspiracy, and all prosecutions were eventually dropped."[79]

DAVIS

Although Johnson's fourth and final pardon absolved former Confederate president Jefferson Davis from federal crimes such as treason and restored his civil and property rights, Davis still could not hold federal office as he had before the Civil War. He was excluded from congressional acts that eliminated the restrictions on most former Confederates. As the National Constitution Center explains, "In 1872, the Amnesty Act was amended to allow almost all former Confederates, except for several hundred former high-ranking officials (such as Davis), to hold public office." Furthermore, "in 1876, Davis was specifically excluded from a universal amnesty bill that restored the full citizenship rights of the remaining former Confederates."[80] Davis could have overcome these disabilities by seeking an individual pardon from the president, but he did not want to do so. In 1884, Davis told the Mississippi legislature, "It has been said that I should apply to the United States for a pardon, but repentance must precede the right of pardon, and I have not repented." Thus, even after the many pardons, the Confederate president was not reconciled and remained at odds with the

U.S. government, both legally and politically. As we will see, resentment over the limitations on Davis would linger until the 1970s.

EXILE

Another respect in which the six presidential mass pardons failed to achieve full reconciliation is that thousands of Confederates chose to leave the country rather than to reconcile with the federal government. By one count, "as many as 10,000 former Confederates would leave the country, to spread out in colonies in Mexico, Venezuela, Belize, Brazil, and even Canada, while the rest simply wandered. A few wound up in the Egyptian army, others spread across Europe."[81] Indeed, 8,000 to 20,000 Confederates left the South for Brazil in the 1860s and 1870s at the invitation of Emperor Dom Pedro II.[82] Brigadier General Joseph Shelby led hundreds of volunteers from his cavalry division to Mexico, where Emperor Maximilian gave them free land near Veracruz. According to the historian George Horne, others fled to Fiji and elsewhere in the Pacific. Some wanted to continue to practice slavery, and others feared they might be prosecuted for treason in the United States despite the presidential pardons.[83]

Many of these former Confederates later ended their self-imposed exile and returned to the United States.[84] For example, John Breckenridge—who had served as James Buchanan's vice president and ran for president in 1860 before becoming the Confederate secretary of war—fled to Cuba, Great Britain, and Canada but returned to the United States after Johnson's final amnesty was issued. Brigadier General Shelby returned to the United States two years after he left. He initially refused to take an oath of loyalty to the Constitution but relented after he took a position as a federal marshal in 1893. Some Confederates who had fled did not return. For example, Judah Benjamin, who held several leadership positions in the Confederate States of America and has been called the "brains of the Confederacy," went into exile in England after the Confederate surrender and remained abroad for the rest of his life.[85]

POSTBELLUM POLITICAL CULTURE

Another way to gauge the limited impact of the six mass pardons is to briefly consider the broader political culture of the United States after the Civil War. Even before the premature end of Reconstruction, efforts were under way to recast the terms of the Civil War and its broader significance. Although the war was fought primarily over what Senator John Calhoun euphemistically called the "peculiar institution" of slavery, shortly after the war's conclusion some Southerners began to regard the war as a noble but failed effort to defend a distinct way of life, which in 1866 editor Edward Pollard of the *Richmond Examiner* called the "lost cause." Depending on one's point of view, the lost-cause narrative was either harmless nostalgia or self-serving revisionism that sought to rewrite the history of the war. Regardless, it suggests that true political reconciliation was not achieved because many Southerners simply reinterpreted the conflict after the fact in order to make it better comport with their self-image and interest.[86]

The historian Nina Silber offers another view of American political culture in the decades after the Civil War. In *The Romance of Reunion*, Silber claims that in the years following the Civil War some Northerners thought that reconciliation had gone too far. For example, she quotes John Logan, who was instrumental in establishing Memorial Day in the late 1860s. Logan complained, "'Conciliation' and 'forgiveness' . . . have gone on the rampage and apologies have been as thick as autumnal leaves." Similarly, Silber quotes a speaker in Philadelphia who "claimed that the Memorial Day 'spirit is violated, and our beautiful ceremonial made either meaningless or a mockery when the same honor is shown to those who died to destroy as those who died to save.'"[87]

However, Silber suggests that such critics of reconciliation were in the minority and had largely faded into obscurity by the time Reconstruction ended. Moreover, she contends that shortly after Reconstruction ended, the nation became infatuated with stories of reconciliation between North and South, or "the romance of reunion." She describes "the late nineteenth century's culture of reconciliation, a movement that had roots in Reconstruction but did not fully blossom until the

1880s and 1890s. In those two decades the reunion theme was strong in many quarters throughout northern society." She says that "numerous groups paid homage to the ideology of reunion" and that "people sought to pay homage to a culture of healing and unity."[88]

Even if the South was not altogether reconciled or reintegrated, the six mass pardons discussed here did help to move the country beyond the violence of the war and to bring many supporters of the Confederacy more or less back into the national fold. Altogether, the multiple pardons of Confederates by two presidents over five years ameliorated the bitter divisions of the Civil War, even in the face of congressional hostility, and they influenced future mass pardons for other matters.[89]

Indeed, the Civil War pardons are not simply a matter of antiquarian interest because the question of pardons for Confederates continued through the nineteenth century and even influenced the debate a century later about amnesty for Vietnam War draft evaders and military deserters. In 1977, Jimmy Carter explained this connection: "I also have an historical perspective about this question. I come from the South. I know at the end of the War Between the States, there was a sense of forgiveness for those who had been not loyal to our country in the past."[9]

For presidents in the 1970s, the Civil War pardons were not just an influence on contemporary debates but also something to be revisited. In August 1975, Gerald Ford signed Senate Joint Resolution 23, which restored full citizenship rights to Robert E. Lee. Three years later, in October 1978, Jimmy Carter approved Senate Joint Resolution 16, which extended similar amnesty to Jefferson Davis. In his signing statement, Carter explained why the measure was appropriate:

In posthumously restoring the full rights of citizenship to Jefferson Davis, the Congress officially completes the long process of reconciliation that has reunited our people following the tragic conflict between the States. Earlier, he was specifically exempted from resolutions restoring the rights of other officials in the Confederacy. He had served the United States long and honorably as a soldier, Member of the U.S.

House and Senate, and as Secretary of War. General Robert E. Lee's citizenship was restored in 1976. It is fitting that Jefferson Davis should no longer be singled out for punishment. Our Nation needs to clear away the guilts and enmities and recriminations of the past, to finally set at rest the divisions that threatened to destroy our Nation and to discredit the principles on which it was founded. Our people need to turn their attention to the important tasks that still lie before us in establishing those principles for all people.[91]

As Francis MacDonnell notes, "The separate measures assured that the two deceased Confederates might legally hold public office and serve jury duty," but their primary impact was of course symbolic. According to MacDonnell, "Their willingness to oppose the federal government because of principle struck a responsive note in a nation disillusioned by Vietnam," and "the two ex-Confederates benefitted from the urge for national reconciliation that followed the divisions of Vietnam."[92] In short, the six Civil War pardons had an impact that extended far beyond their own immediate historical context.

5

VIETNAM WAR RESISTERS

Gerald Ford and Jimmy Carter

As I reject amnesty, so I reject revenge.

—GERALD FORD, 1974

Amnesty means that what you did was right; a pardon means that what you did, right or wrong, is forgiven. So a pardon yes, amnesty no.

—JIMMY CARTER, 1976

T he Vietnam War is arguably the most recent case of a U.S. president using a mass pardon or amnesty for domestic political reconciliation as well as the only one in anyone's living memory or that played out in part on television. More than a century after the Civil War pardons, two presidents once again sought to use a mass pardon to remove the taint of criminality and exclusion from another significantly aggrieved and alienated group within the national community: draft evaders and military deserters from the U.S. war in Southeast Asia.

The American war in Vietnam essentially ended on August 15, 1973, with the cessation of U.S. military involvement after a decade of armed conflict and the deaths of more than 58,000 U.S. military personnel and 2 to 3 million Vietnamese combatants and civilians. Public support for

American military involvement in Vietnam declined steadily through-out the war. In 1965, 61 percent of Americans agreed with the war, but that figure fell to just 28 percent in 1971, which was the last year Gallup polled on the question. By 1967, a majority of Americans thought the war had been a mistake, and 61 percent of respondents in 1971 said that the United States had made a mistake in sending troops to Vietnam.[1]

The Vietnam War was greatly controversial, but there was also con-troversy about military conscription or "the draft." Between 1964 and 1973, 2.2 million people were drafted. Draftees accounted for 25 per-cent of all U.S. forces in Vietnam and 30 percent of combat deaths. The question of who would be drafted was intensely controversial. As the Vietnam veteran and popular author Karl Marlantes puts it, "The draft was unfair. Only males got drafted. And men who could afford to go to college did not get drafted until late in the war, when the fighting had fallen off."[2] Military induction was directed via presidential order until 1969, but between 1969 and 1972 the Selective Service employed a lot-tery based on one's date of birth to determine who would be con-scripted, with provisions for various exemptions and deferments. By one account, "Up to 60 percent of men in the Vietnam generation took active measures to qualify for a deferment from the draft."[3] But it was more difficult for poor people to obtain deferments, for example by going to college. By 1967, "fewer than half of Americans polled believed that the draft operated fairly."[4] And by 1972, there were more conscientious-objector exemptions granted than there were draftees actually inducted into the military.

MASSIVE RESISTANCE

Opposition to the war and the draft led to numerous protests. In April 1967, some 500,000 people demonstrated in New York against the war.[5] During a Stop the Draft Week in October 1967, more than 1,000 men burned or returned their draft cards to the Justice Department, greatly angering President Lyndon Johnson.[6] That same month Philip

Berrigan and three other members of the Baltimore Four poured animal blood on draft records at a Selective Service Board. In May 1968, Berrigan, his brother Daniel, and seven other members of the Catonsville Nine raided a Maryland draft board and burned four hundred draft files with homemade napalm.[7] The antiwar movement grew throughout the late 1960s. On October 15, 1969, more than 2 million Americans participated in a "national moratorium" to end the war, with protests occurring across the country. On November 3, 1969, Richard Nixon told the country that he would not let a "vocal minority" impose its antiwar views on the "silent majority" by "mounting demonstrations in the street."[8] But on November 15, 1969, in one of the largest political rallies in American history, well more than half a million people demonstrated in Washington, DC, against the war.

Many colleges and universities saw protests against the war, and several major universities were forcibly taken over by student protesters in 1968 and 1969. In March 1969, Nixon said of such protests, "It is not too strong a statement to declare that this is the way civilizations begin to die."[9] In April 1970, he again complained about campus protests, telling the country that "great universities are being systematically destroyed."[10] One month later protesters effectively closed hundreds of universities. In May 1972, Nixon described the antiwar movement as "a wild orgasm of anarchists sweeping across the country like a prairie fire."[11]

As elements of the antiwar movement became more radical, some activists moved from protesting the war to taking direct action against it—for example, by damaging military aircraft and bombs and trying to block a naval vessel.[12] At dozens of campuses, Reserve Officers' Training Corps (ROTC) offices and other buildings were vandalized or firebombed. The militant Weathermen group undertook violent acts against police, banks, and companies and bombed governmental buildings, including the U.S. Capitol, the Pentagon, and the State Department.

Beyond protests, hundreds of thousands of Americans resisted, evaded, or violated the draft. Accounts of the numbers of people involved vary widely, but there were roughly 600,000 such people, compared with 2.2 million who were drafted during the war.[13] These people failed to register for the draft, registered but then failed to report for induction, were inducted but then deserted, or failed to complete service programs for conscientious objectors. In addition, many civilians were charged with various crimes for opposing the war.[14]

GOVERNMENTAL RESPONSES

The government responded in several ways to the massive resistance to the war and the draft. One response was mass arrests. When a large protest in Washington, DC, threatened to shut down the city in May 1971, the U.S. attorney general ordered military forces and the National Guard to aid the local police in arresting more than 7,000 people—the largest mass arrest in U.S. history. State governors also made use of the National Guard. For example, Governor Ronald Reagan of California sent in 2,200 National Guard troops to break up a massive rally at the University of California at Berkeley in 1969. One thousand people were subsequently arrested, including two hundred for felonies.

Many other state governors sent the National Guard to campuses to maintain order. In 1970 alone, National Guard units "were activated on 24 occasions at 21 universities in 16 states."[15] Governors' use of the National Guard was often accompanied by strident rhetoric. For example, in March 1970 Reagan threatened, "If it takes a bloodbath to silence the demonstrators, let's get it over with."[16] In May 1970, Governor James Rhodes of Ohio sent nearly a thousand National Guard soldiers to Kent State University to subdue campus protesters, whom he said were "worse than the brown shirt and the communist element and also the night riders and vigilantes. They're the worst type of people."[17] And that same month the armed response to the campus unrest produced deadly results, with four people shot to death at Kent State and two at Jackson State.

Criminal prosecution was another way that government responded because violating the draft was illegal. But some resisters were willing to pay the price, and some even welcomed criminal prosecution as a way to put the war on trial. As David Harris explains, "I picked prison over fighting in Vietnam." Of the hundreds of thousands of Americans who violated the draft, 360,000 were investigated but not charged, and more than 209,000 were accused of a crime, but fewer than 9,000 were convicted. The latter group included the boxer Muhammad Ali, who in 1967 was sentenced to five years for not reporting for induction. According to Harris, "About 25,000 of us were indicted for our disobedience, almost 9,000 convicted and 3,250 jailed." But there were "so many violators that it was impossible to prosecute more than a fraction."[18]

Apart from making mass arrests, calling in the National Guard, and using the criminal justice system, another governmental response was the monitoring and attempted suppression of antiwar protests by major federal intelligence organizations. The Central Intelligence Agency (CIA), in violation of its own charter and against the advice of an internal management advisory group, used its Domestic Operations Division to engage in espionage on American citizens in the United States and eventually compiled files on more than 300,000 Americans.[19] The CIA also created the MH/CHAOS Program to illegally spy on some 10,000 antiwar activists in the United States and even on certain members of Congress who opposed the war.[20] The Federal Bureau of Investigation (FBI) added antiwar activists to its Security Index, "a listing of individuals deemed a threat to internal security" and thus who might be detained in a national emergency.[21] And under J. Edgar Hoover's direct leadership, the FBI's Cold War Counterintelligence Program (COINTELPRO) was expanded to surveil, target, and harass thousands of antiwar groups and individuals, including the musician John Lennon, in order to unsettle protest leaders, sow uncertainty, and "enhance the paranoia endemic in these circles."[22]

EXILE

Beyond those who publicly protested, some 20,000 to 80,000 draft resisters and military deserters went underground in the United States to evade criminal charges.[23] In addition, many Americans who sought to evade the draft went abroad and became exiles. As the well-known journalist Julius Duscha wrote in 1972, "For the first time in the history of the land of the free and the brave . . . a sizable number of citizens have fled their country or gone underground rather than fight in a war that they deemed to be unjust, and that most Americans now agree is unjust, including many of the men who helped propel the United States into Vietnam and set in motion the draft machinery which tens of thousands of young Americans defied."[24]

Many of those who fled went to Canada.[25] Estimates of the numbers of Americans who went to Canada range from 60,000 to 100,000.[26] One of them was Jack Todd, who enlisted in the Marine Corps but deserted in 1970 and moved to Canada. Todd denied that fleeing the United States meant he was a coward, saying, "That was the bravest thing I have ever done." As Todd said of the movement of Americans to Canada, "It has been called the largest politically motivated migration from the U.S. since the Empire Loyalists moved north during the American Revolution."[27]

Repatriation was difficult because the exiles faced prosecution. In addition, "returning to the United States meant facing families and communities who were scornful of their decision to abandon the country. As one woman who came to Canada with her husband to avoid the war reflected, 'My family was so scandalized by our choice to come to Canada . . . going back was never an option.'"[28] Without some sort of amnesty, "most draft dodgers and military deserters could not realistically consider returning to the United States."[29]

HOW TO HEAL?

The war bitterly divided Americans, and it continued to produce political controversy long after the end of military hostilities. As Craig Allen Smith and Kathy Smith explain, "Americans were sharply divided over Vietnam. . . . Americans argued about the fate of those who had dodged or evaded the draft. One interpretive community felt that they should be treated as traitors, another camp felt that the resolution of the war had vindicated their opposition to the war, and animosity between the communities ran high."[30] Obviously, this situation represented a major opportunity for official reconciliation, perhaps via amnesty or some sort of presidential mass pardon.

There were numerous precedents of presidents before the twentieth-century pardoning Americans who had avoided military conscription or had deserted once they were in the military, including during the Revolutionary War, the War of 1812, and the Civil War. In the twentieth century, Woodrow Wilson commuted death sentences for World War I deserters. Warren Harding released Eugene V. Debs and many others who were imprisoned for opposing conscription. In 1923, Calvin Coolidge granted a general pardon to people jailed under wartime draft or espionage laws, and in 1924 he gave amnesty to deserters. In 1933, Franklin D. Roosevelt restored all rights of citizenship to people who had violated the draft. And Harry Truman issued several amnesties for people who had resisted military service during World War II.[31] The resistance to participating in those military conflicts was perhaps less widespread and less politicized than in the Vietnam War case, which saw massive open resistance to the draft and to the war that it served. Regardless of the extent or nature of difference, a president in the 1970s could invoke various precedents to deal with the hundreds of thousands of Americans who had violated mandatory military service in Vietnam.

Debates about some sort of pardon or amnesty for draft resisters were prominent in the 1970s. As Duscha wrote in 1972, "Not since the Civil War has amnesty been as emotional a question as it is today."[32] But recent academic treatments of the period do not always accord amnesty the significance it deserves. For example, writing in 2015, the historian Jason Friedman claimed that the literature on the Vietnam War "largely ignores the debate over amnesty."[33] Indeed, the popular PBS miniseries *The Vietnam War* by Ken Burns and Lynn Novick, aired in 2017, did not discuss it. Nevertheless, this chapter explores the debates about amnesty at some length to demonstrate why and how two presidents in the 1970s sought to use both words and deeds to achieve political reconciliation.

CONGRESS

Members of Congress debated the possibility of pardon or amnesty for draft resisters and others over many years. In 1971, Senator George McGovern (D–SD) came out in favor of amnesty, saying, "I urge that when the war ends amnesty be granted to those who, on the grounds of conscience, have refused to participate in the Vietnam tragedy."[34] Later that year Senator Robert Taft (R–OH) introduced legislation to provide what he labeled a "conditional amnesty." The proposal would have precluded prosecution of draft evaders if they would subsequently serve three years in the military or a federal agency.[35] On the House side, Representative Ed Koch (D–NY) sponsored a bill calling for conditional amnesty in 1971.[36] And in spring 1972, Representative Bella Abzug (D–NY) sponsored a bill for unconditional amnesty called the War Resisters Exoneration Act.[37]

In the course of considering various bills about amnesty, the ninety-second and ninety-third Congresses held hearings on the matter. At a Senate hearing in early 1972, Arlo Tatum of the Central Committee for Conscientious Objectors made the case for amnesty on the grounds that "amnesty is non-judgmental." The historian Henry Steele Commager told the senators, "If the war in Southeast Asia is a mistake from which we are even now extricating ourselves, is it just that we should punish those who—at whatever cost—helped dramatize that mistake?... If we are to restore harmony to our society and unity to our nation we should put aside all vindictiveness, all inclination for punishment, all attempts to cast a balance of patriotism or of sacrifice—a task to which no mortal is competent—as unworthy of a great nation."[38] And David Harris, who served twenty-one months in prison for draft evasion and was the husband of popular singer Joan Baez, presented Congress with a stronger demand: "I told the senators I had no use for their forgiveness, but I would accept their apology."[39] In February 1972, Senator Edward Kennedy (D–MA) framed the debate this way at a hearing: "The issue generates strong emotions across the country. How, some ask, can amnesty be offered to those who fled when others fought? But, others assert, how can amnesty not be offered to those who were right about the war before the rest of us?"[40]

In March 1974, former secretary of the army Robert Froehlke appeared at a House hearing and spoke in favor of a blanket conditional amnesty with a three-month alternate service requirement:

> Amnesty is an act that only a strong, confident and just nation can bestow. You cannot demand amnesty. You cannot threaten amnesty. Amnesty is given. . . . [W]e need to begin mending in every way possible the heartbreak and wounds left by that war. . . . [I]t is clear that right or wrong, Vietnam deeply hurt America. . . . In less than 30 years we have forgiven our former enemies—Germany and Japan. . . . If we will forgive entire nations and hundreds of millions of "enemies," then can't we consider forgiveness, rehabilitation and reinstatement of only a few thousand of our brothers?. . . America is a strong, confident nation of strong, confident and just people who have long demonstrated a capacity to forgive and forget. These people would consider amnesty. The meek, the mean, the insecure cannot forgive and forget. Instead, they would demand recrimination, indulge in devisiveness [*sic*], wallow in self-flagellation. Theirs is to counterattack against those who turned and ran when the nation needed them. Theirs is to punish, and punish again, the men who wronged them. These people would not consider amnesty, but they are not America's people. . . . We should forgive and forget if amnesty will help heal the hurt this nation has suffered. . . . Is there a more noble deed than for a strong, forgiving America to say to those who left, come home now? I think not.[41]

Froehlke also reportedly said, "I want to see an attitude on the part of a vast majority of Americans—a lack of vindictiveness, a generosity and mercy. . . . It should not be, 'Okay, we'll let them come back but we want them to pay': rather, 'We want them back.'"[42]

In 1975, Representative Henry Helstoski (D–NJ) introduced the Vietnam Era Reconciliation Act, which would have provided immunity from prosecution and punishment for draft resisters and military deserters, but the bill did not advance. Despite the many legislative proposals and hearings about amnesty over several years, Congress could not come to a consensus on the issue. As Senator Philip Hart (D–MI) put it in December 1975, "Congress lacks the guts to do anything about amnesty."[43]

THE PRESIDENCY

Beyond Congress, debates about amnesty factored into the presidential campaign of 1972. In August that year, Vice President Spiro Agnew attacked Democratic candidate George McGovern for his support of amnesty. Agnew said, "The President has announced that he is opposed to the granting of any general or unconditional amnesty for those who evaded the draft. . . . He believes that, when the war is over and our prisoners are released, anyone who has evaded the draft must pay a penalty before receiving a pardon."[44] Indeed, during the presidential campaign in 1972, conservatives embraced the slogan of opposition to "amnesty, acid, and abortion."[45] One month before the election, Nixon told the parents of a young man who was killed in Vietnam, "The few hundred that deserted this country, the draft dodgers, are never going to get amnesty when boys like yours died, never. They are going to have to pay a penalty for what they did. That's the way I feel."[46]

The question of amnesty arguably posed difficulties for both of the presidential candidates in 1972 because they initially adopted stances that they later had to temper. Early on, Nixon indicated that although he felt deserters and draft dodgers should have to pay some sort of price, he might nevertheless be "very liberal" in his treatment of them. As the campaign progressed, however, Nixon did not repeat his promise of liberality. In January 1972, when the journalist Dan Rather asked Nixon, "Is there *no* amount of alternative service under which you could foresee granting amnesty?," Nixon replied, "As long as there are any POWs held by the North Vietnamese, there will be no amnesty for those who have deserted their country."[47] And although McGovern had called for general amnesty a year before the election (despite his wife's warning that such a position was not altogether popular), just one month before it he spoke of alternative service as appropriate.[48] According to one newspaper report written soon after the election, in January 1973, "[The candidates'] shifts were a signal that though seven years of war might be over, some of that war's central questions—bitter and divisive ones—remain facing the public and will not go away: Was it a just war? Were the young men who avoided the fighting cowards and traitors who betrayed their country or were they heroes and patriots who showed their country the way to a new high level of morality?"[49] Despite Nixon's landslide victory over McGovern in November 1972, the Vietnam War continued to be controversial, as did the debate about whether or how to reconcile with draft evaders and deserters.

GERALD FORD

Gerald Ford is often regarded as little more than a caretaker president, an unassuming individual who served out the remainder of Nixon's second term and did little of note other than pardon his predecessor. Ford seemed to encourage the view of him as a modest public servant. Upon taking the oath of office to become vice president in December 1973, he declared, "I'm a Ford, not a Lincoln," using the automobile pun to indicate that he was a regular person and not a distinguished figure.

Notwithstanding his claim of being unremarkable, Ford ascended to the presidency in a manner no one else ever had, following the resignation of Nixon on August 9, 1974. The nation was bitterly divided by the events of the 1960s, the Vietnam War, Watergate, and Nixon's presidency. As Donald Rumsfeld wrote several decades later, "What Nixon was passing over to Ford was a government so rocked by turbulence and trauma that it was a very real question whether the American experiment might be wrecked."[50] This situation was challenging for any leader, let alone for one who came into office in so unusual a manner, without a political mandate. Nevertheless, Americans seemed to want to give the new president a chance. As the historian John Robert Greene explains, "People wanted to believe that the Ford administration could heal America."[51]

Ford had served in the U.S. Navy in World War II, and as the House minority leader in the late 1960s he had opposed any form of amnesty for those who sought to evade compulsory military service in the Vietnam War. As Nixon's vice president, Ford had continued to oppose amnesty and said that draft evaders should face criminal charges. However, once he became president, his attitude began to change. As Greene explains,

> Despite entreaties from his three sons, who were vocally in favor of some sort of amnesty, Ford continued to be philosophically opposed to it; however, the political realities of August 1974 led him to soften his beliefs. Faced by a battery of questions from the press about the fate of Richard Nixon, several of Ford's key advisors, including Secretary of Defense James Schlesinger, argued that some sort of reentry plan for Vietnam-era protestors would cement Ford's image as a conciliator, giving him the opportunity to bring to an end one part of the "long national nightmare" of the sixties. Most important, they argued that it was just the sort of dramatic jump start that the new administration needed, allowing Ford to draw a distinction between the Ford and the Nixon administrations.[52]

Other accounts paint a similar picture of Ford's evolving views about amnesty per the idea that some sort of accommodation could help to unify the nation and differentiate Ford's administration from Nixon's.[53] Thus, a variety of political motives influenced Ford's approach to the issue. Despite his previous resistance to any form of pardon, the prospect of helping the divided country to put the war behind it while also advancing his own presidency caused Ford to rethink his position. He ultimately decided to propose a program of limited, earned clemency.

FORD'S ANNOUNCEMENT

Ford announced his plan for clemency for draft evaders on August 19, 1974, just eleven days into his presidency, three weeks before his pardon of Nixon, and well before the actual clemency policy went into effect. He made the announcement in Chicago during his first presidential address outside Washington, DC. And he did it in a dramatic and challenging venue—a convention of the Veterans of Foreign Wars (VFW), which was obviously an unsympathetic audience for the occasion.

As the historian Richard Norton Smith remarks, "Anyone else . . . would have put out a press release on Friday afternoon and headed to Camp David."[54] But Ford had given careful thought to the location for his announcement. Before going to the convention, he told his wife, Betty, "It would have been a little cowardice, I think, if I'd picked an audience that was ecstatic. You can't talk about healing unless you are going to use it in the broadest context."[55] As Greene puts it, "No doubt Ford saw himself as if he were Daniel walking into the lions' den."[56] But as the communications scholar Mary Stuckey explains, Ford purposely chose an unsympathetic crowd for his announcement: "In deciding to face a presumptively hostile audience, the president earned some praise for political courage while potentially taking some of the controversial edge off the announcement. His real audience, then, was the media and the American people. The immediate audience served his larger purpose of conveying a particular kind of image to those larger audiences."[57]

There was no advance indication that Ford would announce his support for any sort of pardon, and the text of his speech made available to reporters beforehand did not mention it, so it was a surprise. Ford began his address by reminding the audience of his membership in the VFW and speaking of the need for better care for veterans. He then noted his public attitude toward amnesty: "As minority leader of the House and recently as Vice President, I stated my strong conviction that unconditional, blanket amnesty for anyone who illegally evaded or fled military service is wrong. It is wrong."[58]

Having thus ingratiated himself with the group, Ford began to prepare it for a shift. He reminded the audience that he had previously referred to divine considerations of justice and mercy: "Yet, in my first words as President of all the people, I acknowledged a Power, higher than the people, Who commands not only righteousness but love, not only justice but mercy." Indeed, in his inauguration speech, immediately after declaring that "our long national nightmare is over," Ford had said, "There is a Power, by whatever name we honor Him, who ordains not only righteousness but love, not only justice but mercy."[59]

After Ford reminded the VFW attendees of the importance of mercy, he spoke of his place in a particular historical juncture: "Unlike my last two predecessors, I did not enter this office facing the terrible decisions of a foreign war, but like president Truman and President Lincoln before him, I found on my desk, where the buck stops, the urgent problem of how to bind up the Nation's wounds. And I intend to do that." He then professed his faith in the justice system, and having thus described the context, he outlined his course of action:

> In my first week at the White House, I requested the Attorney General of the United States and the Secretary of Defense to report to me personally, before September 1, on the status of some fifty thousand of our countrymen convicted, charged, or under investigation, or still sought for violations of Selective Service or the Uniform Code of Military Justice—offenses loosely described as desertion and draft-dodging. . . . [A]ll, in a sense, are casualties, still abroad or absent without leave from the real America. I want them to come home if they want to work their way back.

Ford spoke of how young many of the draft evaders were, as if their youth rendered their actions more excusable and the prospect of their long-term exclusion more problematic. He said, "In my view, these young Americans should have a second chance to contribute their fair share to the rebuilding of peace among ourselves and with all nations."

Ford summed up his position and asked for the audience's support:

> So I am throwing the weight of my presidency into the scales of justice on the side of leniency. I foresee their earned reentry—their earned reentry—into a new atmosphere of hope, hard work, and mutual trust. I will act promptly, fairly, and very firmly in the same spirit that guided Abraham Lincoln and Harry Truman. As I reject amnesty, so I reject revenge. As men and women whose patriotism has been tested and proved—and yours has—I want your help and understanding. I ask all Americans who ever asked for goodness and mercy in their lives, who ever sought forgiveness for their trespasses, to join in rehabilitating all the casualties of the tragic conflict of the past.

Ford thus presented his policy as an attractive midpoint between the extremes of amnesty and revenge, consonant with the approaches of previous presidents, and his plea for support drew on religious themes. As David Veenstra has noted, Ford was a deeply religious man who often invoked religious themes in his speeches. His VFW speech drew on the well-known Psalm 23 and its invocation of "goodness and mercy," and it alluded to the request in the Lord's Prayer to "forgive us our trespasses." According to Veenstra, "The approach was clear: Ford based his policy of forgiveness on the Biblical requirement for forgiveness."[60]

Ford's careful rhetoric did not win over his VFW audience, though. They did not boo him, but "the VFW conventioneers greeted the announcement with stony silence."[61] The day after Ford's address, the VFW passed two resolutions reiterating its long-standing opposition to amnesty.[62]

In late August, Ford met with Attorney General William Saxbe and Secretary of Defense James Schlesinger to work out the details of his conditional pardon program. One of the issues was whether individuals would have to admit wrongdoing or pledge allegiance to the United States in order to be eligible for official forgiveness.[63] Saxbe had previously called for an "act of contrition" on the part of Vietnam war resisters in order for them to gain amnesty or pardon.[64] However, he also reportedly noted the alternative view of Senator Taft and others "that such a requirement would reopen rather than heal the wounds of the Vietnam War."[65] Ultimately, in their report to Ford, Saxbe and Schlesinger recommended that resisters be required only to reaffirm their allegiance to the United States but not to undertake an act of contrition.[66]

PARDONING NIXON

Determinations of what exactly Ford's pardon program would entail were soon caught up in the reaction to another pardon. Three weeks after announcing his support for the conditional-pardon program, the new president issued an even more controversial pardon—one for his disgraced predecessor. Ford pardoned Richard Nixon on September 8, 1974, just one month after Nixon had resigned, ostensibly in order to heal the wounds of Watergate.

The pardon covered "all offenses against the United States which he, Richard Nixon, has committed or may have committed or taken part in." Ford's proclamation said its intent was to avoid "prolonged and divisive debate" and the loss of "the tranquility to which this nation has been restored by the events of recent weeks."[67] In his statement announcing the pardon for Nixon, Ford echoed those justifications, saying that the Watergate affair must be brought to a conclusion and that "someone must write 'The End' to it." Without that sort of closure, Ford said, "ugly passions would again be aroused."[68] Many years later, Ford said of his decision to pardon Nixon, "As a new president under very difficult circumstances, I had an obligation to spend all of my time on the problems of 200 million Americans, and the only way to clear the deck to get to the substantive problems I faced was to pardon Mr. Nixon and get his problems off my desk in the oval office. . . . It was purely practical."[69] Ford's rationale for pardoning Nixon did not convince many Americans, a majority of whom opposed the pardon, though support for it grew over the years, and by 1986 a majority believed that Ford's pardon had been the right thing to do.[70]

Apart from the controversy about the merits of Ford's pardon of Nixon, the pardon sparked new calls for amnesty for draft resisters and deserters. For many people, Ford's indication that his predecessor had made mistakes yet nevertheless should be pardoned suggested that similar treatment would be appropriate for those whose opposition to the Vietnam War had led to legal difficulties. Ronald Docksai, the executive director of Young Americans for Freedom, recognized this parallel but argued against it in September 1974: "I hope this is not a forerunner of the President's policy on amnesty for draft-dodgers and deserters. It would be ironic if Nixon, the most visible opponent of unconditional amnesty, would be responsible for its implementation."[71] From one point of view, the need to further justify the Nixon pardon might have rendered a future pardon for draft evasion more palatable because a pardon for draft evasion would permit Ford to justify the Nixon pardon on the grounds that it was just one instance of his general philosophic commitment to forgiveness.

FORD'S CLEMENCY

Ford issued his formal clemency proclamation for Vietnam draft evaders and deserters on September 16, 1974, a month after his initial announcement at the VFW and just eight days after his pardon of Nixon. Ford's program of "earned reentry" offered amnesty to draft evaders and deserters if they would turn themselves in to authorities by the end of January 1975, acknowledge their allegiance to the United States, and perform up to two years of "alternate service" in public-service positions—all to be overseen by a nine-member clemency review board. On the same day that he issued his clemency proclamation, Ford also issued two executive orders to facilitate his clemency program: one established the Presidential Clemency Board to review applications, and the other enabled the Selective Service to implement the program of alternate service. Ford's clemency proclamation contained the following statement about its motivations:

> Over a year after the last American combatant had left Vietnam, the status of thousands of our countrymen—convicted, charged, investigated

or still sought for violations of the Military Selective Service Act or of the Uniform Code of Military Justice—remains unresolved. In furtherance of our national commitment to justice and mercy these young Americans should have the chance to contribute a share to the rebuilding of peace among ourselves and with all nations. They should be allowed the opportunity to earn return to their country, their communities, and their families, upon their agreement to a period of alternate service in the national interest, together with an acknowledgement of their allegiance to the country and its Constitution. Desertion in time of war is a major, serious offense; failure to respond to the country's call for duty is also a serious offense. Reconciliation among our people does not require that these acts be condoned. Yet, reconciliation calls for an act of mercy to bind the Nation's wounds and to heal the scars of divisiveness.[72]

Ford actually signed the clemency proclamation at the end of a live televised speech in which he explained his action. He referred to his announcement at the VFW convention of his intention "to give these young people a chance to earn their return to the mainstream of American society," and his televised address used some of the same lines from the VFW speech. Ford said he was determined "to do everything in my power to bind up the nation's wounds." He also compared his action to similar actions by Lincoln and Truman and said, "The primary purpose of this program is the reconciliation of all our people and the restoration of the essential unity of Americans." Ford concluded, "My sincere hope is that this is a constructive step toward calmer and cooler appreciation of our individual rights and responsibilities and our common purpose as a nation whose future is always more important than its past."[73]

After issuing his proclamation, Ford continued to echo its themes and to extol the virtues of turning the page and putting the past behind the country. For example, in an address in New Orleans in April 1975, he said: "America can regain the sense of pride that existed before Vietnam. But it cannot be achieved by refighting a war that is finished as far as America is concerned. As I see it, the time has come to look forward to an agenda for the future, to unify, to bind up the Nation's wounds, and to restore its health and its optimistic self-confidence. . . . [W]e can begin a great national reconciliation. . . . I ask that we stop refighting the battles and recriminations of the past."[74]

CONTROVERSY

As the details of Ford's program unfolded, the issue continued to be controversial. A Gallup poll taken just before Ford's announcement in September 1974, found that 59 percent of Americans favored conditional amnesty, 34 percent favored unconditional amnesty, and some opposed any sort of amnesty.[75] Given the divisions in public opinion, it was not surprising that Ford's program evoked a variety of reactions.

Some saw Ford's approach as a "middle-road" policy, which seemed to draw on a moderate proposal that Senator Taft had made in December 1973.[76] According to Nancy Montgomery of Maryland, the mother of a deserter who had fled to Canada, "It's not amnesty. Amnesty means to forget, to wipe the slate clean." And Mrs. Clifford Gaddy of Virginia, whose son had fled to Sweden, said Ford's plan was "not amnesty. It was a form of leniency."[77]

But Ford's clemency program also faced many criticisms from different perspectives.[78] As a *Washington Post* article observed, "Designed to put an end to a bitterly divisive issue, the decision, while generally applauded in Congress, nevertheless was criticized by some veterans' groups as too lenient and by leading opponents of the wartime draft as harsh and unacceptable."[79] Many religious leaders praised Ford's plan, and the 15,000 veterans of the Military Order of the Purple Heart supported it.[80] But many military families, families of those still missing in action, as well as many conservatives were uneasy with Ford's clemency program, which they feared was too forgiving.[81]

Other critics felt that the program was insufficiently generous and too stringent. As Daniel Pollitt and Frank Thompson Jr. noted in the *Washington Post* at the time, "Ford's program to provide clemency for Vietnam War draft evaders and deserters is in some particular respects more demanding and less forgiving than most of the post-war grants of amnesty by his predecessors."[82] According to David Anderson, writing in 1993, "Antiwar spokesmen attacked the failure to grant unconditional amnesty to those who, as civilians or soldiers, had followed their consciences."[83] The *Washington Post* criticized Ford's program as inadequate: "It is not amnesty by any stretch of the definition. It is, instead, a program of contrition and substitution."[84] The American Civil Liberties Union said of Ford's program: "We consider the 'clemency program' . . . offensive in its moral and political assumptions and outrageous in its implementation. The Ford 'clemency' program is worse than no amnesty at all. It is punitive and demeaning. Most of those who fall under the provisions of the 'clemency' have better legal options outside the program than within it."[85]

Americans who had moved abroad to avoid the draft were generally displeased with Ford's clemency offer. Mrs. Douglas Kinsey of Washington, DC, whose son had fled to Canada, said, "I feel that it would have been better to have never brought amnesty up than to offer the boys an amnesty they could not accept. I think the President, rather than healing wounds, has reopened them."[86] Steve Grossman, who had also fled to Canada, said of Ford's program: "At first, I—and others— were buoyed by the prospect of a legal way home, but when Ford spelled out his amnesty program, we found it morally and politically offensive—an extension, in effect, of the very policies that had forced us to leave our country. The offer was made only to a small fraction of those needing amnesty. It required loyalty oaths and years of labor, in return for which deserters would be provided with stigmatizing 'clemency discharges.'"[87] On September 21, 1974, an international conference of Vietnam war resisters sponsored by the exile publication *Amex Canada* voted to reject Ford's conditional clemency program, which it termed "punitive repatriation," and instead to demand unconditional amnesty.[88]

LOW PARTICIPATION

Relatively few people took advantage of Ford's clemency program. According to the head of the Presidential Clemency Board, the response was "greatly disappointing."[89] The board attributed the low level of applications to an allegedly low level of awareness about the program, while attorneys for war resisters claimed it was not clear that the clemency discharge would be better than an undesirable discharge.[90] In late January 1975, Ford issued an executive order to extend the deadline for clemency until March because so few people had taken advantage of the program.[91]

In addition to the low participation rate, many men who started the clemency program did not finish it. In December 1976, the *New York Times* reported that roughly three-quarters of the draft evaders who enrolled in Ford's service program either dropped out or were terminated from their alternative-service positions. Those who left the program generally felt there was no point in remaining in it because Jimmy Carter might soon pardon them.[92]

In December 1976, General William Westmoreland wrote of Ford's program: "Fifty-five percent of the military deserters took advantage of the amnesty program, but only about 16 percent of the draft evaders who had the opportunity to perform alternative service chose to make any effort to re-establish their good standing in our society. This would indicate that what these people were looking for is an apology, not amnesty."[93]

In January 1977, the U.S. comptroller general issued a detailed report on the clemency program, which by then had "nearly run its course." The report said that the pool of people who were eligible for the program numbered "from 113,000 to 300,000 or more," yet only 21,700 people had chosen to participate in it. Of those, 13,750 were assigned to alternate service, 6,052 were pardoned, 911 were denied clemency, and 1,000 had cases pending.[94]

In late December 1976, after Ford lost the election to Jimmy Carter by 2.1 percent of the popular vote, he promised the widow of recently deceased Senator Philip Hart (D–MI) that he would consider an across-the-board amnesty.[95] Yet on January 19, 1977, in one of his last official actions as president, Ford refused to grant a blanket amnesty to draft evaders and deserters. However, he combined his rejection with a directive that the military should upgrade to honorable discharge the records of certain veterans. To be eligible, one had to have previously applied for clemency and received a service medal or been wounded.[96]

Also in January 1977, Lawrence Baskir and William Strauss, who were members of Ford's Clemency Board, authored a 150-page report on Ford's program. They claimed that convicted draft dodgers should be pardoned, charges of draft offenses should be dropped for all so charged, and the status of deserters and veterans with undesirable discharges should be reviewed for a possible change to general discharge status.[97] Baskir and Strauss concluded that Ford's program "offered meaningless relief to people who needed far more."[98] In their report, they made the case for amnesty as follows:

> The amnesty issue is most appropriately viewed as a question of social justice, not antiwar ideology. The burdens of Vietnam were very unevenly imposed. The economically and socially disadvantaged did most of the fighting. They also paid most of the penalties for not fighting. Whether the war was right or wrong, America should seek reconciliation with everyone who was its victim—the dead, the missing, the physically or psychologically wounded, the unemployed veteran, the fugitive or punished offenders, and all their families. No one should be asked to pay any further price.[99]

JIMMY CARTER

Jimmy Carter was not well known nationally before his surprising victory in the Iowa caucuses and subsequent Democratic primaries in early 1976. Carter's record as governor of Georgia from 1971 to 1975 affords no perspective on his general attitude toward pardons and clemency because an amendment to Georgia's constitution had placed the pardon power with a Board of Pardons and Paroles, specifically removing the governor from pardon decisions.[100] But Carter's later writings provide evidence that his religious faith informed his general views about forgiveness. For example, in his book *Living Faith* (1996),

Carter acknowledged that "forgiveness is taught in the Bible," and he spoke of the "forgiving Jesus" of the Gospels. In that book Carter also wrote, "We have to be willing to forgive," and "Forgiveness is not easy, but it is a goal to be sought, a process that should continue throughout our lives."[101]

By some accounts, Carter's position on Vietnam amnesty was the product of the political dynamics of the primary campaign in 1976, which featured more than a dozen major candidates in a wide-open contest. According to an assessment by the *National Review* one month into Carter's presidency, "To win the nomination, Carter defeated the principal candidates of the Democratic left: Udall, Bayh, and Harris. The Vietnam pardon pledge functioned as a device to reconcile this defeated but troublesome faction to an unwelcome candidacy."[102]

After Carter secured enough delegates to win the nomination, Democrats debated how the party's official platform should address amnesty. The antiwar activist Sam Brown and others pushed for a "full and complete pardon" that would cover draft evaders and deserters, but Carter campaign adviser Stuart Eizenstat persuaded Carter to settle for a compromise that would permit him to consider deserters on a case by case basis.[103] According to Tom Wicker in the *New York Times* in late 1976, "In one of the few instances where it overrode Jimmy Carter's wishes, the Democratic platform committee wrote into the platform on which he ran a pledge of clemency to anyone 'in legal or financial jeopardy because of their peaceful opposition to the Vietnam War.'"[104] Amnesty was debated at the Democratic National Convention, where the disabled veteran and author Ron Kovic gave an impassioned plea for amnesty and nominated fugitive draft resister Fritz Efaw for the vice presidency.

After the Democratic and Republican conventions—in which Carter prevailed with three-quarters of the vote, whereas Ford bested Ronald Reagan by just 5 percent—the question of a pardon or amnesty played a role in the general election. The political dynamics were much the same because those who had opposed the war in Vietnam tended to want universal and unconditional amnesty, whereas the war's proponents generally wanted much less accommodation.

CARTER'S ANNOUNCEMENT

On August 24, 1976, five weeks after the Democratic National Convention, Carter announced his intention to issue a blanket pardon for draft evaders if elected president. His announcement came in Seattle during a meeting of the American Legion veterans' service organization, of which the former navy lieutenant was a member. Obviously, it was a setting much like that in which Ford had announced his clemency program two years earlier, with a politician bravely telling his fellow veterans that he favored a policy they did not.

But unlike Ford's address, Carter's was not a surprise. The audience knew what was coming, and Carter knew the crowd would not be supportive. He had conferred with aides about his speech in advance, and he told them that he realized it would not go over well. Nevertheless, he told his aides, "I want to meet it head on."[105] According to Helen Dewar at the *Washington Post*, "Carter told a press conference shortly before the speech that he expected an adverse reaction. He appeared to be consciously courting the image of a bold dissenter carrying an unpopular message to a hostile audience[:] 'I realize that my statements will not be met with approval from members of the American Legion audience, but I want them to understand what I am going to do.' "[106]

Carter told the 15,000 people in attendance, "I would like to speak for a moment about the single hardest decision I have had to make during the campaign. That was on the issue of amnesty." He then extolled the sacrifices of Vietnam veterans:

The Vietnam veterans are our nation's greatest unsung heroes. In my own mind I could never equate what they have done with what those who left this country did to avoid the draft. But I think it's time for the damage and the hatred and the divisiveness of the Vietnam War to be over. I do not favor—and I want you to listen carefully because I don't want you to misunderstand me—I do not favor a blanket amnesty; but for those who violated Selective Service laws, I intend to grant a blanket pardon. To me there's a difference. Amnesty means that what you did was right; a pardon means that what you did, right or wrong, is forgiven. So a pardon yes, amnesty no.[107]

Whereas Ford's surprise announcement was met with silence, Carter's planned announcement provoked a loud chorus of boos. Hundreds of legionnaires in the audience began vigorously to boo him just as soon as he pronounced the word *but* in saying "I do not favor a blanket amnesty; but. . . ."[108] By one account, "the audience of more than fifteen thousand legionnaires and their wives reacted violently."[109] Cries of "no, no, no" immediately erupted, and Carter was loudly booed for more than forty-five seconds. The legion's national commander had to gavel the crowd back to order. While Carter was being booed, he kept his gaze down, then raised it with his trademark wide grin when the crowd's reaction had finally dissipated.[110]

After the boos stopped, Carter continued:

> I realized before I made my statement to you, that everybody would not agree. I'm a veteran myself, a member of the American Legion. But I want to spell out my position to you because of this: Our nation is still divided. There's still a lot of hatred, there's still a lot of division, there's still an absence of support for our military personnel left over from the Vietnamese War. I think it's time to get that behind us. . . . We must bind up our wounds. We simply cannot afford to let them fester any longer. . . . I believe that there is no one in this country, certainly there is no one in this auditorium, who does not want to heal our wounds.[111]

According to the journalist Jules Witcover, "The reaction was expected; Carter obviously had chosen to throw his plan in the teeth of the Legion as a means of demonstrating to the wider national audience his courage as a campaigner. It was a pointed refutation of the allegation that he always tailored his speeches to please his audiences. But the question here was, which audience was the prime one, the legion or the country beyond?"[112]

CONTROVERSY

The day after Carter's speech, Ford's vice presidential nominee, Senator Bob Dole (R–KS), spoke at the same American Legion convention. Dole referred to Carter's distinction between amnesty and pardon: "I am confused by such semantics. Webster's New World dictionary makes no such distinction. It defines 'amnesty' as 'a general pardon.'" He said Ford's position was "unequivocal" and promised that Ford would give "no blanket pardon, no blanket amnesty, no blanket clemency."[113] The legionnaires gave Dole a standing ovation, a sharp contrast to their booing of Carter.

In contrast, the *Wall Street Journal* defended Carter's distinction between pardon and amnesty: "On Vietnam amnesty . . . we would love to put the matter behind us, incorporating back into society those who divorced themselves from it, but only provided that this can be done in a way that does not suggest they were right and society was wrong. This, we take it, is what Mr. Carter is driving at in the semantic distinction between 'amnesty' and 'pardon.' We think the distinction a good one; even those who quote the similar dictionary definitions do so precisely because they intuitively recognize the different connotations."[114]

The question of a broader pardon factored in the presidential campaign through the fall of 1976. According to the historian Jason Friedman, it was "a decisive election issue."[115] For example, Ford and Carter discussed amnesty during their televised debate on September 23 in Philadelphia. Marvin Kalb and Deborah Kalb comment in their book about the "haunting legacy" of Vietnam, "It was no surprise that the amnesty/pardon issue was raised."[116] The debate began with questions about unemployment, taxes, and the budget. Then moderator Frank Reynolds of ABC News asked President Ford:

> Mr. President, when you came into office, you spoke very eloquently of the need for a time for healing. And very early in your administration you went to Chicago and you announced, you proposed a program of case-by-case pardons for draft resisters and to restore them to full

citizenship. Some 14,000 young men took advantage of your offer, but another 90,000 did not. In granting the pardon to former President Nixon, sir, part of your rationale was to put Watergate behind us, to, if I may quote you again, truly end "our long national nightmare." Why does not the same rationale apply now, today, in our Bicentennial year to the men who resisted in Vietnam, many of them still in exile abroad?[117]

Ford answered: "The amnesty program I recommended in Chicago in September of 1974 would give to all draft evaders and military deserters the opportunity to earn their good record back. About 14 to 15,000 did take advantage of that program. We gave them ample time. I am against an across-the-board pardon of draft evaders or military deserters."

Ford then briefly discussed his pardon of Nixon, after which the moderator asked: "I take it, then, sir, that you do not believe that you are going to reconsider and think about those 90,000 who are still abroad? Have they not been penalized enough? Many of them have been there for years." Ford replied: "Well, Mr. Carter has indicated that he would give a blanket pardon to all draft evaders. I do not agree with that point of view. I gave in September of 1974 an opportunity for all draft evaders, all deserters, to come in voluntarily, clear their records by earning an opportunity to restore their good citizenship. I think we gave them a good opportunity. I don't think we should go any further." The moderator then turned to Carter, who said:

> Well, I think it's very difficult for President Ford to explain the difference between the pardon of President Nixon and his attitude toward those who violated the draft laws. As a matter of fact now, I don't advocate amnesty; I advocate pardon. There is a difference, in my opinion, and in accordance with the ruling of the Supreme Court and in accordance with the definition in the dictionary. Amnesty means that what you did was right. Pardon means that what you did, whether it's right or wrong, you are forgiven for it. And I do advocate a pardon for draft evaders. I think it's accurate to say that two years ago, when Mr. Ford put in this amnesty, that three times as many deserters were

excused as were the ones who evaded the draft. But I think that now is the time to heal our country after the Vietnam war.

Three years later, in his autobiography *A Time to Heal,* Ford admitted that Carter had handled the exchange well: "He no doubt scored some points when I was asked how I could justify pardoning Nixon while refusing a blanket pardon for all draft dodgers and deserters. I explained my reasoning and discussed the earned amnesty program. Carter jumped all over that."[118]

The controversy continued throughout the remaining six weeks of the campaign, and the public remained divided over the question of a more generous pardon, even after Carter's close victory in November 1976. The details of Carter's policy continued to evolve during his presidential transition as his team debated how broadly the new president's action might reach.[119] According to Tom Wicker, the fact that Ford considered issuing a broader pardon after the election put pressure on Carter to pardon not just draft resisters but others too.[120]

Public opinion remained mixed after the election. In early 1977, Helen Frazelle of Virginia, whose son had been killed in Vietnam in 1971, said of Carter's promise of a blanket pardon for draft evaders who had fled the United States: "Let them stay where they are. They'll never be any good to you here. They didn't take it [Ford's clemency offer,] so it shows they don't want to have anything to do with this country." In contrast, Theresa Cavanaugh of Virginia supported Carter's approach: "Oh, how long can you go on with this?. . . Carter is trying to start anew, to get the people together."[121] Also in early 1977, Reverend Barry W. Lynn wrote, "Granting an amnesty would not heal all the wounds of the Vietnam war. It is, however, a critical prerequisite for reconciliation."[122]

CARTER'S PARDON

Carter's Inaugural Address in January 1977 was much more limited and humbler than those of many of his predecessors. The goals he stated in it included mercy, justice, and respect for law. At the start of the address, Carter paid tribute to Ford's efforts to heal the nation's wounds: "For myself and for our nation, I want to thank my predecessor for all he has done to heal our land." Carter then shook hands with Ford, who appeared genuinely moved by the praise.[123] According to the biographer Victor Lasky, that praise "obviously constituted an apologetic gesture" toward the opponent whom Carter had beaten in the election.[124]

In his first full day in office—January 21, 1977—Carter granted a full and unconditional pardon to those who had evaded the Vietnam draft. The pardon proclamation was issued without any statement from the president. The document was unusually brief, almost even terse; its substantive section was only 210 words long. It thus broke with the norm of previous presidents' mass pardons, which were generally promulgated and promoted with relatively voluminous rhetoric. The pardon proclamation did not characterize the conflict and division to which it responded, did not invoke the virtues of mercy or compassion, did not reference Ford's clemency program, and gave no reason or justification for the action.

The proclamation merely referenced the president's constitutional authority, then granted a "full, complete, and unconditional pardon" to people who had violated draft regulations between August 1964 and March 1973. It "explicitly exempted" those whose violations involved "force or violence" and employees of the Military Selective Service. And implicitly, by omission it did not cover the thousands of men who joined the military but then deserted, nor did it cover soldiers who received less than an honorable discharge.[125] On the same day that Carter issued his amnesty proclamation, he also issued an executive order to facilitate it. The order directed the U.S. attorney general to dismiss pending indictments and to terminate and not initiate further investigations for violations of the Selective Service Act, except for cases involving violence or employees of the Selective Service system.

The rhetorical minimalism of Carter's amnesty proclamation suggested it was simply a necessary and overdue final step in moving beyond an issue that had divided the country for too long. The conservative *National Review* offered a similar interpretation: "Carter himself attempted to limit the moral significance of the pardon, stressing merely a desire to wipe the slate clean, but the pardon is and will be understood to be part of the debate about the war itself. It will appear to give official approval to the position that the war was a mistake, wrong, immoral and even illegal, and that the draft evaders were 'right.' The pardon does not assert this explicitly, of course, but it may be so understood inferentially and symbolically."[126] This attitude might explain why the amnesty proclamation was so terse.

Carter's own subsequent comments confirmed the pragmatic nature of his action. In early March 1977, Carter elaborated on his motives in issuing the amnesty during a meeting with Department of Defense employees:

> I know that my own position on granting pardon to the violators of the Selective Service laws during the Vietnam conflict was not a popular one for many Americans to accept . . . I also felt that those who had fled our country during the Vietnam War and had been living overseas for 10, 12, 15 years, had been punished enough. It was a matter of judgment. I made my judgment clear during the campaign. I never misled anyone. I made the major announcement of my plan to grant this pardon at an American Legion convention in Seattle, perhaps one of the most antagonistic audiences that I could have chosen. But I didn't want to mislead anyone about it, and I was elected either because of it or in spite of it. . . . I don't have any apology to make about it. I made my decision clear before the election. The first week I was in office, I carried out my commitment.[127]

And many years later, in an interview in 2006, Carter said of his amnesty: "I was just following up, basically, on the heroic action that President Gerald Ford had taken in trying to heal our nation, and to give us a chance to move beyond the Vietnam War and obsession with Vietnam into another era of life," thus evoking both moral and practical reasons for his action.[128]

REACTION

Carter's pardon was essentially a middle ground between Ford's conditional amnesty and the total amnesty that many demanded.[129] Like many compromises, it struck some as sensible but drew criticism from others who favored one side or the other. A Harris poll published a month after Carter's amnesty proclamation found that a 46–42 percent plurality of Americans opposed it and a 52–38 percent majority gave him a negative rating on his handling of the pardon issue, but for diametrically opposed reasons. A 46–43 percent plurality approved of his action as a way of "burying the past" and agreed that Carter "was right to issue the pardon so that Vietnam could be left behind us in the past."[130]

Major newspapers characterized Carter's action as a sensible middle ground. For example, the *Wall Street Journal* said, "If it is any consolation to President Carter, the general and varied discontents over his pardon of Vietnam draft evaders suggest that he has at least succeeded in striking a rough balance. To have expected more than that on such a divisive and emotional issue would have been unrealistic."[131] And the *New York Times* remarked, "President Carter's pardon for draft resisters drew sharp denunciations yesterday from major veterans' organizations and only qualified praise from pro-amnesty groups, which called it insufficient because of its exclusion of deserters and veterans with less-than-honorable discharges."[132] The *Times* also said, "The pardon is considerably more than the conditional amnesty program under the Ford Administration but considerably less than the total amnesty demanded by many."[133]

For people who thought that Ford's program had been too generous, Carter's was a further step in the wrong direction. And some felt that it asked too little of the people it covered. For example, eighteen-year-old Sheila Cavanaugh, whose father was killed in Vietnam in 1971, and whose mother supported the pardon, said, "They should do something to redeem themselves."[134] One day after Carter proclaimed the mass pardon, Tim Marlow of the VFW said, "We were very displeased with the pardon."[135] The American Legion officially opposed Carter's amnesty plan, and some members even tried to have Carter ousted from the organization. William Rogers, the national commander of the 2.8-million-member American Legion said, "We deeply and strongly protest the President's action," which he predicted would be "more divisive than healing." In January 1977, four hundred delegates at a Wisconsin state American Legion convention unanimously approved a resolution calling for Carter's ouster.[136] The executive director of the VFW said, "This is probably one of the saddest days in the history of our country."[137] Senator Bob Dole said, "It's distressing to see conscious disobedience condoned on a blanket basis."[138] And prominent conservative Senator Barry Goldwater (R–AZ) called it "the most disgraceful thing that a President has ever done."[139]

Whereas some thus felt that Carter's policy went too far, others felt that it did not go far enough. For example, shortly before Carter's inauguration, the New York Times voiced criticism of anything less than the broadest possible amnesty, saying less would run "the risk of not healing the nation's wounds."[140] Similarly, Representative Elizabeth Holtzman (D–NY) said, "I would have liked to have seen it broader, I would have liked to have seen it extended to some of the people who are clearly not covered."[141] And Pat Simon, head of the group Gold Star Parents for Amnesty, said, "There are 1 million more who need amnesty—veterans with less than honorable discharge; deserters still at large, and this may be from 5,000 to 40,000; civilian resisters who have court records because they participated in demonstrations; and nonregistrants, who the draft board says were anywhere from 8 to 10 percent a year."[142]

Apart from politics, the issue of the amnesty's timing—specifically whether it came too soon—seems to have influenced how some people viewed it. Time may or may not heal all wounds, but when the issue remains ongoing or has yet to fade, reconciliation seems premature or inappropriate. Thus, reactions to the amnesty may have turned on people's emotional distance from the conflict. For example, Corrine Hayword, whose husband had been killed in Vietnam in 1968, noted that other military widows opposed amnesty, yet she asked, "But what does it matter at this point? Enough time has passed."[143]

In spring 1977, Carter announced a second part of his program to reconcile with opponents of the Vietnam War. His initial amnesty had addressed only those who had violated draft laws, but now he sought to include the hundreds of thousands of veterans who had less-than-honorable discharges. Carter invited such veterans to apply to have their discharges reviewed for possible upgrades.[144] Later, in October 1977, Carter signed into law S-1307, a measure to allow veterans whose discharges had been upgraded to receive veterans' benefits if they passed a case-by-case review.[145]

Congress sought to respond to Carter's amnesty, though the plenary nature of the presidential pardon power limited Congress's ability to counter the chief executive's action. Senator James Allen (D–AL) tried for weeks in early 1977 to pass a resolution to formally disavow Carter's amnesty, but the resolution failed to garner enough support to come up for a vote.[146] In the House, Representative John Myers (R–IN) succeeded in amending the supplemental appropriations bill for fiscal year 1977 to stipulate that no funds could be used to carry out Carter's program, even though the program's efficacy did not require administrative funding. When Carter signed the appropriations bill into law, he issued a signing statement objecting to the provisions that sought to deny funds for his amnesty program.[147] He contended that two aspects of the measure were ineffective because his policy required no funds to be implemented.

As happened with previous mass pardons, some who might have benefited from Carter's pardon chose not to take advantage of it and instead to remain beyond the reach of the federal government, in this case by not coming home to the United States from exile abroad. For example, although most Americans who had fled to Canada returned to the United States after Carter's pardon, many thousands chose to remain abroad.[148]

DENOUEMENT?

Beyond those who thought that Carter's amnesty went either too far or not far enough, many Americans seemed satisfied with it and welcomed the chance to finally put the war behind the country. The Vietnam case is now more than four decades in the past, but tens of millions of Americans have some living memory of it, and the issue remains divisive even today.

Anyone trying to get a sense of how this played out in U.S. political culture in the 1970s could do worse than to consider Norman Lear's television show *All in the Family*. Following an oddly likable bigot named Archie Bunker in Queens, New York, the sitcom ran from 1971 to 1979. It was the most popular TV show for five consecutive years, with tens of millions of viewers watching every episode. It was also critically acclaimed and won a number of awards.

One of the show's most poignant episodes was "The Draft Dodger" (season 7, episode 15). It aired on Christmas Day in 1976 and depicts a Christmas dinner at Archie's house with his friend Pinky Peterson, whose son, Steve, was killed while serving in Vietnam. Archie's son-in-law's friend David Brewster also stops by unexpectedly, after living in Canada while wanted by U.S. authorities for evading the draft. The holiday dinner is tense, and soon Archie yells at David for avoiding the draft and then praises Pinkie's late son for doing what his country asked him to do, even if he did not want to go to war. David is about to leave, when Pinkie says to Archie, "I understand how you feel, Arch. My kid hated the war, too. But he did what he thought he had to do, and David here did what he thought he had to do. But David's alive to share Christmas dinner with us. And if Steve were here, he'd want to sit down with him. And that's what I wanna do." Pinkie and David awkwardly shake hands and tell each other, "Merry Christmas." Archie is shaken and mumbles, "I gotta work this out." As the credits start to roll, the camera focuses on the word *peace* on the Bunkers' Christmas wreath. It is a remarkably moving episode, and it dramatically underscores just how raw feelings about the war remained in the mid-1970s and how unsettled the issue of reconciliation remained after Ford's clemency and the election of Carter.

The sense of controversy about an unresolved conflict has persisted. A *New York Times* report from January 1973 had presciently noted, "Like the Vietnam war itself, the issue of amnesty for those who refused to fight seems likely to be a divisive and emotional part of the American political scene for many years."[149] Forty years later Karl Marlantes wrote in the *New York Times*, "The Vietnam War continues to define us, even if we have forgotten how."[150] Also writing in 2017, the documentary filmmakers Ken Burns and Lynn Novick commented, "We have been unable to put that war behind us. . . . Nothing will ever make the tragedy of the Vietnam War all right."[151] The conclusion to their popular PBS miniseries on the war aired in 2017 said, "More than four decades after the war ended, the divisions it created between Americans have not yet wholly healed."[152] As a review of Geoffrey Ward's companion book to the miniseries put it, "Vietnam divided Americans 50 years ago. It continues to divide us today."[153]

Even today, more than four decades after Carter's amnesty, the Department of Justice's website still has a page with instructions for how people may apply for a certificate indicating that they are covered by Carter's pardon, as if there are still people who might benefit from it so many years later. The site carefully explains whom Carter's amnesty does and does not cover:

> President Carter's Pardon Proclamation applies *only* to violations of the Military Selective Service Act by civilians. If you were a member of the armed forces during the relevant period, and you were convicted for a violation of military law, *your offense does not qualify for treatment under the Proclamation*. A person wishing to seek a presidential pardon for a military conviction may apply for a pardon from the current President under the regular pardon procedure. In addition, the Carter Proclamation *does not apply* to Military Selective Service Act violations involving force or violence, or to offenses committed by agents, officers, or employees of the Military Selective Service system in connection with duties or responsibilities arising out of their employment.[154]

It is not clear how many Americans might still desire a pardon for their actions during the Vietnam War.

This chapter has examined the presidential use of clemency and amnesty for Vietnam War resisters. As we have seen, the issue evolved over many years and involved many different actors, including Congress. A pardon was controversial at the time and perhaps remains so even today. The two presidential actions discussed here resulted from a variety of motives, and they also varied in their scope, nature, and impact. By most accounts, Ford's demanding and limited clemency program was inadequate, and even Carter's relatively broad amnesty could not entirely overcome the divisions of the Vietnam War.

CONCLUSION

Presidents through the country's history have seen fit to grant clemency to rebels or evaders as part of the process of binding the emotional wounds of war. Whatever the injustices, it is a way of putting past divisions behind. . . . [A] government must at some point remove its censure.

—WALL STREET JOURNAL, 1977

Remember that forgiveness too is a power. To beg for it is a power, and to withhold or bestow it is a power, perhaps the greatest.

—MARGARET ATWOOD, *THE HANDMAID'S TALE*

This book has endeavored to provide an accessible historical account of U.S. presidents' efforts to overcome rebellions and serious resistance to governmental authority and to reintegrate their partisans. The foregoing chapters have in some detail covered the history of presidents using mass pardons and amnesties to facilitate domestic political reconciliation for major disruptions, with attention to their political context and rhetoric.

Even if some of these actions are unfamiliar to many people today, they are nevertheless important historical episodes, and they demonstrate a particular way in which the deployment of presidential power may advance broad national purposes. Had presidents not issued and promoted these pardons, the conflicts that they sought to address would surely not have been ameliorated to the extent that they were and thus would have continued to strain national unity more than they did. As the *Wall Street Journal* approvingly said of Jimmy Carter's amnesty for Vietnam War draft resisters in early 1977, "Presidents through the country's history have seen fit to grant clemency to rebels or evaders as part of the process of binding the emotional wounds of war. Whatever the injustices, it is a way of putting past divisions behind. . . . [A] government must at some point remove its censure."[1]

There are disputes about some of the facts of the cases covered here, especially about the numbers, motivations, and conduct of the rebellious groups involved in them as well as about the degree of seriousness of the conflicts and the motives and efficacy of the pardons. Indeed, much more could be said about the details and nuances of these conflicts and their resolutions. But beyond the particular details of these episodes, what broader lessons may be gleaned from this discussion of four major political ruptures, nine presidents, and thirteen proclamations of mass pardon or amnesty across 183 years? This conclusion briefly considers a number of implications of this book.

Before that, however, it might be noted that this study is arguably already too broad, at least probably for scholars committed to studying discrete historical events in their own unique contexts.[2] That view is not without its merits, and it is certainly the case that each of the various events discussed here is in some sense unique or sui generis, such that any attempt to treat them as somehow equal or as comparable units of analysis necessarily ignores important differences. Obviously, there are important differences both within and across the four complex cases. For example, despite their considerable similarities, George Washington and John Adams were responding to different crises. And treating late eighteenth-century tax rebellions in Pennsylvania as comparable to the great convulsion of the Civil War more than six decades later is in some respects a stretch.

In addition to the differences within and across the cases, there is also the matter of differences in the presidency, in terms of both the individual presidents and the presidency as an institution. It is undeniable that different presidents act in different ways in part because of their own personal or political inclinations and in part because of the context of the times in which they govern. In the cases discussed here, Washington and Adams, despite their temporal proximity, were different people who approached the presidency differently, as were Lincoln and Johnson, Ford and Carter. And as an institution, the presidency has certainly changed over the centuries in ways too numerous to be contemplated here, such that the same office occupied by Washington and Carter had very different capacities and expectations.

Given these and other differences, any attempt to delineate similarities or to place these actions into general categories may neglect some details and differences in order to discern broader meanings. Nevertheless, that is what much historically minded social science does. Although cognizant of the dangers inherent in such a task, historical social science often seeks to step back from the particulars so as to discern generalities, to focus not just on the story but on the moral of the story or its broader significance, and to consider generalizability, portability, or whether the dynamics of one case might be relevant for understanding other cases and other issues, too. Those are the motivations for the discussion in this conclusion.

The analysis presented in this book is not merely a matter of antiquarian interest but rather has significant implications for multiple academic debates in political science and related fields and perhaps even for real-world politics, as discussed here. Specifically, an appreciation of the presidential use of mass pardons or amnesties for alienated groups is important for scholarly understandings of at least seven significant issues: (1) the incidence of domestic rebellions and the power of the U.S. federal government, (2) the use of mass pardons as distinct from individual pardons, (3) the role of rhetoric in some unilateral presidential directives, (4) the character of that rhetoric, (5) the broader phenomena of official governmental actions for political belonging and reconciliation, (6) the efficacy of presidential rhetoric, and (7) the future of presidential pardons. The rest of this conclusion briefly sketches the implications of this book for each of these issues.

RESISTING THE STATE

One implication of this book is historical and essentially empirical. Although the focus here has been on how presidents have responded to domestic unrest, the discussion of that unrest is significant. This book has demonstrated that serious, principled resistance to the U.S. federal government is not altogether rare. On the contrary, the United States has a substantial history of real resistance and in fact outright armed rebellion against the federal government. American rebellion is not limited just to the well-known case of the Civil War. Time and again Americans have resisted the state and its policies in a sustained and even violent fashion. This book may thus contribute to the small academic literature that documents and chronicles America's considerable history of rebellion. Although the primacy and indeed hegemony of the American national state survived these challenges, the state has had to contend with multiple episodes of serious resistance.

That fact can be important for understandings—both American and foreign—of American exceptionalism and political development. America's history of insurrection and resistance demonstrates that the hegemony of the American state is not altogether a given but rather something that has been contested, albeit unsuccessfully. This conception may perhaps occupy a middle ground between older scholarly interpretations of the American national state as shadowy and weak and more recent scholarly accounts of the American state as ever present and potent.[3] In terms of comparative political development, an awareness of America's history of rebellion and reconciliation suggests that the United States is perhaps not altogether an outlier but rather may be compared with other countries that have at times struggled to assert and maintain their control in the face of popular dissent, resistance, and rebellion. The eminent sociologist Charles Tilly suggested this point in 1969, and more than five decades later this analysis supports that suggestion.[4]

PARDONS FOR GROUPS

Another empirically significant aspect of this account is that it has demonstrated that presidential pardons are not just for individuals; there is a significant history of plural or mass pardons or amnesties. Indeed, this book has addressed only part of the broader phenomenon of mass pardons, specifically those pertaining to domestic rebellions and similar occurrences. In the aggregate, it appears that far more Americans have been pardoned via group pardons than via individual pardons, although the incomplete historical record necessarily renders such a claim imprecise. And unlike many individual pardons, the group pardons discussed here were arguably for more significant wrongs that posed more significant threats to the nation than the crimes addressed by most individual pardons. A journalist's account of Donald Trump's controversial pardons for white-collar criminals in February 2020 said, "The world will not change much because of these actions," but, in contrast, mass pardons offer the possibility of enacting great change.[5] Even though the use and politics of mass pardons no doubt often differ from those of individual pardons, scholarly accounts of the president's pardon power should be attentive to this important genre of pardons. Any conclusions or understandings of the president's pardon power based only on individual pardons are significantly incomplete.

Beyond the assertion that mass pardons matter, however, it should also be said that more could be said about the topic. Although this book constitutes an initial effort to address the relatively unexamined topic of presidential mass pardons and to raise awareness of it and its importance, scholars of pardons may well find that the topic of group pardons could benefit from further exploration, particularly of mass pardons that have addressed matters other than rebellion.

PARDONS AS RHETORICAL ACTS

Although the previous two implications are largely empirical and amount to calls for scholars to be more aware of certain phenomena (i.e., domestic resistance and mass pardons), the next several implications are more analytical and somewhat related. The discussion of the four complex cases of mass pardons and amnesties in the four previous chapters indicates that these actions generally have a significant rhetorical element and that presidents have been attentive to it. In their proclamations of pardons and in their efforts to defend and promote them, presidents have evidently felt the need to carefully employ rhetoric. In many of the cases discussed here, presidents solicited input from their cabinets and advisers and carefully crafted the pardon proclamations and supporting statements over time before actually issuing them.

Jimmy Carter's amnesty of early 1977 was the only one discussed here that was just a pro forma, legalistic document, without much in the way of rhetorical persuasion either contained in it or issued separately from it. It is the exception to the rule that mass pardons are not communicated in just basic legal fashion. And as discussed in the previous chapter, the minimalism of Carter's amnesty arguably was a rhetorical statement of sorts, as if to say that by 1977 nothing more remained to be said about the issue of resistance to the Vietnam War and that it was therefore appropriate to issue a simple amnesty without fanfare, explanation, or justification.

Carter's quasi-counterexample notwithstanding, the cases examined here have addressed a particular policy area in which unilateral presidential directives have incorporated and been accompanied by persuasive presidential rhetoric. Although the fact that presidents carefully used rhetoric in these cases is important, it remains to explain why rhetoric was used. The discussion here indicates that rhetorical persuasion was needed to convince those who could choose whether to accept a conditional pardon or to take an oath or to undertake a term of public service that they should do so, to convince the recipients of unconditional pardons that the measures were reasonable, and to convince other Americans that the pardons and their terms were appropriate and thereby to enhance the reconciliatory effect of the proclamations. In other words, presidents sought to persuade both the target group and the broader nation of the merits of these acts. In the cases discussed here, the presidents evidently believed that the pardons would be less effective if they were not to include persuasive rhetoric: the presidential deeds also needed presidential words.

It is entirely understandable that presidents have used rhetoric to promote political reconciliation. Minor administrative changes may be effectively enacted by a simple, bare-bones unilateral presidential directive unadorned with superfluous rhetoric, but national political reconciliation via a presidential proclamation of pardon or amnesty is a far more complicated matter. Bringing about true political reconciliation can require more than the stroke of a president's pen; it may well also require presidential persuasion. Unlike other unilateral presidential directives, which may require the assent of just a few employees within the executive bureaucracy to be effective, mass pardons require the assent of the people to be truly effective. Therefore, the efficacy of mass pardons and amnesties depends on the persuasiveness of presidential rhetoric. The ways in which a mass pardon is presented, promoted, administered, and defended matter, and they may even be as important as the legal change conferred by the pardon.

Gerald Ford invoked this point regarding his clemency program. When the Clemency Board named the first group of Vietnam War resisters to qualify for clemency, Ford held a signing ceremony in the White House Cabinet Room to formally approve the board's recommendations. He noted that although presidential signing ceremonies typically "mark the end of a project," this one marked "the beginning" or the first steps on a long road to reconciliation. Ford also said, "These first few clemencies do not end the unfinished business of clemency. The controversy is not stopped with the stroke of a pen. But the task of formal forgiveness is underway. I hope it marks the beginning of personal forgiveness in the hearts of all Americans troubled by Vietnam and its aftermath."[6] Thus, Ford recognized that the legal change conferred by his unilateral directive was but a necessary first step in a longer process of reconciliation in which communication and persuasion would be crucial.

Again, this book has demonstrated that some major unilateral presidential directives contained significant rhetorical components. Insofar as the pardon power is one of the few explicit and most plenary of presidential powers, the fact that even some pardons have a persuasive rhetorical element is striking. Although the pardon power is significant and little constrained, it is not omnipotent, and it cannot blithely overcome all obstacles; its broader efficacy in helping to overcome a problematic past depends in part on rhetorical persuasion. At least in the cases discussed here, unilateral presidential directives did not entirely afford presidents "power without persuasion" because the presidents employed rhetoric to persuade people about the merits of the mass pardons. In short, mass pardons are less strictly unilateral than some scholarship would lead us to expect.

This view comports with recent work by other scholars that has found that unilateral presidential directives might in fact require some persuasion.[7] The findings here might therefore contribute to that broader debate, but, strictly speaking, they are limited to the particular dynamics of the set of unilateral presidential directives comprising mass pardons for rebellions. The rhetorical or persuasive elements of mass pardons might be just an idiosyncrasy of such pardons, so it must remain for future scholarship to ascertain just how common the nonunilateral aspects of unilateral presidential directives really are.

VARIED RHETORIC

Another implication of this book for broader scholarly debates concerns not just the presence of intentional presidential rhetoric in these actions but its character. The main scholarly works on pardon rhetoric are by Karlyn Kohrs Campbell and Kathleen Hall Jamieson, who claim that pardons have a crucial rhetorical element but that it is rather limited and even formulaic. According to Campbell and Jamieson, "An analysis of pardoning rhetoric suggests that no presidential power is wholly unfettered. Even the unilateral and discretionary act of pardoning needs to be performed properly if presidential power is to be maintained." This is so, they contend, because "were any presidential power wholly unfettered, it would be impossible to claim that the rhetoric involved in its exercise was constitutive either of the institution or of a particular presidency. But because power is always limited, the rhetorical exercise thereof is constitutive in that such power will always be exercised wisely or unwisely, with care for or indifference to the institution and with concern for or apathy to the future of the presidency and future presidents."[8]

In other words, Campbell and Jamieson claim that a pardon must adhere to legalistic norms that articulate or at least allude to the pardon's proper place in the constitutional order. Otherwise, the president could simply declare, "I hereby pardon this person" or "I hereby grant amnesty to this group," with no explanation or justification whatsoever, an action that the authors suggest would be unsustainable. Beyond the need for a pardon to be firmly grounded in constitutional norms, Campbell and Jamieson also claim that a president's pardon rhetoric must cover three elements: "(1) acting in the presidential role as symbolic head of state; (2) demonstrating that this is an opportune time for action; and (3) justifying the pardon as for the public good."[9]

Since every pardon must address those things, Campbell and Jamieson find that pardons tend to be very similar and even formulaic. As noted in the introduction to this book, they maintain that presidential pardons are a rhetorical genre in which "the impersonal tone, the archaic language, reliance on legalistic terminology, and the formality of the document overpower individual style and give these documents a quaint sameness." In short, they contend that "as they recur through time, these forms of rhetorical action become ritualistic," and individual style is suppressed.[10]

For the most part, however, the pardons examined in this book call into question the accuracy of that assessment. The pardons discussed here do contain many of the elements that Campbell and Jamieson describe, and they do tend to follow a rough formula: they generally describe a problematic situation and enumerate the wrongs committed; sometimes they recount how the government responded to the situation; they often allude to some greater good to be served; they invoke the president's authority to act (per the Constitution or legislation or both); they proffer or confer a pardon, sometimes contingent upon the recipients undertaking some sort of loyalty action; and sometimes they threaten future action if the would-be recipients do not submit. Not every mass pardon follows this basic form, but many do.

But this does not mean that the mass pardons considered here were formulaic or that their rhetorical content was limited to legalistic invocations of constitutional norms. Some of the pardons omitted some of the elements listed. Some required detailed oaths, whereas others did not; some threatened, whereas others encouraged; some contained lengthy accounts of the wrongs done and detailed legalistic justifications of governmental action, whereas others were more limited; and some had voluminous and grandiloquent prose about the benefits of reconciliation, but others did not.[11] Furthermore, the pardons analyzed here vary considerably in their presentation as well as in their tone and justification. Lincoln's first mass pardon was contained in his Annual Message to Congress, and Ford dramatically signed his pardon on live television after justifying it, but Carter's amnesty was issued without any notice at all.

These pardons were far from uniform. For the presidents who crafted them, formulating and issuing them were not merely a matter of adapting a template and making only minor adjustments; they were not boilerplate forms with small differences. The legalistic norms of such pardons may somewhat constrain the scope for radically original or varied content, but within those loose constraints there is room for great variation, as we have seen in the previous chapters. And the different circumstances and scopes of these pardons are reflected in their varied rhetoric. In short, it appears that presidential pardons are a more varied rhetorical type than Campbell and Jamieson contend.

Again, not only was there presidential attention to rhetoric in the cases examined here, but that rhetoric also varied considerably. This view comports with previous scholarly work that has found rhetorical diversity in other unilateral presidential directives.[12] What accounts for the differences in rhetoric in these pardons? As this book has shown, different presidents and different political contexts drive differences in pardon rhetoric. The nature of the conflict and the president's relation to it determine much. But the rhetoric also depends on how limited or wide the pardon is in terms of the target group, whether the pardon is conditional, and how others view the pardon and the episode to which it responds.

PARDONS, PEOPLEHOOD, AND POLITICAL RECONCILIATION

It is not surprising that presidential mass pardons and amnesties tend to carefully employ rhetoric because these actions often amount to negotiating or asserting the nature of membership in the national political community. And as Rogers Smith has argued, conceptions of citizenship, political identity, or peoplehood are forged, sustained, and transformed by rhetorical narratives of belonging.[13] A political community might be created and to some extent policed by coercion, but its long-term maintenance and modification require rhetorical appeals that render plausible and even intuitive the various rights, obligations, and allegiance on which the community is based.

Some of the mass pardons considered here functioned in these ways. For example, as the historian John Rodrigue states of Abraham Lincoln's "Proclamation of Amnesty and Reconstruction," "The presidential pardon, requiring an oath of future loyalty, could be used to rebuild a political community."[14] Again, insofar as mass pardons and amnesties involve the maintenance or reestablishment of membership in a political community, the role of rhetoric in them accords with that of similar efforts to sustain political community.

The rhetorical aspect of mass pardons not only corresponds to that of the construction and maintenance of conceptions of peoplehood but also reflects the rhetorical aspects of other governmental actions for reconciliation. There is a large scholarly literature on political reconciliation and apology (broadly construed) in comparative politics and transitional justice, and it often focuses on the rhetoric of reconciliatory actions, including pardons and amnesties. This literature explores how governments use political apologies and other measures to try to reconcile aggrieved groups with the state, atone for historical wrongs, heal political divides, and move beyond a problematic past to a more inclusive future. Mass pardons or amnesties are a primary type of this action and can help to achieve political reconciliation by officially affirming the acceptance of the wayward group. Moreover, the acceptance of some conditional pardons may constitute a sort of apology in that the wrongdoers may effectively acknowledge the error of their ways or pledge their (past or future) loyalty.

Again, this book's contention that persuasive rhetoric is important for presidential mass pardons accords with the attention to rhetoric in the broader scholarship on political reconciliation and apology. Scholars may have neglected this connection because the United States, compared to other countries, has made relatively few official governmental apologies.[15] Nevertheless, it makes sense to consider U.S. mass pardons and amnesties as similar to such actions. Indeed, presidential proclamations of mass pardon share a number of basic traits with political apologies and other official governmental actions for reconciliation, which it may be useful to note here.

VARIETY OF MOTIVES

Despite their rhetoric of reconciliation, mass pardons and other reconciliatory actions such as political apologies can be driven by motivations that are less than altruistic. Indeed, although all of the pardons considered here were ostensibly aimed at achieving some sort of reconciliation, they nevertheless reflect a wide range of presidential motives, including instrumental ones. They were arguably driven by motivations that ranged from seeking to avoid armed confrontation (Buchanan's pardon) to aiding a military campaign (Lincoln's pardons), to other narrow political reasons (Ford seeking to differentiate himself from Nixon), to trying to avoid awkward alternatives (Johnson and the trial of Jefferson Davis), to truly trying to be merciful. Even though the legal and political changes brought by these pardons may be quite similar, and although the pardons tend to utilize rhetoric that extolls reconciliation, their motivations can be quite different.

ORIGINS: REQUESTED BEFORE GRANTED

Another commonality between mass pardons and other governmental actions for reconciliation is their origin. In some cases, it is the aggrieved group that initiates discussion about future governmental action to resolve the dispute; the potential subjects of a possible pardon or apology may be the first to broach the topic or to ask for the pardon. Thus, presidential action may be reactive rather than proactive. Some of the mass pardons discussed here were requested and did not entirely originate with the president. For example, some of the Pennsylvania rebels actively sought pardons; Andrew Johnson's many early pardons for individual Confederates informed his later mass pardons, as the various pardons of individual Mormons in the late nineteenth century informed the later mass pardon of Mormons in general; and the idea of some sort of amnesty for Vietnam War resisters was actively promoted for years before Ford acted. Like other pardons and apologies, some of the pardons discussed here demonstrate that mass pardons often are actively sought by the would-be recipients before they are granted by the government. The president's action is primary and fundamental, but the president's decision to issue a mass pardon does not occur in a vacuum and often involves crucial input from the pardon's would-be beneficiaries.

LOWER-LEVEL ACTIONS

Like many political apologies, mass pardons often have to contend with the phenomenon of lower-level actions. Indeed, some of the major mass pardons discussed here occurred in a milieu that also saw other, lesser reconciliatory actions, from individual pardons to lower-level pardons. Thus, there is the question of the relationship between pardons at different levels in that subordinates or lower-level political actors may issue pardons in furtherance of or in anticipation of presidential pardons. This occurred in three of the cases discussed here: General Henry Lee for George Washington, Governor Alfred Cumming for James Buchanan, and Governor Andrew Johnson for Abraham Lincoln. Mass pardons or apologies that do not come from the president may seem less significant than those that do, and they raise questions about the relationship between the actions of the political actors at the different levels.

TIMING

Another trait that several of the mass pardons discussed here share with political apologies is the timing of their issuance. As in the case of many state apologies, presidents often chose to issue mass pardons on significant dates, such as Independence Day and Christmas Day, in order to take advantage of the themes of nationalism, community, and generosity that those holidays evoke. This accords with the philosopher Kathleen Dean Moore's observation that major individual pardons are often granted on holidays: "Pardons granted on days of celebration—Christmas, Thanksgiving, Good Friday, the birthday of the Governor of Oklahoma—might seem to make no sense at all. But if pardons increase the popularity of the ruler, and if a popular ruler is in the public interest, then holiday pardons are in the public interest, and an attempt to justify them may be made on that ground." Moore notes that a century ago Governor James Withycombe of Oregon articulated a persuasive objection to such a practice: "If a man is entitled to a pardon, he is entitled to it regardless of whether or not it is due him during the holiday season. If he is not entitled to it, the fact that it is during the holiday season is no reason why leniency should be extended."[16] Nevertheless, mass pardons for political reconciliation may benefit from this sort of timing because the themes of the holiday might make the pardon more meaningful or palatable.

In addition, Adams's last-minute pardon for the participants in Fries's Rebellion and Carter's decision to confer amnesty on his first day in office suggest that presidents might gauge the timing of such actions for dramatic effect. And like other broadly apologetic gestures, pardons that are issued either too soon (Lincoln's first pardon might be such an example) or too late (Cleveland's pardon for polygamists might qualify) might be less likely to be effective in terms of achieving real political reconciliation. In short, the question of timing can be important for mass pardons, as it is for political apologies.

ITERATION

Many of the presidential acts here built upon earlier attempts to reconcile, and many were in some sense repeated or rearticulated in different forms. Furthermore, these pardons reflect something of the common quality of apologies that are iterated: if at first you don't succeed, try again. Each of the iterated pardons discussed here grew more encompassing and less restrictive or conditional, essentially growing from contingent pardons for some to blanket amnesties for (nearly) all. For example, George Washington expanded Governor Henry Lee's pardon; Andrew Johnson's four pardons followed this trajectory; and Jimmy Carter's amnesty expanded Gerald Ford's clemency in the same fashion. Like apologies and other official acts of reconciliation, these pardons suggest that the reconciliatory impulse, once activated, appears to grow stronger and more generous rather than stingier and more limited.

POWER REVERSAL

As acts of reconciliation, presidential pardons reflect the standard apologetic trope of mercy in which a powerful entity (i.e., the U.S. president if not also the entire federal government) bestows leniency and forgiveness on the (soon to be) conquered wrongdoers. But like some other apologetic acts, some of the mass pardons discussed here also demonstrate the odd phenomenon of reversing power roles as the would-be beneficiaries are empowered to decide whether to accept or reject the terms of reconciliation. Just as the recipient of a personal apology may choose to reject it as inappropriate or inadequate and thus opt not to reconcile but rather remain at odds, someone who is offered a pardon may choose to reject it as being overly demanding or otherwise undesirable, as many Vietnam War draft evaders dismissed Ford's clemency offer. This suggests that perhaps part of the process of effectively reintegrating an alienated group involves that group's actively questioning the conditions of its own readmission. In other words, reconciliation with the broader community may at times be a mutually interpretative act.

This may be easiest to see for conditional pardons: if the party who is offered a pardon rejects its conditions, then the pardon fails. But a similar dynamic may also obtain for pardons that are not conditional. If a pardon is not conditional, then the wrongdoers cannot refuse the pardon, as might be done in response to other apologetic acts; they are pardoned whether they consent to it or not. Yet even if the wrongdoers cannot reject the pardon, they may require that the pardon meet certain criteria for it to be truly effective. The president must persuade the pardon's recipients and the nation that it is appropriate. And this is where the rhetoric of pardon is crucial: the deed alone might not be enough; the particular words can matter, too. Again, the point is that although pardons confer a benefit given by someone in a position of great power, their recipients also have power to determine their efficacy. As the acclaimed author Margaret Atwood wrote, "Remember that forgiveness too is a power. To beg for it is a power, and to withhold or bestow it is a power, perhaps the greatest."[17]

REJECTING RECONCILIATION

When a mass pardon is not conditional, such that its recipients cannot formally reject it, they may nevertheless opt to flee rather than submit. Like some political apologies and related actions, mass pardons can fail to achieve reconciliation when some people spurn them by fleeing.

Regardless of how well the president manages the granting of a mass pardon, some recipients may effectively reject it by going elsewhere. Sometimes the target group moves away; members of the aggrieved community may choose to leave the country rather than reconcile. Relevant examples discussed here include David Bradford's flight to Spanish territory after the Whiskey Rebellion, the Mormon "Move South" in 1858, Confederates such as Judah Benjamin moving abroad after the Civil War, and Vietnam War resisters staying in Canada and elsewhere even after Carter's amnesty. Mass pardons aim to reestablish the recipients' place within the national community, so recipients who have left the country and choose to remain outside it may undermine the pardons' efficacy.[18]

COUNTERAPOLOGIES

As with political apologies, the actions of other political actors regarding presidential mass pardons can complicate things. This may be seen in terms of counterapologetic actions that undermine the reconciliatory impact of a pardon, either before or after its issuance. For example, Alexander Hamilton's letter criticizing John Adams, Brigham Young's actions after 1858, radical Republicans in Congress during Andrew Johnson's administration, and Senator Bob Dole's address to legionnaires after Carter's announcement—all posed challenges to presidential efforts to achieve reconciliation. These types of pushback obviously constitute a challenge to reconciliation via amnesty, and they arguably also constitute their own distinct rhetorical category.

EFFICACY

Having now argued that presidential mass pardons for major political ruptures have a significant rhetorical element, that their rhetoric varies, and that they are broadly similar to articulations of peoplehood and other official acts of political reconciliation such as governmental apologies, one might well ask whether any of it really matters or whether these actions are truly effective. In short, did and do these mass pardons work?

In some cases, the mass pardons examined here were obviously effective in that they avoided or decreased large-scale violence. This was the case with Buchanan's pardon and the short-lived Utah War, and it is also clear that Lincoln's pardons helped to hasten the Union's victory in the Civil War. Had those pardons not been issued, there would almost certainly have been much more violence than there was. Other pardons were clearly effective insofar as they removed the taint of criminality and ensured that their recipients could return to the status of regular citizenship with its various benefits. Clear examples include some of the Civil War pardons and those by Harrison, Cleveland, Ford, and Carter. In other words, regardless of whether these pardons facilitated deep and lasting reconciliation, at a minimum they were a crucial part of stopping armed hostilities and criminal exclusion and helped to bring about peace.

Even if some of the pardons clearly led to less conflict, however, that result might be due to the legal changes conferred by the pardons rather than to their rhetoric. Beyond the legal changes brought by the pardons, did the presidents' words enhance the efficacy of their actions? As noted in the introduction to this book, on one view presidential rhetoric is not nearly as effective as we might assume it is. If, as George Edwards has argued in *On Deaf Ears: The Limits of the Bully Pulpit* (2003), presidential rhetoric is generally ineffective,[19] then how can one expect presidents to persuade the government's foes to accept its terms or to persuade the American people to forgive lawbreakers, rebels, and traitors?

Edwards's critique is largely empirical, and the cases discussed here do not easily permit a precise empirical assessment because most of them are too deeply historical for polling data to shed any light on the pardons' efficacy. One cannot go back to the 1790s or the 1860s to survey the American people concerning what they thought about the particulars of these events. It is therefore not possible to gauge these pardons' efficacy with much empirical precision. As discussed in the previous chapter, polls about Carter's amnesty showed that public opinion was sharply divided, and there is no easy way to ascertain if a change in Carter's rhetoric would have led to greater or lesser approbation.

One might, however, mine the historical record for quotations attesting to the efficacy of the presidential rhetoric contained in the mass pardons examined here. As we have seen, major newspaper accounts of some mass pardons spoke of their efficacy. And it is tempting to invoke a quote from a committed Confederate or an exiled draft evader, for example, saying that a particular rhetorical turn of phrase or some point that Lincoln or Ford invoked in or about a mass-pardon proclamation made all the difference and convinced them to change their mind and embrace the president's terms. Findings of that sort would support the claim that presidential rhetoric was effective.

But such an exercise could also lead to legitimate criticisms of selectively picking data to support a particular view. Furthermore, there may be reason to doubt the sincerity of some pronouncements of rhetorical efficacy: as this study has indicated, public professions of reconciliation can mask a variety of stronger, more instrumental motives. For example, some of the whiskey rebels who signed the oath of submission were reportedly not truly repentant. Similarly, Brigham Young's acceptance of Buchanan's pardon was clearly not sincere. And many Confederates reportedly took the loyalty oath in Lincoln's first mass pardon just to advance their personal situation rather than to truly affirm their support for the Union.

These points suggest that Edwards's challenge about the efficacy of presidential rhetoric can be difficult to directly rebut. But there is some evidence that some particular rhetoric in some mass pardons dissuaded some people from accepting them. For example, Mormon leaders were initially put off by how Buchanan's proclamation characterized their behavior; Jefferson Davis was opposed to Johnson's first two mass pardons because of how they treated the Emancipation Proclamation; and some Vietnam War resisters opposed Ford's clemency offer because of how it was framed.

The best evidence of the efficacy of the rhetoric of the mass pardons examined here may be that so many of their recipients embraced them.

The subjects of these actions surely would not have accepted them had they not been presented and promoted in appealing terms. Moreover, the fact that presidents and their advisers evidently felt they had to utilize rhetoric in undertaking these actions suggests that the rhetoric served some purpose, and the fact that presidents often repeated the relevant rhetoric suggests that it had the desired effect. For example, had Ford not perceived some efficacy in his remarks to the VFW, he surely would not have repeated them to the American people on live television before issuing his clemency proclamation. Given these considerations, it seems reasonable to conclude that the persuasive rhetoric involved in issuing the mass pardons highlighted in this book did not fall altogether "on deaf ears."

Ultimately, it is difficult to say exactly how much of the efficacy of these actions derived from their rhetoric and how much came from just the legal changes they conferred. The most that can be fairly said is that in the aggregate these actions did foster peace and reconciliation. And that may well be enough. Had presidents not issued and promoted these pardons as they did, the conflicts that they sought to address would surely not have been ameliorated to the extent that they were and thus would have continued to strain national unity more than they did.

This book also indicates that Edwards's critique may fail to give sufficient credit for the efficacy of presidential rhetoric in two other respects. First, via mass pardons presidents can (re-)create an entire discursive community; they can (re)establish full citizenship and membership in the national community and help to put the past behind the nation. Apart from moving the people toward their desired point of view, presidents may essentially reconstitute the people. Second, Edwards's critique pertains mainly to presidents' (in)ability to move the public on concrete policy proposals, but an awareness of mass pardons suggests that presidents can use rhetoric to put different issues on the agenda and to massage the public's views of broader political matters. Regardless of whether the pardons' recipients were placated by the presidents' rhetoric, that rhetoric helped to frame the actions for the broader public and to set the terms of the postconflict eras. In other words, mass pardons point to the potential efficacy of presidential rhetoric on a more fundamental level than Edwards addresses.

In the years since Edwards first published his critique of presidential rhetoric, numerous scholars have argued against it and have claimed that presidential rhetoric can be effective in one way or another.[20] Various journalists have also found that the president's words can have a real impact.[21] Beyond academics and journalists, courts have also claimed that presidential rhetoric matters.[22] Thus, the evidence here of the efficacy of presidential rhetoric for mass pardons, even if mixed and limited, may add to various other claims about its efficacy.

Yet in the attempt to redeem some efficacy for presidential rhetoric, the point should not be overstated. As Justice Stephen Field noted in *Knote v. United States* (95 U.S. 149 [1877]), a pardon "does not make amends for the past," meaning that it cannot undo all that was done. The pardon power is great, and presidential rhetoric can make mass pardons more politically effective, but sometimes even effective rhetoric may not be enough. The overall political context can limit the ability of both words and deeds to achieve significant political reconciliation. Congress and the courts can try to thwart or limit effective reconciliation via presidential pardon. Even if the president's pardon power is plenary, such that the other branches have little formal means of checking or balancing it, their criticisms need not be altogether impotent, at least politically. They can challenge the purposes for which the pardons are issued and can push back against presidential claims about the general desirability of reconciliation or the particular means toward that end. Indeed, symbolic counterapologetic actions can significantly diminish the efficacy of reconciliatory gestures such as mass pardons. Public sentiment plays a key role in reconciliation after rebellion, and the president's voice is not the only by which people are influenced.

AMNESTY'S FUTURE

Apart from the implications this book has for academic debates on mass pardons, such as the half dozen mentioned in the previous sections, there is also the question of what if anything the analysis here means for real-world politics and public policy. In particular, can this book's historical discussion help us to better understand pardons today or even tomorrow? This book has indicated that mass pardons can do a great deal of good, so perhaps this will provide advocates of pardons with more reasons to advocate for more pardons. However, the odds of seeing more mass pardons of this sort in the near future are likely not good, for two reasons.

First, it is arguably the case that at present there are no large aggrieved groups in the United States that have resisted the state for principled reasons and that might now stand to benefit from a mass pardon or amnesty. Most of the cases discussed here are somewhat removed from contemporary political life and involved groups that strenuously resisted the federal government and were met with a forceful or even military response from the government, but arguably there is no similarly situated large group of domestic rebels in the United States today. Without a ready population of recent insurgents, the opportunities for an amnesty like those discussed here are perhaps correspondingly limited.

However, it is not the case that there are *no* groups that might benefit from a mass pardon today. Insofar as the president's pardon power has few limits and mass pardons may reach vast groups, the president has the ability to unilaterally change the lives of thousands or even millions of Americans via a quick pardon. For example, there are presently more than 150,000 inmates in the U.S. federal criminal justice system, tens of thousands under federal indictment, and many millions with a federal criminal record. Even if those people are not members of a principled group that engaged in violent confrontation with the government, they are nevertheless people who stand to benefit from a pardon. More and more Americans have come to embrace the idea of criminal-sentencing reform and rehabilitation, so presidential action to release inmates or to forgive former ones might well find a receptive audience. A mass pardon of federal criminal offenders today would likely not entail the sort of political reconciliation that the four cases here did, but it could nevertheless constitute a major instance of forgiveness and transformation.

Apart from ameliorating the harshness of the criminal justice system, a mass pardon or amnesty may perhaps also address the millions of undocumented immigrants in the United States. By most estimates, more than 11 million unauthorized immigrants are currently living in the United States, or more than 3 percent of the total population, and two-thirds of them have been in the country for more than a decade.[23] The daily lives of undocumented immigrants are constantly subject to a host of uncertainties and difficulties, including access to education and health care as well as the possibility of being deported. For years, the president and Congress have failed to agree on a course forward. Instead of a legislative or administrative solution, some argue that the president could simply use the office's pardon power to help undocumented immigrants. A pardon for undocumented immigrants would not confer citizenship, but it could remove the possibility of deportation.

However, such a course of action is potentially problematic. Although several million undocumented immigrants entered the United States unlawfully and thereby violated the federal criminal code, most undocumented immigrants initially entered the country legally but then overstayed their tourist or business visas. And simply being in the United States unlawfully is not itself a crime per se but rather a civil offense subject to a penalty of deportation. As discussed in chapter 2, there is some dispute about whether a presidential pardon can address civil wrongs rather than criminal ones. If courts were to uphold such a distinction, then presumably the president would be able pardon only the minority of undocumented immigrants who entered illegally, not the majority who entered legally.[24] Insofar as there is a real question about whether presidential pardons may address civil offenses, the ability of a mass pardon to resolve the undocumented immigrant issue is uncertain.

The second reason that the odds for a future mass pardon are low is politics. This book has shown that well-executed mass pardons can do much good, but they are subject to a host of political factors. One of those political factors is blowback, or the criticism that a president can face from citizens who believe that a granted pardon is inappropriate. For example, in the cases explored here, Adams and Buchanan experienced such criticism, as did Johnson, Ford, and Carter. Of course, a mass pardon could also please people (beyond its recipients) and thus offer a political benefit to the president. But as Susan Hennessey and Benjamin Wittes note, "Pardons seldom result in substantial political benefit."[25] And the odds of political criticism for a pardon outweighing public praise for it might well be greater when the target group is a disaffected minority violently at odds with the national majority.

Arguably, the political barriers to national reconciliation via mass pardons are even greater today than they were in decades past. The contemporary era is characterized by elevated levels of partisanship, low levels of public trust in government and democratic processes, and the dissipation of common news media, none of which augurs well for the political benefits of a president pardoning a large group of rebels. Moreover, the idea of invoking presidential action to forgive large groups of recalcitrant citizens is at odds with the recent vogue for "cancel culture" or forever shunning and ostracizing wrongdoers. In short, politics might well render a president hesitant to grant a mass pardon for rebels.

In *Commentaries on the Constitution of the United States* (1833), Justice Joseph Story discussed how political considerations might affect pardons: "If the [pardon] power should ever be abused, it would be far less likely to occur in opposition than in obedience to the will of the people. The danger is not, that in republics the victims of the law will too often escape punishment by a pardon, but that the power will not be sufficiently exerted in cases where public feeling accompanies the prosecution, and assigns the ultimate doom to persons who have been convicted upon slender testimony or popular suspicions."[26] Thus, Story worried in the early nineteenth century that popular politics might prevent a president from granting a deserved pardon.

The evidence over the past several decades suggests that Story was correct. By most accounts, presidents since Gerald Ford have been reticent to issue many pardons because of fear of political blowback for appearing to be overly generous or even tolerant of serious wrongdoing.[27] There has been a clear trend of presidents issuing fewer and fewer pardons. Former U.S. pardon attorney Margaret Colgate Love noted that Franklin Roosevelt issued more than 3,000 pardons and 557 commutations and that "until 1980, each president granted well over a hundred post-sentence pardons and sentence commutations almost every year, without fanfare or scandal."[28] But she bemoaned that after 1980, "presidential pardoning went into a decline."[29] Similarly, in 2013 law professor Marc Miller said of pardons, "That practice has decayed almost to the point of oblivion in the federal system, and in most states."[30] And even though Barack Obama made extensive use of commutations, giving 1,715 of them (330 of them on his last day in office), which was more than his twelve predecessors combined, on several occasions the *New York Times* chided him for not granting more pardons.[31]

The foregoing considerations suggest that it is unlikely that the United States will soon see another mass pardon or amnesty for political reconciliation like those examined in this book. Nevertheless, the practice is well established, and the tool remains there for future presidents to use if and when the occasion arises. Sooner or later such an occasion will surely arise, and when it does, the president can defend a mass pardon by invoking the country's rich history of similar actions and the broader purposes that they served.

Reconciliation and forgiveness are basic to many major religious traditions, and they comport with the long-running American valorization of second chances and pragmatic solutions. As George W. Bush said in his State of the Union Address in 2004, "America is the land of second chance, and when the gates of the prison open, the path ahead should lead to a better life."[32] And as we saw in chapter 1, even the arch Federalist Alexander Hamilton argued that government should avoid overly cruel outcomes and be prepared to foster "the tranquility of the commonwealth." Clearly, the nine presidents whose pardon proclamations were explored here also believed in the value of forgiveness, as did most of the recipients of those pardons and much of the national audience. This book has demonstrated that the American people can be willing to forgive, but it might fall to the president to convince them that they should do so.

In conclusion, this book has attempted to address an important yet understudied topic and to engage with several different strands of academic literature. It has covered the presidential use of mass pardons in some detail by analyzing four complex cases in which multiple presidents issued pardons to try to foster domestic reconciliation. Future academic work—and, more importantly, future presidents—will undoubtedly challenge and change the themes discussed here. But this book should encourage scholars, citizens, politicians, and perhaps even presidents to consider how the president can employ both words and deeds to overcome divisions and rebellion and to facilitate political reconciliation.

EPILOGUE

I submitted the final manuscript for this book to the press shortly
after Election Day in 2020, but the final months of Donald Trump's
presidency produced several actions that are sufficiently relevant to
this book to warrant a brief mention here.

In late 2020, Trump pardoned several associates who had been convicted of making false statements during the Mueller Investigation; he
pardoned several private military contractors who had been convicted
of killing civilians; and the Department of Justice began an investigation of an alleged "bribery-for-pardon" scheme at the White House.
The majority of the relatively few clemency actions that Trump undertook while president occurred on his last full day in office, when he
issued seventy-three pardons and seventy commutations, and most of
them did not go through regular channels but were granted only after
their recipients leveraged connections and paid insiders to intercede on
their behalf. Trump publicly mused about possibly issuing preemptive
pardons for himself and his family members, but shortly before the end
of his term the White House counsel and attorney general convinced
him not to do so.

But the most relevant action of the end of the Trump presidency
occurred on January 6, 2021, when a mob of hundreds of people who
supported Trump's efforts to overturn the presidential election of 2020

violently stormed the U.S. Capitol and disrupted Congress's official certification of the election. For some, it was an impromptu riot, but others
saw it as a deliberate attempt at a putsch, coup, insurrection, or rebellion. I had concluded this book by noting that the odds of a new mass
pardon or amnesty like those discussed in chapters 2–5 were low
because of the contemporary lack of a group of aggrieved rebels, but the
Capitol attackers arguably are such a group. There are, of course, many
questions about whether this group is in any meaningful way analo-
gous to the groups discussed here, whether it is deserving of presidential forgiveness, and whether a pardon for them would help or hinder
national unity and peace. Regardless, their actions suggest that the concerns of this book are not merely historical but will be continue to be
relevant going forward. The United States is unlikely to be forever
rebellion free, so the possibility of mass pardons for rebels will surely be
an issue in the future.

APPENDIX

OTHER MASS PARDONS AND AMNESTIES
IN THE UNITED STATES

T his book has analyzed four complex cases of presidential mass pardons or amnesties for political reconciliation involving rebellions and major domestic political ruptures: George Washington and John Adams for insurrectionists in Pennsylvania; James Buchanan, Benjamin Harrison, and Grover Cleveland for Mormon insurrectionists and polygamists; Abraham Lincoln and Andrew Johnson for Confederates during and after the Civil War; and Gerald Ford and Jimmy Carter for Vietnam War resisters. Those cases appear to constitute the main instances of mass pardons for sustained political resistance and rebellion throughout U.S. history.

However, those cases do not comprise the complete set of all American mass pardons or amnesties; presidents have issued other mass pardons for various other issues, and some of them might appear to be similar to those analyzed here.[1] Nevertheless, the other mass pardons may be distinguished and excluded from the group discussed in this book on various grounds. For example, some predated the formal creation of the United States, and others addressed wrongs that were comparatively narrower in scope in the sense that they were not part of broader political disruptions or threats to the national community. This appendix briefly describes some of these other mass pardons, listing them in chronological order.

THE COLONIAL ERA

There were a variety of group pardons in the colonial era.[2] For example, Nathaniel Bacon's rebellion in Jamestown in 1676–1677 led to a pardon by Governor William Berkeley of Virginia. And during Shays's Rebellion of 1786–1787, Governor James Bowdoin of Massachusetts granted a pardon to citizens who had been involved in the insurgency but explicitly excluded Shays and three others. Although pardons for rebellions in the colonial era informed later ones, they took place before the U.S. Constitution formalized the president's pardon power.

LOYALISTS

By many estimates, roughly one in five people in the American colonies at the time of the Revolutionary War—roughly half a million people—remained loyal to Great Britain. In 1776, General George Washington considered issuing a generous amnesty for Loyalists to try to win them over to the revolutionary cause.[3] In 1777, Washington offered to pardon Loyalists who would change their allegiance to the United States, and in 1782 he recommended that the Congress pardon Loyalist regiments among the British forces, subject to certain restrictions.[4] Also during the war, some states issued pardons and amnesties for Loyalists, often specifically excluding certain individuals.[5]

The issue of amnesty for Loyalists was debated among the commissioners who negotiated the Treaty of Paris, which ended the Revolutionary War in 1783, and both England and France favored amnesty. Ultimately, the treaty did not provide amnesty, but it contained two articles that addressed Loyalists. It said the Congress of Confederation would "earnestly recommend" that state legislatures recognize the rights of Loyalists and provide restitution of their confiscated property, and it stipulated that the new country would prevent any future confiscations of Loyalists' property. State policies against Loyalists ceased, and some states offered to grant amnesty in return for the Loyalists' taking an oath of allegiance to the United States. For example, the North Carolina General Assembly passed several conciliatory measures between 1784 and 1790 to reimburse Loyalists whose property had been confiscated.[6] Despite these policies, tens of thousands of loyalists fled the United States, many of them permanently settling in eastern Canada. Like the colonial pardons noted earlier, most of the governmental responses to loyalists occurred before the U.S. Constitution came into effect.

SEDITION

The Alien and Sedition Acts were four measures passed by Congress in 1798 and signed into law by John Adams. Their ostensible purpose was to protect the republic from foreign powers, chiefly France, but Democratic-Republicans claimed that the acts stifled legitimate political dissent and curtailed the freedom of the press. The laws were unpopular and arguably helped Thomas Jefferson defeat Adams in the election of 1800. Shortly after Jefferson took office in 1801, he pardoned the ten people who had been convicted under the Alien and Sedition Acts and were still in prison. They included David Brown, who evidently did not hear about his pardon by Jefferson because he petitioned the president for a pardon two weeks after Jefferson had pardoned him.[7] Also, Congress repaid their fines. Most of the Alien and Sedition Acts' measures expired or were repealed by 1802.

BARATARIAN PIRATES

Jean Lafitte was a pirate, a privateer, and a smuggler in the early nine-teenth century in southern Louisiana, particularly in and around Barataria Bay, where the Mississippi River meets the Gulf of Mexico. He oversaw hundreds of men and dozens of armed vessels and plundered many Spanish ships. In September 1814, British forces tried to enlist Lafitte's aide in capturing New Orleans and offered to pardon him for past offenses and to pay him if he agreed. Lafitte demurred but eventually declined and instead offered to assist General Andrew Jackson and the American forces on the condition that they urge the president to pardon him. Jackson was initially suspicious and even attacked Lafitte's forces. However, Jackson soon changed his mind, and he and Governor Jacques Villeré of Louisiana agreed to make peace with Lafitte in order to gain his assistance against the British. In January 1815, Lafitte and his men helped defeat the British in the Battle of New Orleans. Jackson praised Lafitte in his report to the secretary of war, and James Madison then pardoned Lafitte in February 1815.[8]

Madison's proclamation noted that "the offenders have manifested a sincere penitence" and that the State of Louisiana had recommended a pardon. The pardon was contingent: "*Provided,* That every person claiming the benefit of this full pardon in order to entitle himself thereto shall produce a certificate in writing from the governor of the State of Louisiana stating that such person has aided in the defense of New Orleans and the adjacent country during the invasion thereof as aforesaid."[9] Ultimately, only one pirate sought the certification of military service that was a condition of Madison's pardon, yet authorities ceased prosecution of the pirates.[10]

DAKOTA SIOUX

The Dakota Sioux Uprising of August–September 1862 (also known as the Dakota War) grew out of long-standing disputes between several Native American tribes and American settlers in southwestern Minnesota regarding land, treaty violations, annuity payments, and trading. It culminated in a series of battles over several weeks that left hundreds of settlers and dozens of Dakota Sioux warriors dead. Some 1,400 federal troops entered the conflict, and by late September more than 2,000 Dakota Sioux were taken into custody. Over the next several weeks, 393 of them faced military trials, and on November 8 convictions were announced for 323 men, of whom 303 were given death sentences.[11]

In early November, President Abraham Lincoln received a list of the convicted Dakota Sioux. He decided to review the convictions, and his advisers found that most of the condemned Sioux had been sentenced after only ten minutes of consideration. Many Minnesotans and public officials were eager to have them executed, but some religious leaders pushed for pardons. By one account, "The execution problem haunted Lincoln."[12] He wanted to ascertain which of the convicted Sioux were more clearly guilty, and he was under great political pressure. On December 1, 1862, in his Second Annual Message to Congress, Lincoln appeared to validate the desire for vengeance when he noted that the Dakota Sioux had killed eight hundred people in the conflict and that "the State of Minnesota has suffered great injury from this Indian War."[13]

That same day Lincoln sought legal advice from Judge Advocate General Joseph Holt: "I wish your legal opinion whether if I should conclude to execute only a part of them, I must myself designate which, or could I leave the designation to some officer on the ground?" Holt replied to Lincoln, "The power cannot be delegated."[14] This suggests that the president was reluctant to decide who would live and die.

According to the historian David Nichols, "Lincoln apparently believed that the situation demanded a blood sacrifice if emotions were to be calmed."[15] But he chose a "middle-road" solution, ultimately deciding to pardon all but 39 of the 303 condemned prisoners. One more prisoner was pardoned at the last minute, and on December 26 the remaining 38 men were executed by hanging. Months after the hangings, Lincoln issued individual pardons for several of the remaining Dakota Sioux prisoners, and on April 30, 1864, he pardoned 26 of them.[16]

For some critics, Lincoln's pardons indicate that he could and perhaps should have done more. As Nichols explains,

Arguments have raged since as to whether Lincoln acted humanely or whether he could have prevented bloodshed altogether. Those favoring the humanity of the decision can argue that Lincoln acted in an atmosphere of hatefulness. Without him, all of the three hundred three probably would have been executed. On the other hand, Lincoln still ordered the largest official mass execution in American history in which guilt of the executed cannot be positively determined. He also acquiesced in concession to Minnesotans that resulted in further injustice to the Indians. Nevertheless, viewed in context, Lincoln's actions were relatively humanitarian. By the time the problem reached Lincoln's desk, no ideal decision was possible. Given the demands of the War for the Union, there may have been very little else he could do.[17]

Lincoln later explained his review of the convictions to the U.S. Senate: "Anxious to not act with so much clemency as to encourage another outbreak on one hand, nor with so much severity as to be real cruelty on the other, I ordered a careful examination of the records of the trials to be made."[18] The pardons were politically unpopular, but Lincoln said, "I could not afford to hang men for votes."[19] Whatever Lincoln's motives were, they likely did not include an effort to reconcile with the Sioux more generally, let alone also with the great many other Native Americans who had been wronged or mistreated by the American government.[20]

THE PHILIPPINE-AMERICAN WAR

The United States gained control of the Philippines in 1898, after the Spanish-American War. But from 1898 to 1902, the Tagalog Revolt against U.S. authorities in the Philippines led to thousands of deaths on both sides. On July 4, 1902, Theodore Roosevelt issued a proclamation "granting pardon and amnesty" to forces led by Emilio Aguinaldo, who had fought the United States for control of the Philippines, saying that the pardon was "wise and humane." The pardon was contingent on rebels taking the following oath: "I solemnly swear (or affirm) that I recognize and accept the supreme authority of the United States of America in the Philippine Islands and will maintain true faith and allegiance thereto; that I impose upon myself this obligation voluntarily without mental reservation or purpose of evasion so help me God." Roosevelt's pardon excluded some groups of people, such as those convicted of serious crimes and Moro tribesmen, yet it stipulated that they could individually apply for a pardon.[21]

PROHIBITION

After Congress overrode Woodrow Wilson's veto of the National Prohibition (or Volstead) Act of 1919, Wilson pardoned or granted clemency to some five hundred people who were convicted under the law. According to Marie Gottschalk, "His pardons were widely understood at the time as an indictment of Prohibition," much as Jefferson's pardon of those convicted under the Alien and Sedition Acts was driven by his opposition to those laws.[22]

ESPIONAGE IN WORLD WAR I

On December 23, 1921, Warren Harding released two dozen people convicted under the Espionage Act of 1917, including Eugene V. Debs. Debs had been sentenced to ten years in prison in 1918 for criticizing the country's involvement in World War I, and in 1920 he ran for president while incarcerated, garnering 3.5 percent of the vote. Woodrow Wilson had rejected calls to pardon Debs, but Harding commuted his sentence. On Christmas Day in 1923, Calvin Coolidge released the remaining prisoners who were convicted under the Espionage Act.[23]

JAPANESE AMERICANS

On Christmas Eve in 1947, Harry Truman pardoned several hundred Japanese Americans who had resisted military conscription during World War II on the grounds that they should not have to fight for a country that interned them because of doubts regarding their loyalty. More than three hundred people from ten internment camps— especially Heart Mountain Relocation Camp in Wyoming—were jailed for draft evasion. The trial of sixty-three resisters from Heart Mountain in June 1944 was the largest mass trial for draft resistance ever in the United States.[24]

DRUG OFFENDERS

From 1961 to 1963, John F. Kennedy pardoned more than 100 people who were first-time drug offenders but serving long mandatory-minimum sentences stipulated by the Narcotics Control Act of 1956. Lyndon Johnson pardoned 226 similarly sentenced drug offenders. By one account, the two presidents' actions laid "the groundwork for repeal of mandatory minimum sentencing laws in the 1970s."[25]

PUERTO RICAN TERRORISTS

On August 11, 1999, Bill Clinton offered to commute the sentences of sixteen members of the Fuerzas Armadas de Liberación Nacional (FALN), a terrorist group that sought independence for Puerto Rico. The group had engaged in violence and conducted more than 120 bombings in the United States between 1974 and 1982, resulting in six deaths and many serious injuries. The sixteen men were convicted of conspiracy and sedition and sentenced to lengthy prison terms, of which they had served nineteen years when Clinton acted. Clinton offered clemency on the condition that the prisoners renounce violence. Congress condemned Clinton's action by votes of 95–2 in the Senate and 311–41 in the House. Two men rejected Clinton's clemency offer, including Oscar Lopez, but in 2017 Barack Obama commuted the remaining twenty years of Lopez's fifty-five-year sentence for seditious conspiracy.[26]

MILITARY DESERTION

There are numerous instances of presidents pardoning Americans who avoided military conscription or deserted once in the military. For example, during the Revolutionary War, George Washington repeatedly offered to pardon deserters who returned to duty. During the War of 1812, the American military suffered a great many desertions. According to one account, "Madison had to pardon the deserters in order to fill the ranks."[27] In February 1812, Madison offered to pardon deserters if they turned themselves in to the U.S. military within four months. He issued a similar pardon in October, with another four-month timeframe. Madison issued a third proclamation of pardon for deserters in June 1814, provided they return to duty within three months. The Civil War also saw pardons for deserters.

In the twentieth century, Woodrow Wilson commuted death sentences for World War I deserters. Warren Harding released Eugene V. Debs and many others who were imprisoned for opposing conscription. In 1923, Calvin Coolidge granted a general pardon to people jailed under wartime draft laws, and in 1924 he gave amnesty to deserters. In 1933, Franklin Roosevelt restored all rights of citizenship to people who had violated the draft or espionage laws. And Harry Truman issued several amnesties for people who had resisted military service during World War II.[28]

NOTES

INTRODUCTION

1. Gerald R. Ford, "Proclamation 4313—Announcing a Program for the Return of Vietnam Era Draft Evaders and Military Deserters, American Presidency Project, ed. Gerhard Peters and John T. Woolley, https://www.presidency.ucsb.edu/node/256605.

2. Judy Keen, "Bush Grants Pardons Less Than Predecessors," *USA Today*, December 30, 2005.

3. John Gramlich and Kirsten Bialik, "Obama Used Clemency Power More Often Than Any President Since Truman," Pew Research Center, January 20, 2017.

4. Thomas B. Edsall, "The Savage Injustice of Trump's Military Pardons," *New York Times*, December 4, 2019.

5. As Edward Corwin once put it, with regard to certain powers the Constitution "is an invitation to struggle" (*The President: Office and Powers, 1787–1957*, 5th rev. ed. [New York: New York University Press, 1984], 201).

6. Craig Allen Smith and Kathy B. Smith, *The White House Speaks: Presidential Leadership as Persuasion* (Westport, CT: Praeger, 1994), 63.

7. Harold J. Krent, "Conditioning the President's Conditional Pardon Power," *California Law Review* 89, no. 6 (December 2001): 1668 n. 14.

8. Barack Obama, remarks at White House press conference, January 17, 2017, quoted in Bill Chappell, "Chelsea Manning, Once Sentenced to 35 Years, Walks Free After 7 Years," NPR, May 17, 2017.

9. Anthony Ripley, "Amnesty for Draft Resisters Is Expected to Be Divisive Political Issue for Years," *New York Times*, January 30, 1973.

10. Jonathan Truman Dorris, *Pardon and Amnesty Under Lincoln and Johnson: The Restoration of the Confederates to Their Rights and Privileges, 1861–1898* (1953; reprint, Westport, CT: Greenwood Press, 1977), xvii.

11.   Edward S. Corwin, *The Constitution and What It Means Today* (Princeton, NJ: Princeton University Press, 1948), 97–98.

12.   As Margaret Colgate Love states, "Even sixty years ago when pardoning was frequent and routine, the only systematic study of the federal pardon power noted [that] the 'persistence of erroneous ideas, the lack of exact information, and the absence of publicity concerning the acts of the pardoning authority envelop the power in a veil of mystery'" ("The Twilight of the Pardon Power," *Journal of Criminal Law and Criminology* 100, no. 3 [2010]: 1173 n. 13).

13.   The rationale for a pardon may be seen in the distinction in analytic philosophy between the "act" and "rule" types of utilitarianism: the former says that in a given case you may (or should) violate the general rule if doing so would lead to greater utility. In contrast to the idea that a pardon constitutes an aberration or a departure from the norm, on some accounts it is entirely normal. The journalist Amanda Taub claims, "If you define amnesty broadly, as a rule for discretionary decision that exempts certain people from the legal consequences of their wrongdoing, then the American legal system is amnesties all the way down." For example, the legal system regularly accepts departures from a rigid adherence to the law, as in by granting some discretion to prosecutors and judges. More broadly, Taub argues, "the ways that laws are not enforced . . . can be as vital to the legal system's effectiveness as enforcing them" ("The Word May Be Toxic, but Amnesty Is Everywhere," *New York Times*, October 15, 2017). In contrast, the law professor Martha Minow offers another version of the idea that pardons do not constitute a departure from legal norms, suggesting that pardon or forgiveness should be seen as central to the administration of law, which should always be open to forgiveness, compassion, and reconciliation (*When Should Law Forgive?* [New York: Norton, 2019]).

14.   U.S. House of Representatives, Committee on Government Reform, *Justice Undone: Clemency Decisions in the Clinton White House*, House Report 107-454, 107th Cong., 2nd sess., May 14, 2002 (Washington, DC: U.S. Government Printing Office, 2002).

15.   Jackie Steele, quoted in Kayla Epstein, "Defeated GOP Governor Pardoned Violent Criminals in a Spree Lawyers Are Calling an 'Atrocity of Justice,'" *Washington Post*, December 12, 2019.

16.   "The Moral Injury of War Crimes Pardons," *New York Times*, November 24, 2019.

17.   Carol Williams, "End-of-Term Clemency Is a Centuries-Old, Often Vilified Tradition," *Los Angeles Times*, January 10, 2011.

18.   P. S. Ruckman Jr., "'Last-Minute' Pardon Scandals: Fact and Fiction," paper presented at the Midwest Political Science Association conference, Chicago, April 2004, 6.

19.   Smith and Smith, *The White House Speaks*, 24.

20.   See, for example, Charles Tilly, "Collective Violence in European Perspective," in *Violence in America: Historical and Comparative Perspectives*, ed. Hugh Davis Graham and Ted Robert Gurr, National Commission on the Causes and Prevention of Violence (Washington, DC: U.S. Government Printing Office, 1969), 4–45.

21. Significant treatments of America's history of rebellion include the following twelve books (listed chronologically), three of which are essentially different versions of the same volume: Graham and Gurr, *Violence in America*; Thomas Rose, ed., *Violence in America: A Historical and Contemporary Reader* (New York: Random House, 1969); Richard Hofstadter and Michael Wallace, eds., *American Violence: A Documentary History* (New York: Knopf, 1970); Richard Maxwell Brown, *Strain of Violence: Historical Studies of American Violence and Vigilantism* (New York: Oxford University Press, 1975); Hugh Davis Graham and Ted Robert Gurr, eds., *Violence in America: Historical and Comparative Perspectives*, rev. ed. (Thousand Oaks, CA: Sage, 1979); Ted Robert Gurr, ed., *Violence in America: Protest, Rebellion, Reform* (Thousand Oaks, CA: Sage, 1989); Clayton D. Laurie and Robert H. Cole, *The Role of Federal Military Forces in Domestic Disorders, 1877–1945* (Washington, DC: Center of Military History, 1997); Christopher Waldrep and Michael Bellesiles, eds., *Documenting American Violence: A Sourcebook* (New York: Oxford University Press, 2006); Steven Lawrence Danver, ed., *Revolts, Protests, Demonstrations, and Rebellions in American History*, 3 vols. (Santa Barbara, CA: ABC-CLIO, 2011); Ted Robert Gurr, *Political Rebellion: Causes, Outcomes, and Alternatives* (London: Routledge, 2015); James T. Sparrow, William J. Novak, and Stephen Sawyer, eds., *Boundaries of the State in U.S. History* (Chicago: University of Chicago Press, 2015); Connor K. Whitmore and Preston Boggs, *Rebellions of the United States* (North Charleston, SC: CreateSpace Independent Publishing Platform, 2016).

22. Hofstadter and Wallace, *American Violence*; Christopher Waldrep and Michael Bellesiles, introduction to *Documenting American Violence*, ed. Waldrep and Bellesiles, 4.

23. Tilly, "Collective Violence in European Perspective," 6–10, 29, 33.

24. Waldrep and Bellesiles, introduction to *Documenting American Violence*, 5.

25. Richard Hofstadter, "Reflections on Violence in the United States," in *American Violence*, ed. Hofstadter and Wallace, 3–4.

26. Alexander Hamilton, Federalist No. 9, "The Union as a Safeguard Against Domestic Faction and Insurrection" (1787), in *The Federalist Papers*, Avalon Project, Yale Law School, https://avalon.law.yale.edu/18th_century/fed09.asp; James Madison, Federalist No. 9, "The Same Subject Continued: The Union as a Safeguard Against Domestic Faction and Insurrection" (1787), in *The Federalist Papers*, Avalon Project, Yale Law School, https://avalon.law.yale.edu/18th_century/fed09.asp.

27. Madison would articulate much the same point with regard to factions eleven months later in Federalist No. 10.

28. Thomas Jefferson to James Madison, January 30, 1787, Founders Online, National Archives, https://founders.archives.gov/documents/Jefferson/01-11-02-0095.

29 Hofstadter, "Reflections on Violence in the United States," 3.

30. Simon Schama, "Mourning in America: A Whiff of Dread for the Land of Hope," *New York Times*, September 15, 2002.

31. Hofstadter, "Reflections on Violence in the United States," 27.

32. Jefferson to Madison, January 30, 1787.

33. Alexander Hamilton, Federalist No. 74, "The Command of the Military and Naval Forces, and the Pardoning Power of the Presidency," in *The Federalist Papers*, Avalon Project, Yale Law School, https://avalon.law.yale.edu/18th_century/fed74.asp.
34. Hofstadter, "Reflections on Violence in the United States," 27.
35. The phrase "stroke of a pen" is familiar to scholars as the title of Kenneth Mayer's book on executive orders. Mayer notes that although many people date the phrase to Kennedy's campaign promise in 1960 to end housing discrimination via an executive order, it had origins in the nineteenth century. See Kenneth R. Mayer, *With the Stroke of a Pen: Executive Orders and Presidential Power* (Princeton, NJ: Princeton University Press, 2001), 8.
36. Books on the general topic of unilateral presidential directives include (chronologically): Ruth Morgan, *The President and Civil Rights: Policy-Making by Executive Order* (New York: St. Martin's, 1970); Mayer, *With the Stroke of a Pen*; Phillip J. Cooper, *By Order of the President: The Use and Abuse of Executive Direct Action* (Lawrence: University Press of Kansas, 2002); William G. Howell, *Power Without Persuasion: The Politics of Direct Presidential Action* (Princeton, NJ: Princeton University Press, 2003); Adam L. Warber, *Executive Orders and the Modern Presidency* (Boulder, CO: Lynne Rienner, 2006); Ricardo Jose Pereira Rodrigues, *The Preeminence of Politics: Executive Orders from Eisenhower to Clinton* (New York: LFB Scholarly, 2007); Graham G. Dodds, *Take Up Your Pen: Unilateral Presidential Directives in American Politics* (Philadelphia: University of Pennsylvania Press, 2013); Michelle Belco and Brandon Rottinghaus, *The Dual Executive: Unilateral Orders in a Separated and Shared Power System* (Palo Alto, CA: Stanford University Press, 2017); Daniel Gitterman, *Calling the Shots: The President, Executive Orders, and Public Policy* (Washington, DC: Brookings Institution Press, 2017); Fang-Yi Chiou and Lawrence S. Rothenberg, *The Enigma of Presidential Power: Parties, Policies, and Strategic Uses of Unilateral Action* (Cambridge: Cambridge University Press, 2017).
37. One exception is Raymond T. Williams, "A Simple Twist of the Wrist: Presidential Use of Executive Orders and Proclamations in Times of Crisis, 1861–2012," PhD diss., University of Maryland, 2017.
38. Richard E. Neustadt, *Presidential Power: The Politics of Leadership from FDR to Carter* (1960; reprint, New York: Wiley, 1980), 10.
39. Howell, *Power Without Persuasion,* 22.
40. Matthew Dickinson, "We All Want a Revolution: Neustadt, New Institutionalism, and the Future of Presidency Research," *Presidential Studies Quarterly* 39, no. 4 (December 2009): 736–70.
41. Andrew Rudalevige, "Executive Orders and Presidential Unilateralism," *Presidential Studies Quarterly* 42, no. 1 (March 2012): 138–60.
42. Matthew Dickinson and Jesse Grub, "The Limits to Power Without Persuasion," *Presidential Studies Quarterly* 46, no. 1 (March 2016): 48–72.
43. Christopher S. Kelley, Bryan W. Marshall, and Deanna J. Watts, "Assessing the Rhetorical Side of Presidential Signing Statements," *Presidential Studies Quarterly* 43, no. 2 (June 2013): 274–98.

44. Karlyn Kohrs Campbell and Kathleen Hall Jamieson, *Deeds Done in Words: Presidential Rhetoric and the Genres of Governance* (Chicago: University of Chicago Press, 1990); Karlyn Kohrs Campbell and Kathleen Hall Jamieson, *Presidents Creating the Presidency: Deeds Done in Words* (Chicago: University of Chicago Press, 2008).

45. Marie Gottschalk, *Caught: The Prison State and the Lockdown of American Politics* (Princeton, NJ: Princeton University Press, 2016), 191.

46. "Gerald R. Ford's Pardon of Richard Nixon (1974)," in *The Evolving Presidency: Landmark Documents*, 6th ed., ed. Michael Nelson (Washington, DC: Congressional Quarterly Press, 2019), 237.

47. Kyle Sammin, "Why We Should Amend the Constitution to Restrict the President's Power to Pardon," *Federalist*, February 8, 2019.

48. Alan Dershowitz, "What's Mercy Got to Do with It?," *New York Times*, July 16, 1989.

49. Significant scholarship on pardons includes (chronologically): William Duker, "The President's Power to Pardon: A Constitutional History," *William and Mary Law Review* 18 (1977): 475–538; Mark J. Rozell, "The Presidential Pardon Power: A Bibliographic Essay," *Journal of Law and Politics* 5, no. 2 (Winter 1989): 459–67; David Gray Adler, "The President's Pardon Power," in *Inventing the American Presidency*, ed. Thomas E. Cronin (Lawrence: University Press of Kansas, 1989), 209–35; Daniel T. Kobil, "The Quality of Mercy Strained," *Texas Law Review* 69 (1991): 569–641; P. S. Ruckman Jr., "Presidential Character and Executive Clemency: A Reexamination," *Social Science Quarterly* 76, no. 1 (March 1995): 213–21; Margaret Colgate Love, "Of Pardons, Politics, and Collar Buttons: Reflections on the President's Duty to Be Merciful," *Fordham Urban Law Journal* 27, no. 5 (2000): 1483–513; Margaret Colgate Love, "Reinventing the President's Pardon Power," American Constitution Society, October 2007, https://www.acslaw.org/wp-content/uploads/old-uploads/originals /documents/Presidential%20Pardons%20Issue%20Brief%20-%20October%202007 .pdf; Jeffrey P. Crouch, *The Presidential Pardon Power* (Lawrence: University Press of Kansas, 2009); Love, "The Twilight of the Pardon Power." In contrast to the popular view that the literature on pardons is limited, see P. S. Ruckman Jr.'s bibliography of more than forty political science studies of U.S. presidential pardons: "The Study of Mercy: What Political Scientists Know (and Don't Know) About the Pardon Power," *University of St. Thomas Law Review* 9 (2012): 783–868.

50. Rozell, "The Presidential Pardon Power," 462.

51. Crouch, *The Presidential Pardon Power*; Andrew Novak, *Comparative Executive Clemency: The Constitutional Pardon Power and the Prerogative of Mercy in Global Perspective* (London: Routledge, 2015).

52. See, for example (in chronological order), Nicholas Tavuchis, *Mea Culpa: A Sociology of Apology and Reconciliation* (Palo Alto, CA: Stanford University Press, 1991); Dann Bronkhorst, *Truth and Reconciliation: Obstacles and Opportunities for Human Rights* (Washington, DC: Amnesty International, 1995); Roy L. Brooks, ed., *When Sorry Isn't Enough: The Controversy Over Apologies and Reparations for Human Injustice* (New York: New York University Press, 1999); Martha Minow, *Between*

Vengeance and Forgiveness: Facing History After Genocide and Mass Violence (Boston: Beacon, 1998); Robert R. Weyeneth, "The Power of Apology and the Process of Historical Reconciliation," *Public Historian* 23, no. 3 (Summer 2001): 9–38; John B. Hatch, "Reconciliation: Building a Bridge from Complicity to Coherence in the Rhetoric of Race Relations," *Rhetoric and Public Affairs*, Winter 2003, 737–64; Erik Doxtader, "The Potential of Reconciliation's Beginning: A Reply," *Rhetoric and Public Affairs*, Fall 2004, 378–90; Kirt H. Wilson, "Is There Interest in Reconciliation?," *Rhetoric and Public Affairs*, Fall 2004, 367–77; Aaron Lazare, *On Apology* (New York: Oxford University Press, 2005); Elazar Barkan and Alexander Karn, eds., *Taking Wrongs Seriously: Apologies and Reconciliation* (Palo Alto, CA: Stanford University Press, 2006); John B. Hatch, "The Hope of Reconciliation: Continuing the Conversation," *Rhetoric and Public Affairs*, Summer 2006, 259–77; Melissa Nobles, *The Past Is Present: Official Apologies and Multicultural Citizenship* (Cambridge: Cambridge University Press, 2007); Austin Sarat and Nasser Hussain, eds., *Forgiveness, Mercy, and Clemency* (Palo Alto, CA: Stanford University Press, 2008); Jennifer Lind, *Sorry States: Apologies in International Politics* (Ithaca, NY: Cornell University Press, 2008); John B. Hatch, "Dialogic Rhetoric in *Letters Across the Divide*: A Dance of (Good) Faith Toward Racial Reconciliation," *Rhetoric and Public Affairs*, Winter 2009, 482–532; Jennifer Lind, "Apologies in International Relations," *Security Studies* 18, no. 3 (2009): 517–56; Adam Ellwager, "Apology as *Metanoic* Preference: Punitive Rhetoric and Public Speech," *Rhetoric Society Quarterly* 42, no. 4 (2012): 307–29; Francesca Lessa and Leigh A. Payne, *Amnesty in the Age of Human Rights Accountability* (Cambridge: Cambridge University Press, 2012); Edwin Battistella, "The Art of the Political Apology," *Politico*, May 7, 2014; Loramy Gerstbauer, *U.S. Foreign Policy and the Politics of Apology* (London: Routledge, 2016); Catherine Lu, *Justice and Reconciliation in World Politics* (Cambridge: Cambridge University Press, 2017). My own contributions to this literature include Graham G. Dodds, "Political Apologies and Public Discourse," in *Public Discourse in America: Conversation and Community in the Twenty-First Century*, ed. Judith Rodin and Stephen P. Steinberg (Philadelphia: University of Pennsylvania Press, 2003), 135–60; "Political Apologies and Racial Reconciliation," in *Racism and Justice: Dialogue on the Politics of Inequality and Change*, ed. Sean P. Hier and B. Singh Bolaria (Black Wood, NS, Canada: Fernwood, 2009), 137–51; "Governmental Apologies and Political Reconciliation: Promise and Pitfalls," in *Peacebuilding, Memory, and Reconciliation: Bridging Top-Down and Bottom-Up Approaches*, ed. Bruno Charbonneau and Genevieve Parent (London: Routledge, 2011), 130–45.

53. See (in chronological order) James W. Ceaser, Glen E. Thurow, Jeffrey K. Tulis, and Joseph M. Bessette "The Rise of the Rhetorical Presidency," *Presidential Studies Quarterly* 11, no. 2 (1981): 158–71; Robert E. Denton and Dan F. Hehn, *Presidential Communication: Description and Analysis* (Westport, CT: Praeger, 1986); Jeffrey Tulis, *The Rhetorical Presidency* (Princeton, NJ: Princeton University Press, 1987); Roderick P. Hart, *The Sound of Leadership: Presidential Communication in the Modern Age* (Chicago: University of Chicago Press, 1987); Campbell and Jamieson, *Deeds*

Done in Words; Mary E. Stuckey, *The President as Interpreter-in-Chief* (Chapel Hill: University of North Carolina Press, 1991); Jeffrey E. Cohen, "Presidential Rhetoric and the Public Agenda," *American Journal of Political Science* 39, no. 1 (1995): 87–107; Jeffrey E. Cohen, *Presidential Responsiveness and Public Policy-Making* (Ann Arbor: University of Michigan Press, 1997); Kim Quaile Hill, "The Policy Agendas of the President and the Mass Public," *American Journal of Political Science* 42, no. 4 (1998): 1328–334; Cynthia G. Emrich, Holly H. Brower, Jack M. Feldman, and Howard Garland, "Images in Words: Presidential Rhetoric, Charisma, and Greatness," *Administrative Sciences Quarterly* 26 (2001): 527–57; Adam Lawrence, "Does It Really Matter What Presidents Say? The Influence of Presidential Rhetoric on the Public Agenda, 1946–2002," paper presented at the American Political Science Association conference, Boston, 2002; Mary E. Stuckey, *Defining Americans: The Presidency and National Identity* (Lawrence: University Press of Kansas, 2004); David A. Frank and Mark Lawrence McPhail, "Barack Obama's Address to the 2004 Democratic National Convention," *Rhetoric and Public Affairs*, Winter 2005, 571–93; Colleen Shogan, *The Moral Rhetoric of American Presidents* (College Station: Texas A&M University Press, 2006); Douglas L. Wilson, *Lincoln's Sword: The Presidency and the Power of Words* (New York: Vintage, 2006); Elvin T. Lim, *The Anti-intellectual Presidency: The Decline of Presidential Rhetoric from George Washington to George W. Bush* (New York: Oxford University Press, 2008); Campbell and Jamieson, *Presidents Creating the Presidency*; Vanessa B. Beasley, "The Rhetorical Presidency Meets the Unitary Executive: Implications for Presidential Rhetoric on Public Policy," *Rhetoric and Public Affairs*, Spring 2010, 7–35. Texas A&M University Press alone has published more than a dozen books on presidential rhetoric.

54. Campbell and Jamieson, *Deeds Done in Words*, 190; Campbell and Jamieson, *Presidents Creating the Presidency*, 135.

55. Campbell and Jamieson, *Deeds Done in Words*, 190, 170, 4–5; Campbell and Jamieson, *Presidents Creating the Presidency*, 135, 109–10, 7.

56. George C. Edwards, *On Deaf Ears: The Limits of the Bully Pulpit* (New Haven, CT: Yale University Press, 2003).

57. Hillary Clinton, quoted in Glenn Thrush, "Clinton's '08 Slaps Still Sting Obama," *Politico*, August 1, 2013.

58. Adam Clymer, "When Presidential Words Led to Swift Action," *Washington Post*, June 8, 2013.

59. See Charles Shanor and Marc Miller, "Pardon Us: Systematic Presidential Pardons," *Federal Sentencing Reporter* 13, nos. 3–4 (2000–2001): 140.

1. MASS PARDONS IN HISTORY, LAW, AND POLITICS

1. Edward Coke, *Institutes of the Laws of England*, part 3 (London: Clarke, 1817), 233; Thomas Hobbes, *Leviathan*, ed. Richard Tuck (Cambridge: Cambridge University Press, 1996), 106 (chap 15, part 1, "Of Man").

2. Daniel T. Kobil, "The Quality of Mercy Strained," *Texas Law Review* 69 (1991): 569–641.

3. Sir William Blackstone, quoted in Harold J. Krent, "Conditioning the President's Conditional Pardon Power," *California Law Review* 89, no. 6 (December 2001): 1672. Just as Blackstone supported placing the pardon power with the monarch, in the French tradition Jacques Necker called the pardon power "the most august prerogative" of the king and "the most precious, honourable and imposing of all the ancient privileges of the Crown" (*On Executive Power in Great States*, ed. Aurelian Craiutu [Indianapolis, IN: Liberty Fund, 2020], 9, 207).

4. Kobil, "The Quality of Mercy Strained;" Krent, "Conditioning the President's Conditional Pardon Power," 1672; Mary Kathleen Quigley, "Pardons in Major Cases of Insurrections in Colonial America, 1675–1773," PhD diss., Ohio State University, 1970.

5. Akhil Reed Amar, *America's Constitution: A Biography* (New York: Random House, 2005), 133.

6. Alan Taylor, *American Revolutions: A Continental History, 1750–1804* (New York: Norton, 2016), 3.

7. Leonard L. Richards, *Shays's Rebellion: The American Revolution's Final Battle* (Philadelphia: University of Pennsylvania Press, 2003); Massachusetts Historical Society, "'This Convulsed Commonwealth': Daniel Shays Attempts to Call a Truce During Shays' Rebellion, the Agrarian Revolt Named for Him," May 2013, http://www.masshist.org/object-of-the-month/may-2013.

8. Alexander Hamilton, Federalist No. 74, "The Command of the Military and Naval Forces, and the Pardoning Power of the Executive" (1788), in *The Federalist Papers*, Avalon Project, Yale Law School, https://avalon.law.yale.edu/18th_century/fed74.asp

9. Alexander Hamilton, Federalist No. 69, "The Real Character of the Executive" (1788), in *The Federalist Papers*, Avalon Project, Yale Law School, https://avalon.law.yale.edu/18th_century/fed69.asp.

10. Hamilton, Federalist No. 74.

11. Hamilton, Federalist No. 74.

12. George Mason, quoted in D. W. Buffa, "The Pardon Power and Original Intent," FIXGOV, Brookings Institution, July 25, 2018, https://www.brookings.edu/blog/fixgov/2018/07/25/the-pardon-power-and-original-intent/.

13. James Iredell, North Carolina ratifying convention, July 28, 1788, in *The Founders' Constitution*, ed. Philip B. Kurland and Ralph Lerner (Chicago: University of Chicago Press, 1987), online at https://press-pubs.uchicago.edu/founders/documents/a2_2_1s22.html.

14. According to Kathleen Moore, almost every other constitution in the world also includes a provision for pardons (*Pardons: Justice, Mercy, and the Public Interest* [New York: Oxford University Press, 1989], 7).

15. Leon Ulman, testimony, U.S. House of Representatives, Subcommittee on Courts, Civil Liberties, and the Administration of Justice, *Amnesty: Hearings Before the Subcommittee on Courts, Civil Liberties, and the Administration of Justice, Committee*

on the Judiciary, House of Representatives, March 8, 11, and 13, 1974, 93rd Cong., 2nd sess. (Washington, DC: U.S. Government Printing Office, 1974), 29. See also Ford Foundation, "Vietnam Veterans, Deserters, and Draft-Evaders: The Vietnam Decade," September 1974, 36, https://www.fordlibrarymuseum.gov/library/document /0193/1505994.pdf.

16. Ford Foundation, "Vietnam Veterans, Deserters, and Draft-Evaders: A Summer Study," September 1974, II-4, https://www.fordlibrarymuseum.gov/library/document /0067/1562799.pdf; see also Anthony Ripley, "Amnesty for Draft Resisters Is Expected to Be Divisive Political Issue for Years," *New York Times*, January 30, 1973.

17. Ford Foundation, "Vietnam Veterans, Deserters, and Draft-Evaders: A Summer Study," II-5.

18. U.S. House of Representatives, Subcommittee on Courts, Civil Liberties, and the Administration of Justice, *Information on H.R. 9568: The Vietnam Era Reconciliation Act*, 94th Cong., 1st sess. (Washington, DC: U.S. Government Printing Office, October 1975), 5.

19. Marie Gottschalk, *Caught: The Prison State and the Lockdown of American Politics* (Princeton, NJ: Princeton University Press, 2016), 191.

20. Governor Ryan was moved to act after reading a series in the *Chicago Tribune* on questionable verdicts in capital punishment cases (Alex Kotlowitz, "A Quarter of a Century Behind Bars, for a Crime He Didn't Commit," review of *Ghost of the Innocent Man: A True Story of Trial and Redemption*, by Benjamin Rachlin [Little, Brown, 2017], *New York Times Book Review*, October 27, 2017). Yet Ryan's action was motivated by concerns with the fairness of the way the death penalty was administered, not by the morality of the death penalty itself (Gottschalk, *Caught*, 191).

21. Katie Rose Quandt, "The Largest Commutation in U.S. History," *Slate*, November 8, 2019.

22. Stephen Greenspan, "Posthumous Pardons in American History," Death Penalty Information Center, March 2011.

23. Civil Rights and Restorative Justice Project, Northeastern University School of Law. "Civil Rights–Related Pardons," n.d., https://crrj.northeastern.edu/home/about-us /pardons/.

24. *Howell v. McAuliffe*, 788 S.E.2d 706 (Va. 2016).

25. Justice Hugo Black, *Solesbee v. Balkom*, 339 U.S. 9, 12, 70 S.Ct. 457, 94 L. Ed. 604 (1950).

26. For a good overview of jurisprudence on pardons, see Kenneth R. Thomas, ed., "Pardons and Reprieves," in *The Constitution of the United States of America: Analysis and Interpretation* (Washington, DC: Congressional Research Service, June 28, 2012), 510–17, http://law.justia.com/constitution/us/article-2/16-pardons -and-reprieves.html.

27. In a later case, Calvin Coolidge pardoned a prisoner who refused it; Coolidge then ordered the prisoner removed from the prison and "the doors locked behind him" ("Constitutional Topic: Presidential Pardons," U.S. Constitution, n.d., http://www .usconstitution.net/consttop_pard.html).

28. *Ex parte Garland*, quoted in Jonathan Truman Dorris, *Pardon and Amnesty Under Lincoln and Johnson: The Restoration of the Confederates to Their Rights and Privileges, 1861–1898* (Westport, CT: Greenwood Press, 1977), 397.

29. *Ex parte Garland*, quoted in Glendon A. Schubert, *The Presidency in the Courts* (Minneapolis: University of Minnesota Press, 1956), 293, 300 n. 49.

30. *Ex parte Garland*, quoted in Moore, *Pardons*, 80.

31. *Ex parte Garland*, quoted in Charles Shanor and Marc Miller, "Pardon Us: Systematic Presidential Pardons," *Federal Sentencing Reporter* 13, nos. 3–4 (2000–2001): 145 nn. 8 and 9.

32. Schubert, *The Presidency in the Courts*, 294.

33. *Armstrong v. United States*, quoted in Frank W. Klingberg, *The Southern Claims Commission* (New York: Octagon Books, 1978), 91. Although the decision in *Armstrong* said a presidential pardon is "a public act," the public nature of a pardon might be different at the state level: Governor Paul LePage of Maine pardoned 112 people between 2011 and 2019, but a full list of those pardoned was kept secret until the Associated Press made a request for it under the Freedom of Information Act of 1966. See Nicholas Bogel-Burroughs, "Matt Bevin Drew Outrage Over His Pardons. These Governors Have, Too," *New York Times*, December 21, 2019.

34. As to whether a pardon erases the offense, in William Shakespeare's play *Hamlet* Claudius asks, "May one be pardoned and retain th' offense?"

35. *Burdick v. United States*, quoted in Eugene Volokh, "If You're Pardoned, Can You Be Compelled to Testify About Your Crime?," *Washington Post*, June 2, 2017.

36. Scott Shane, "For Ford, Pardon Decision Was Always Clear-Cut," *New York Times*, December 29, 2006; Donald Rumsfeld, "How the Nixon Pardon Tore the Ford Administration Apart," *Politico*, May 20, 2018.

37   *Biddle*, quoted in Edward S. Corwin, *The Constitution and What It Means Today* (Princeton, NJ: Princeton University Press, 1948), 98.

38. *Biddle*, quoted in Corwin, *The Constitution and What It Means Today*, 98, and in Moore, *Pardons*, 64, 80, 193.

39. Michael A. Foster, *Presidential Pardons: Overview and Selected Legal Issues* (Washington, DC: Congressional Research Service, January 14, 2020), 15.

40. James Pfiffner, "The President's Broad Power to Pardon and Commute," Heritage Foundation, July 9, 2007. Additional cases of note here include *Ex parte Wells*, 59 U.S. (18 How) 307 (1855); *Osborn v. US*, 19 U.S. 474 (1875); *Burdick v. U.S.*, 236 U.S. 79 (1915); *Hoffa v. Saxbe*, 387 F. Supp. 1221 (D.D.C. 1974).

41. However, there is some jurisprudential support for the view that Congress may have its own pardon power. See *The Laura*, 114 U.S. 411, 413–14 (1885), and *Brown v. Walker*, 161 U.S. 591, 601 (1896).

42. Judge Susan Bolton, quoted in John Gerstein, "House Democrats Ask Judge to Reject Arpaio Pardon," *Politico*, September 27, 2017. See also *New York Times* Editorial Board, "The Perils of a Pardon for Joe Arpaio." *New York Times*, August 24, 2017.

43. Donald Trump, quoted in "National Thanksgiving Turkey Pardon," C-SPAN, November 21, 2017, https://www.c-span.org/video/?437626-1/president-trump-pardons-thanksgiving-turkey.

44. *In re De Puy*, 7 F. Cas. 506 (1869).

45. Ken Belson and Eric Lichtblau, "A Father, a Son, and a Short-Lived Presidential Pardon," *New York Times*, December 25, 2008 (quote); Jeffrey Crouch, "The Toussie Pardon, 'Unpardon,' and the Abdication of Responsibility in Clemency Cases," *Congress and the Presidency* 38, no. 1 (2011): 77–100; Karen Tumulty, "More on Pardons," *Time*, December 25, 2008; "Reversal of Presidential Pardon Analyzed," NPR, December 25, 2008, https://www.npr.org/templates/story/story.php?storyId=98711226.

46. Donald J. Trump, "Statement by the Press Secretary Regarding Executive Grants of Clemency," American Presidency Project, ed. Gerhard Peters and John T. Woolley, https://www.presidency.ucsb.edu/node/334414.

47. A further distinction is that in a criminal case a jury can find someone guilty, and the court can then direct that the defendant be imprisoned, but in a civil case a judge can find that someone is liable and that this person must pay compensation or damages.

48. Some argue that the president's pardon power may encompass civil offenses. See, for example, Noah A. Messing, "A New Power? Civil Offenses and Presidential Clemency," *Buffalo Law Review* 64, no. 4 (2016): 661–743; and Peter L. Markowitz and Lindsay Nash, "Pardoning Immigrants," *New York University Law Review* 93 (April 2018): 58–106.

49. Donald Trump, tweet, June 2018, quoted in Foster, *Presidential Pardons*, 13, emphasis in original.

50. Frank O. Bowman III, *High Crimes and Misdemeanors: A History of Impeachment for the Age of Trump* (Cambridge: Cambridge University Press, 2019), 263.

51. Foster, *Presidential Pardons*, 14.

52. Bowman, *High Crimes and Misdemeanors*, 263.

53. From 2001 to 2005, the U.S. Justice Department investigated whether Bill Clinton's pardon of Marc Rich, whose spouse had given $450,000 to Clinton's presidential library, might have been issued in response to a bribe. See Daniel Hemel and Richard Posner, "If Trump Pardons, It Could Be a Crime," *New York Times*, July 21, 2017.

54. Hemel and Posner, "If Trump Pardons."

55. Gerstein, "House Democrats Ask Judge to Reject Arpaio Pardon."

56. Kyle Cheney, "House Dems Push Legislation to Criminalize Quid-pro-Quo Pardons," *Politico*, July 22, 2020.

57. Nicholas Fandos, "House Democrats Advance New Checks on Presidential Pardon Power," *New York Times*, July 23, 2020.

58. Bowman, *High Crimes and Misdemeanors*, 264. Apart from the possibility that the president could be impeached for misusing the pardon power, this has occurred at the state level for a governor. In 1932, Governor Jack Walton of Oklahoma was impeached in part because of his supposedly overly generous use of pardons (David Grann, *Killers of the Flower Moon: The Osage Murders and the Birth of the FBI* [New York: Vintage, 2017], 102).

59. "The President and His Power to Pardon," *New York Times*, May 19, 2019.

60. *New York Times* Editorial Board, "The Perils of a Pardon for Joe Arpaio."

2. PENNSYLVANIA INSURRECTIONS IN THE LATE
EIGHTEENTH CENTURY

1. Alexander Hamilton was central to the response to both Pennsylvania insurrections because he was George Washington's secretary of the Treasury and John Adams's senior officer of the army, and U.S. attorney William Rawle was a prosecutor for both rebellions. In addition, some scholars claim that the two uprisings in 1794 and 1798 drew on the same broader tradition of principled political dissent. See Terry Bouton, *Taming Democracy: "The People," the Founders, and the Troubled Ending of the American Revolution* (New York: Oxford University Press, 2007); and Alan Taylor, *American Revolutions: A Continental History, 1750–1804* (New York: Norton, 2016).

2. Alexander Hamilton, Federalist No. 12, "The Utility of the Union in Respect to Revenue" (1787), in *The Federalist Papers*, Avalon Project, Yale Law School, https://avalon.law.yale.edu/18th_century/fed12.asp.

3. Joseph J. Ellis, *His Excellency: George Washington* (New York: Knopf, 2005), 224; John C. Miller, *Alexander Hamilton and the Growth of the New Nation* (New York: Harper and Row, 1964), 396–37.

4. Ron Chernow, *Alexander Hamilton* (New York: Penguin Books, 2004), 468.

5. Miller, *Alexander Hamilton and the Growth of the New Nation*, 397.

6. Miller, *Alexander Hamilton and the Growth of the New Nation*, 397.

7. Taylor, *American Revolutions*, 413.

8. Taylor, *American Revolutions*, 413.

9. U.S. National Park Service, "Whiskey Rebellion," Friendship Hill National Historical Site, Pennsylvania, February 26, 2015, https://www.nps.gov/frhi/learn/historyculture/whiskeyrebellion.htm.

10. Taylor, *American Revolutions*, 413.

11. Thomas P. Slaughter, *The Whiskey Rebellion: Frontier Epilogue to the American Revolution* (New York: Oxford University Press, 1986), 89.

12. Taylor, *American Revolutions*, 413.

13. Bouton, *Taming Democracy*, 218.

14. Even Shays's Rebellion was arguably also part of this revolutionary tradition. Indeed, some academics argue that it was a grassroots protest that Federalists strategically recharacterized for their own purposes as a more sinister and organized campaign. See, for example, Charles U. Zug, "Daniel Shays and the Question of Oligarchy at the Founding," paper presented at the American Political Science Association conference, Boston, 2018.

15. Taylor, *American Revolutions*, 6–7; see also John R. Alden, *George Washington: A Biography* (Baton Rouge: Louisiana State University Press, 1984), 261.

16. Bouton, *Taming Democracy*, 217–20.

17. See, for example, James Roger Sharp, "The Whiskey Rebellion and the Question of Representation," in *The Whiskey Rebellion: Past and Present Perspectives*, ed. Steven R. Boyd (Westport, CT: Greenwood Press, 1985), 119–33; Pauline Maier, "Popular

Uprisings and Civil Authority in Eighteenth-Century America," *William and Mary Quarterly* 27 (1970): 3–35; Jacob E. Cooke, "The Whiskey Insurrection: A Reevaluation," *Pennsylvania History*, July 1963, 316–64; Slaughter, *The Whiskey Rebellion*.

18. Bouton, *Taming Democracy*, 218. See also Gregory H. Nobles, "Historians Extend the Reach of the American Revolution," in *Whose American Revolution Was It?*, ed. Alfred F. Young and Gregory H. Nobles (New York: New York University Press, 2011), 219.

19. Forrest McDonald, *Alexander Hamilton: A Biography* (New York: Norton, 1979), 297.

20. Perhaps ironically, western Pennsylvania is exactly the same place where George Washington's military career "had begun forty years earlier" (Ellis, *His Excellency*, 224).

21. Chernow, *Alexander Hamilton*, 343.

22. Donna Scanlon, "The Whiskey Rebellion," Library of Congress, Business Reference Services, December 2009, https://www.loc.gov/rr/business/businesshistory/August/whiskeyrebellion.html.

23 Washington County, Pennsylvania, resolution, August 23, 1791, quoted in Steven R. Boyd, "Hugh Henry Brackenridge, *Incidents of the Insurrection*," in *The Whiskey Rebellion*, ed. Boyd, 75 n. 25. Almost a year later, on August 21, 1792, tax resisters in Pittsburgh adopted the same resolution.

24. Cooke, "The Whiskey Insurrection," 317.

25. Ellis, *His Excellency*, 224.

26. Alden, *George Washington*, 262; Robert C. Lieberman and Suzanne Mettler, *Four Threats: The Recurring Crises of American Democracy* (New York: St. Martin's, 2020), 37.

27. Bouton, *Taming Democracy*, 227.

28. Chernow, *Alexander Hamilton*, 468.

29. "An Exciseman," 1791, Teaching American History, https://teachingamericanhistory.org/library/document/an-exciseman/; "An Exciseman, Anonymous, 1792," Explore PA History, https://explorepahistory.com/displayimage.php?imgId=1-2-70E. See also Cynthia L. Krom and Stephanie Krom, "The Whiskey Tax of 1791 and the Consequent Insurrection: 'A Wicked and Unhappy Tumult,'" *Accounting Historians Journal* 40, no. 2 (December 2013): 91–114.

30. Chernow, *Alexander Hamilton*, 469.

31. Taylor, *American Revolutions*, 413–14.

32. Alexander Hamilton to George Washington, September 1, 1792, Founders Online, National Archives, https://founders.archives.gov/documents/Washington/05-11-02-0030.

33. George Washington, "Proclamation 3B—Cessation of Violence and Obstruction of Justice in Protest of Liquor Laws," September 15, 1792, American Presidency Project, ed. Gerhard Peters and John T. Woolley, https://www.presidency.ucsb.edu/node/200718.

34. Miller, *Alexander Hamilton and the Growth of the New Nation*, 399.

35. McDonald, *Alexander Hamilton*, 297–98.

36. McDonald, *Alexander Hamilton*, 298.

37. Miller, *Alexander Hamilton and the Growth of the New Nation*, 405.

38. Alden, *George Washington*, 263.

39. Taylor, *American Revolutions*, 413.

40. Major General John Gibson, quoted in Richard A. Ifft, "Treason in the Early Republic: The Federal Courts, Popular Protest, and Federalism During the Whiskey Insurrection," in *The Whiskey Rebellion*, ed. Boyd, 170.

41. Sharp, "The Whiskey Rebellion and the Question of Representation," 122.

42. See Bouton, *Taming Democracy*, 217; McDonald, *Alexander Hamilton*, 299.

43. Ellis, *His Excellency*, 224.

44. Forrest McDonald, *The Presidency of George Washington* (Lawrence: University Press of Kansas, 1974), 147.

45. Miller, *Alexander Hamilton and the Growth of the New Nation*, 406; William Hogeland, *The Whiskey Rebellion: George Washington, Alexander Hamilton, and the Frontier Rebels Who Challenged America's Newfound Sovereignty* (2006; reprint, New York: Simon and Schuster, 2010), 203.

46. Jonathan Keane, "History of an American Uprising," review of *The Whiskey Rebellion*, by William Hogeland (Scribner, 2006), World Socialist website, October 5, 2006, http://www.wsws.org/articles/2006/oct2006/whis-005.shtml.

47. Leland D. Baldwin, *Whiskey Rebels: The Story of a Frontier Uprising*, rev. ed. (Pittsburgh: University of Pittsburgh Press, 1968), 188.

48. Keane, "History of an American Uprising."

49. Bouton, *Taming Democracy*, 228.

50. Governor James Bowdoin of Massachusetts granted a pardon to citizens who had been involved in the Shays insurgency but explicitly excluded Shays and three others.

51. Hogeland, *The Whiskey Rebellion*, 189.

52. Hogeland, *The Whiskey Rebellion*, 189.

53. Hogeland, *The Whiskey Rebellion*, 189.

54. Ryan J. Barilleaux, "Foreign Policy and the First Commander in Chief," in *Patriot Sage: George Washington and the American Political Tradition*, ed. Gary L. Gregg and Matthew Spalding (Wilmington, DE: ISI Press, 1999), 145.

55. McDonald, *Alexander Hamilton*, 299.

56. Alexander Hamilton to George Washington, August 5, 1794, Founders Online, National Archives, https://founders.archives.gov/documents/Hamilton/01-17-02 -0017.

57. George Washington, "Proclamation—Cessation of Violence and Obstruction of Justice in Protest of Liquor Laws in Pennsylvania," August 7, 1794, American Presidency Project, ed. Gerhard Peters and John T. Woolley, https://www.presidency.ucsb .edu/node/206668.

58. Ellis, *His Excellency*, 225.

59. Keane, "History of an American Uprising."

60. Ellis, *His Excellency*, 225.

61. Baldwin, *Whiskey Rebels*, 191–93.

62. Declaration of submission, September 11, 1794, quoted in Baldwin, *Whiskey Rebels*, 199.

63. Hogeland, *The Whiskey Rebellion*, 204.

64. H. G. Cutler, "The Nation's First Rebellion," *Magazine of American History with Notes and Queries* 12 (1884): 345.

65. Baldwin, *Whiskey Rebels*, 255.

66. Commissioners James Ross, J. Yates, and W. M. Bradford, "From the Commissioners Sent to Western Pennsylvania," September 24, 1794, Founders Online, National Archives, https://founders.archives.gov/documents/Washington/05-16-02-0488. See also Michael Hoover, "The Whiskey Rebellion," Alcohol and Tobacco, Tax and Trade Bureau, U.S. Department of the Treasury, August 21, 2014, https://www.ttb.gov/public-information/whiskey-rebellion.

67. McDonald, *Alexander Hamilton*, 86.

68. Tully, "No. III," *American Daily Advertiser*, August 28, 1794, in Alexander Hamilton, *Selected Writings and Speeches of Alexander Hamilton*, ed. Morton J. Frisch (Washington, DC: AEI Press, 1985), 409.

69. Tully, "No. IV," *American Daily Advertiser*, September 2, 1794, in Hamilton, *Selected Writings and Speeches of Alexander Hamilton*, 412.

70. George Washington, "Proclamation—Authorizing Military Intervention to End Violence and Obstruction of Justice in Protest of Liquor Laws in Pennsylvania," September 25, 1794, American Presidency Project, ed. Gerhard Peters and John T. Woolley, https://www.presidency.ucsb.edu/node/207275.

71. Ellis, *His Excellency*, 225.

72. Scholars disagree about the exact number of troops involved, with figures ranging from 12,000 to 15,000. Forrest McDonald says it was 12,950 (*The Presidency of George Washington*, 145). Jonathan Keane says 13,000 ("History of an American Uprising"). Others say 15,000 (e.g., Sharp, "The Whiskey Rebellion and the Question of Representation," 122–23).

73. Chernow, *Alexander Hamilton*, 475.

74. George Washington to Henry Lee, October 20, 1794, Founders Online, National Archives, https://founders.archives.gov/documents/Washington/05-17-02-0061.

75. Miller, *Alexander Hamilton and the Growth of the New Nation*, 408; McDonald, *Alexander Hamilton*, 302.

76. Miller, *Alexander Hamilton and the Growth of the New Nation*, 409.

77. Governor Henry Lee, "A Proclamation," November 29, 1794, reproduced in Kevin T. Barksdale, "Our Rebellious Neighbors: Virginia's Border Counties During Pennsylvania's Whiskey Rebellion," *Virginia Magazine of History and Biography* 111, no. 1 (2003): 26.

78. Ifft, "Treason in the Early Republic," 171, 177; McDonald, *The Presidency of George Washington*, 146; Baldwin, *Whiskey Rebels*, 143.

79. Hogeland, *The Whiskey Rebellion*, 235.

80. Keane, "History of an American Uprising."

81   George Washington, Sixth Annual Message, November 19, 1794, Avalon Project, Yale Law School, http://avalon.law.yale.edu/18th_century/washs06.asp; all subsequent quotations from the message come from this source.

82. On this point, see Baldwin, *Whiskey Rebels*, 261.

83. McDonald, *Alexander Hamilton*, 298.

84. Sharp, "The Whiskey Rebellion and the Question of Representation," 126.

85   Lieberman and Mettler, *Four Threats*, 45.

86   Baldwin, *Whiskey Rebels*, 135, 173; Hogeland, *The Whiskey Rebellion*, 165.

87. George Washington, "Proclamation—Granting Pardon to Certain Persons Formerly Engaged in Violence and Obstruction of Justice in Protest of Liquor Laws in Pennsylvania," July 10, 1795, American Presidency Project, ed. Gerhard Peters and John T. Woolley, https://www.presidency.ucsb.edu/node/206665.

88. George Washington, Seventh Annual Address, December 8, 1795, Avalon Project, Yale Law School, https://avalon.law.yale.edu/18th_century/washs07.asp.

89. Gary L. Gregg, "The Symbolic Dimensions of the First Presidency," in *Patriot Sage*, ed. Gregg and Spalding, 176.

90. McDonald, *Alexander Hamilton*, 302.

91. Slaughter, *The Whiskey Rebellion*, 223–24.

92. Alden, *George Washington*, 265.

93. Taylor, *American Revolutions*, 414.

94. Alexander Hamilton, *Letter Concerning the Public Conduct and Character of John Adams*, pamphlet, October 24, 1800, Founders Online, National Archives, https://founders.archives.gov/documents/Hamilton/01-25-02-0110-0002.

95. Chernow, *Alexander Hamilton*, 478.

96. John Adams to Thomas Jefferson, June 30, 1813, Founders Online, National Archives, https://founders.archives.gov/documents/Adams/99-02-02-6084.

97. See Fred I. Greenstein, "Presidential Difference in the Early Republic: The Highly Disparate Leadership Styles of Washington, Adams, and Jefferson," *Presidential Studies Quarterly* 36, no. 3 (September 2006): 373–90; Fred I. Greenstein, *Inventing the Job of President: Leadership Style from George Washington to Andrew Jackson* (Princeton, NJ: Princeton University Press, 2009).

98. Stephen Skowronek, *The Politics Presidents Make: Leadership from John Adams to George Bush* (Cambridge, MA: Harvard University Press, 1993), 66, 67, 74.

99. Chernow, *Alexander Hamilton*, 578.

100. Birte Pfleger, review of *Fries's Rebellion*, by Paul Douglas Newman (University of Pennsylvania Press, 2004), *Pennsylvania Magazine of History and Biography*, July 2006, 336–37.

101. For these different accounts, see Paul Douglas Newman, "Fries's Rebellion and American Political Culture, 1798–1800," *Pennsylvania Magazine of History and Biography* 119, nos. 1–2 (January–April 1995): 37 n. 1.

102. On the controversy about Hamilton supposedly fomenting Fries's Rebellion, see McDonald, *The Presidency of George Washington*; McDonald, *Alexander*

Hamilton; Keane, "History of an American Uprising"; Miller, *Alexander Hamilton and the Growth of the New Nation*, 411–12; Cooke, "The Whiskey Insurrection," 317.

103. Bouton, *Taming Democracy*, 245, 244.

104. Paul Douglas Newman, *Fries's Rebellion: The Enduring Struggle for the American Revolution* (Philadelphia: University of Pennsylvania Press, 2004); Pfleger, review of *Fries's Rebellion*.

105. Frank Whelan, "Angry Taxpayers, U.S. Clashed in Fries Rebellion," *Morning Call*, November 25, 1984.

106. Ralph Adams Brown, *The Presidency of John Adams* (Lawrence: University Press of Kansas, 1975), 127; Chernow, *Alexander Hamilton*, 578.

107. Newman, "Fries's Rebellion and American Political Culture," 38.

108. Miller, *Alexander Hamilton and the Growth of the New Nation*, 506.

109. John Adams, "Proclamation on Insurrection in Pennsylvania," March 12, 1799, Founders Online, National Archives, https://founders.archives.gov/documents/Adams/99-02 -02-3377.

110. Chernow, *Alexander Hamilton*, 578.

111. Bouton, *Taming Democracy*, 255.

112. "The Fries Rebellion of 1799 Historical Marker," Explore PA History, n.d., http:// explorepahistory.com/hmarker.php?markerId=1-A-28E.

113. See Brown, *The Presidency of John Adams*, 128; Miller, *Alexander Hamilton and the Growth of the New Nation*, 507; Chernow, *Alexander Hamilton*, 578.

114. *Case of Fries*, 9 Fed. Cas. 826, 924, Nos. 5, 126, 5, 127 (C.C.D.Pa. 1799, 1800).

115. Newman, *Fries's Rebellion*, 180.

116. Brown, *The Presidency of John Adams*, 128.

117. Newman, *Fries's Rebellion*, 183.

118. Newman, *Fries's Rebellion*, 183.

119. Samuel Chase, quoted in Miller, *Alexander Hamilton and the Growth of the New Nation*, 507.

120. Jane Shaffer Elsmere, "The Trials of John Fries," *Pennsylvania Magazine of History and Biography* 103, no. 4 (October 1979): 432–45.

121. In a letter to James McHenry on May 6, 1799, Uriah Tracy wrote, "If some executions are not had of the most notorious offenders I shall regret the events of leniency in '94 & '99 as giving a fatal stroke to government" (quoted in Newman, "Fries's Rebellion and American Political Culture," 66 n. 102).

122. Newman, *Fries's Rebellion*, 180.

123. Timothy Pickering to John Adams, May 10, 1799, Founders Online, National Archives, https://founders.archives.gov/documents/Adams/99-02-02-3499, emphasis in original.

124. Hamilton, *Letter Concerning the Public Conduct and Character of John Adams*.

125   John Adams, autobiography (1802–1807), quoted in Claude Halstead Van Tyne, *The Loyalists in the American Revolution* (New York: Macmillan, 1902), 287.

126. Adams, autobiography (1802–1807), quoted in Van Tyne, *The Loyalists in the American Revolution*, 287.

127. David McCullough, *John Adams* (New York: Simon and Schuster, 2001), 158. The first and second Continental Congresses had sought some form of reconciliation with King George III, and in late 1775 the British Parliament passed legislation that would permit royal representatives to pardon colonists who returned to loyal service. Five months later, Richard Howe and William Howe were appointed as the commissioners who could issue such pardons, but their effort to end hostilities and reconcile with the colonies via pardons was short-lived and unsuccessful. General George Washington informed a British emissary that there was no need for pardons because the colonists had done nothing wrong, and Benjamin Franklin indicated that the colonists were the injured party and hence not appropriate recipients of a royal pardon. A subsequent meeting of the parties on Staten Island in September 1776 lasted only three hours before adjourning in failure (Weldon Amzy Brown, "The Howe Peace Commission of 1776," *North Carolina Historical Review* 13, no. 2 [1936]: 122–42). Nevertheless, the Howe brothers issued a proclamation on November 30, 1776, offering a pardon to colonists who would swear an oath of loyalty to the British Crown. On January 25, 1777, George Washington responded with his own proclamation directed at colonists who had taken up the British offer and made an oath of loyalty to the king in order to receive a pardon, in which he ordered them either to report to the Continental army or militia and take an "oath of allegiance to the United States of America" or else move with their families to enemy territory and be "treated as common enemies of the American States" (George Washington, "Proclamation Concerning Persons Swearing British Allegiance, 25 January 1777," Founders Online, National Archives, https://founders.archives.gov/documents/Washington/03-08-02-0160).

128. John Adams, pardon of David Bradford, March 9, 1799, quoted in Whitman H. Ridgway, "Fries in the Federalist Imagination: A Crisis of Republican Society," *Pennsylvania History* 67, no. 1 (Winter 2000): 150, 158 n. 32.

129. McCullough, *John Adams*, 540.

130. Brown, *The Presidency of John Adams*, 128.

131. John Adams, quoted in McCullough, *John Adams*, 540.

132. John Adams, quoted in Page Smith, *John Adams*, vol. 2 (New York: Doubleday, 1962), 1007.

133. Brown, *The Presidency of John Adams*, 128–29.

134. John Adams, list of questions sent to cabinet, May 20, 1800, quoted in Smith, *John Adams*, 1033.

135. John Ferling, *John Adams: A Life* (Knoxville: University of Tennessee Press, 1992), 395.

136. John Adams to Charles Lee, May 21, 1800, Founders Online, National Archives, https://founders.archives.gov/documents/Adams/99002-02-4356.

137. John Adams, "Proclamation of May 21, 1800, Regarding the Insurrection in Pennsylvania in 1799," Avalon Project, Yale Law School, https://avalon.law.yale.edu/19th_century/japroc04.asp.

138. John Adams to James Lloyd, March 31, 1815, Founders Online, National Archives, https://founders.archives.gov/documents/Adams/99-02-02-6445.

139. Newman, *Fries's Rebellion*, 184.
140. Ferling, *John Adams*, 395; McCullough, *John Adams*, 540–41; Chernow, *Alexander Hamilton*, 579.
141. Newman, *Fries's Rebellion*, 183–84.
142. Smith, *John Adams*, 1034.
143. Newman, *Fries's Rebellion*, 187.
144. Newman, *Fries's Rebellion*, 184.
145. McCullough, *John Adams*, 549.
146. Hamilton, *Letter Concerning the Public Conduct and Character of John Adams*.
147. Newman, *Fries's Rebellion*, 187.

3. MORMON RESISTANCE IN THE NINETEENTH CENTURY

1. Daniel Boorstein, *The Americans: The National Experience* (New York: Vintage Books, 1967), 64; David L. Bigler and Will Bagley, *The Mormon Rebellion: America's First Civil War, 1857–1858* (Norman: Oklahoma University Press, 2012).
2. Bigler and Bagley, *The Mormon Rebellion*, 363.
3. John Eldredge, quoted in Lee Davidson, "America's Forgotten War," *Deseret News*, July 9, 2006.
4. Gene Deerman, review of *The Mormon Rebellion: America's First Civil War, 1857–1858*, by David L. Bigler and Will Bagley (Oklahoma University Press, 2013), Faculty Research and Creative Activity Paper no. 7, http://thekeep.eiu.edu/sociology_fac/7.
5. Bigler and Bagley, *The Mormon Rebellion*, ix.
6. Bigler and Bagley, *The Mormon Rebellion*, x.
7. For other critical accounts of the Mormon War, see Howard R. Lamar, *The Far Southwest, 1846–1912*, rev. ed. (Albuquerque: University of New Mexico Press, 2000); and Norman F. Furniss, *The Mormon Conflict: 1850–1859* (New Haven, CT: Yale University Press, 1960).
8. Will Bagley, "President Pardoned All Utahns," *History Matters* blog, February 18, 2001, http://historytogo.utah.gov/salt_lake_tribune/history_matters/021801.html.
9. See, for example, Marvin S. Hill and James B. Allen, introduction to *Mormonism and American Culture*, ed. Marvin S. Hill and James B. Allen (New York: Harper and Row, 1972), 1.
10. Hill and Allen, introduction to *Mormonism and American Culture*, 1–2.
11. J. Michael Hunter, "Preface and Acknowledgments," in *Mormons and Popular Culture: The Global Influence of an American Phenomenon*, vol. 1, ed. J. Michael Hunter (Santa Barbara, CA: Praeger, 2013), vii–viii.
12. David Roberts, "The Brink of War," *Smithsonian*, June 2008.
13. Governor Liburn W. Boggs, Executive Order 44, October 27, 1838, Office of the Missouri Secretary of State, https://www.sos.mo.gov/cmsimages/archives/resources/findingaids/miscMormRecs/eo/18381027_ExtermOrder.pdf#sos. In 1976, Governor

Kit Bond of Missouri rescinded this order, which had authorized the extermination or expulsion of Mormons from Missouri. Bond's order said he was "expressing on behalf of all Missourians our deep regret for the injustice and undue suffering which was caused by the 1838 order." In 2010, the Mormon History Association gave Bond an award for his action. See R. Scott Lloyd, "Former Missouri Governor Honored for Rescinding Mormon 'Extermination Order,'" *Deseret News*, May 31, 2010.

14. In his campaign, Smith argued that the president should be able to send in troops to put down local disorder without first having to be asked by the governor.

15. In 2004, the Illinois House expressed "official regret" for the historical violence against Mormons, and Illinois state officials went to Salt Lake City to apologize for the murder of Joseph Smith in 1844 and the expulsion of Mormons from the state. See Melissa Sanford, "Illinois Tells Mormons It Regrets Expulsion," *New York Times*, April 8, 2004.

16. Susan Easton Black, "Faces Turned West," in Glenn Rawson, Dennis Lyman, and Bryant Bush, *History of the Saints: The Great Mormon Exodus and the Establishment of Zion* (American Fork, UT: Covenant Communications, 2014), 3.

17. Orson Pratt, quoted in Lorin K. Hansen, "Voyage of the *Brooklyn*," *Dialogue: A Journal of Mormon Thought* 21 (Autumn 1988): 47.

18. William G. Hartley, "Exodus from Nauvoo," in Rawson, Lyman, and Bush, *History of the Saints*, 18.

19. Eugene Young, "Revival of the Mormon Problem," *North American Review* 168, no. 509 (April 1899): 476.

20. Roberts, "The Brink of War."

21. Thomas B. H. Stenhouse, *The Rocky Mountain Saints: A Full and Complete History of the Mormons* (New York: Appleton, 1873), 269.

22. Mormon constitution, March 1848, quoted in Peter Crawley, "The Constitution of the State of Deseret," *Brigham Young University Studies* 29, no. 4 (Fall 1989): 9.

23. James B. Allen and Glen M. Leonard, *The Story of the Latter-day Saints* (Salt Lake City, UT: Deseret Book, 1976), 258.

24. Allen and Leonard, *The Story of the Latter-day Saints*, 259.

25. Brigham Young, quoted in John Krakauer, *Under the Banner of Heaven: A Story of Violent Faith* (New York: Anchor Books, 2003), 208.

26. Will Bagley, *Blood of the Prophets: Brigham Young and the Massacre at Mountain Meadows* (Norman: University of Oklahoma Press, 2012), 43.

27. Roberts, "The Brink of War."

28. William W. Drummond, quoted in Ronald W. Walker, "'Proud as a Peacock and Ignorant as a Jackass': William W. Drummond's Unusual Career with the Mormons," *Journal of Mormon History* 42, no. 3 (July 2016): 7.

29. Harold Schindler, *In Another Time: Sketches of Utah History* (Logan: Utah State University Press, 1998), 69; Brigham Young, quoted in Walker, "'Proud as a Peacock and Ignorant as a Jackass'" 34.

30. Walker, "'Deseret' and Utah's Early Governments," 193.

31. Chief Justice John F. Kinney to James Buchanan, March 20, 1857, quoted in William P. MacKinnon, *At Sword's Point, Part 1: A Documentary History of the Utah War* (Norman: University of Oklahoma Press, 2008), 108–9.

32. Judge William Drummond, letter of resignation, March 30, 1857, reproduced in Edward W. Tullidge, *The History of Salt Lake City and Its Founders* (Salt Lake City, UT: E. W. Tullidge, 1886), 132–34. See also Thomas L. Kane to Brigham Young, May 21, 1857, in *The Prophet and the Reformer: The Letters of Brigham Young and Thomas L. Kane*, ed. Matthew F. Grow and Ronald W. Walker (New York: Oxford University Press, 2015), 219; Walker, "'Proud as a Peacock and Ignorant as a Jackass,'" 25–26; Allen and Leonard, *The Story of the Latter-day Saints*, 24.

33. Elbert B. Smith, *The Presidency of James Buchanan* (Lawrence: University Press of Kansas, 1975), 66.

34. Roberts, "The Brink of War."

35. Brigham Young, quoted in Bagley, *Blood of the Prophets*, 43.

36. Furniss, *The Mormon Conflict*, 80.

37. Church of Jesus Christ of Latter-day Saints, "Plural Marriage in Kirtland and Nauvoo," Gospel Topics, 2016, https://www.churchofjesuschrist.org/topics/plural-marriage-in-kirtland-and-nauvoo?lang=eng.

38. Allen and Leonard, *The Story of the Latter-day Saints*, 296.

39. Allen and Leonard, *The Story of the Latter-day Saints*, 296.

40. Stephen Douglas, quoted in Stenhouse, *The Rocky Mountain Saints*, 347.

41. Allen and Leonard, *The Story of the Latter-day Saints*, 297.

42. Republican Party platform, 1856, quoted in Allen and Leonard, *The Story of the Latter-day Saints*, 297.

43. R. Scott Lloyd, "1856 Election Sowed the Seeds of Utah War, Y. Scholar Says," *Deseret News*, June 30, 2012; Jerald Ray Johansen, *After the Martyrdom: What Happened to the Family of Joseph Smith?* (Springville, UT: Cedar Fort, 1997), 86.

44. Krakauer, *Under the Banner of Heaven*, 208.

45. Robert Tyler, quoted in Krakauer, *Under the Banner of Heaven*, 210.

46. Krakauer, *Under the Banner of Heaven*, 209.

47. Krakauer, *Under the Banner of Heaven*, 210.

48. See, for example, Thomas G. Alexander, *Brigham Young and the Expansion of the Mormon Faith* (Norman: University of Oklahoma Press, 2019), 130.

49. See, for example, Smith, *The Presidency of James Buchanan*, 67.

50. Allen and Leonard, *The Story of the Latter-day Saints*, 300.

51. Heber Kimball, quoted in Juanita Brooks, *The Mountain Meadows Massacre* (Norman: University of Oklahoma Press, 1962), 19.

52 Allen and Leonard, *The Story of the Latter-day Saints*, 303.

53. Brigham Young, proclamation, August 5, 1857, reissued September 15, 1857, Digital Collections, Brigham Young University Library, https://contentdm.lib.byu.edu/digital/collection/NCMP1820-1846/id/17393; the reissuing of the proclamation is explained at the site Mormon Publications: 19th and 20th Centuries, https://lib.byu.edu/collections/mormon-publications-19th-20th-centuries/p/.

54. Stenhouse, *The Rocky Mountain Saints*, 365–66.

55. Allen and Leonard, *The Story of the Latter-day Saints*, 303.

56. Allen and Leonard, *The Story of the Latter-day Saints*, 306. In 1961, the LDS Church posthumously reinstated Lee as a member of the church. And in September 2007, on the 150-year anniversary of the massacre, the LDS Church issued an apology for the massacre.

57. Roberts, "The Brink of War."

58 James Buchanan, First Annual Message to Congress on the State of the Union, December 8, 1857, American Presidency Project, ed. ed. Gerhard Peters and John T. Woolley, https://www.presidency.ucsb.edu/documents/first-annual-message-congress-the-state-the-union.

59. Brigham Young, quoted in Bigler and Bagley, *The Mormon Rebellion*, 292.

60. Brigham Young, quoted in Leonard J. Arrington, *Brigham Young: American Moses* (New York: Knopf, 1985), 252–53.

61. Roberts, "The Brink of War."

62. Thomas L. Kane to Brigham Young, February 25, 1858, in *The Prophet and the Reformer*, ed. Grow and Walker, 239; Roberts, "The Brink of War"; Stenhouse, *The Rocky Mountain Saints*, 382; William P. MacKinnon, " 'Full of Courage': Thomas L. Kane, the Utah War, and BYU's Kane Collection as Lodestone," *Brigham Young University Studies* 48, no. 4 (2009): 98, 105–7; Richard E. Bennett, "Raising Kane," review of *Liberty to the Downtrodden: Thomas L. Kane, Romantic Reformer*, by Matthew J. Grow (Yale University Press, 2009), *Review of Books on the Book of Mormon* 23, no. 1 (2011): 127.

63. Allen and Leonard, *The Story of the Latter-day Saints*, 307.

64. Church of Jesus Christ of Latter-day Saints, "The Utah War," chap. 29 in *Church History in the Fullness of Time Student Manual*, note 26, https://www.churchofjesuschrist.org/manual/church-history-in-the-fulness-of-times/chapter-twenty-nine?lang=eng#note26; Brigham Young to Elder W. I. Appleby, January 6, 1858, in Brigham Young Letterpress copybooks, typescript, LDS Historical Department, Salt Lake City, UT.

65. Bigler and Bagley, *The Mormon Rebellion*, 292–95.

66. Richard D. Poll, "Utah Expedition," in *Encyclopedia of Mormonism*, ed. Daniel H. Ludlow (New York: Macmillan, 1992), 1501.

67. Allen and Leonard, *The Story of the Latter-day Saints*, 308.

68. David Vaughn Mason, *Brigham Young: Sovereign in America* (London: Routledge, 2014), 114.

69. James Buchanan, "Proclamation on the Rebellion in the Territory of Utah," April 6, 1858, American Presidency Project, ed. Gerhard Peters and John T. Woolley, https://www.presidency.ucsb.edu/node/202635; all quotations from the proclamation come from this source.

70. Bigler and Bagley, *The Mormon Rebellion*, 298.

71. Bagley, "President Pardoned All Utahns."

72. Wilford Woodruff, quoted in Tullidge, *The History of Salt Lake City and Its Founders*, 214.

73. Robert Kent Fielding, *The Unsolicited Chronicler: An Account of the Gunnison Massacre, Its Causes and Consequences* (Taos, NM: Redwing Book, 1992), 443.

74. Brigham Young, quoted in Richard D. Poll and Ralph W. Hansen, "Buchanan's Blunder," *Military Affairs* 25, no. 3, part 1 (Autumn 1961): 130.

75. MacKinnon, *At Sword's Point, Part 1*, 534.

76. "Proclamation of Governor Cumming, June 14, 1858," reproduced in Frederick T. Wilson, *Federal Aid in Domestic Disturbances, 1787–1903* (Washington, DC: U.S. Government Printing Office, 1903), 295–96; see also Fielding, *The Unsolicited Chronicler*, 445.

77. "Proclamation of Governor Cumming, June 14, 1858," 295–96; see also "Governor Cummings Reports and Correspondence," in *Mormon Resistance: A Documentary Account of the Utah Expedition, 1857–1858*, ed. LeRoy Hafen and Ann Woodbury Hafen (Lincoln: University of Nebraska Press, 2005), 318–19.

78. Allen and Leonard, *The Story of the Latter-day Saints*, 309; Roberts, "The Brink of War."

79. Poll, "Utah Expedition," 1501.

80. Mason, *Brigham Young*, 114.

81. Lemuel Filmore, "How Peace Was Made," *New York Herald*, July 19, 1858, quoted in Bigler and Bagley, *The Mormon Rebellion*, ix.

82. *New York Times*, June 17, 1858, quoted in R. Scott Lloyd, "Pioneer Women Left Accounts of Hardships Suffered in 'Move South' During Utah War," Church of Jesus Christ of Latter-Day Saints, 2016, https://www.lds.org/church/news/pioneer-women-left-accounts-of-hardships-suffered-in-move-south-during-utah-war?lang=eng.

83. Allen and Leonard, *The Story of the Latter-day Saints*, 309.

84. Allen and Leonard, *The Story of the Latter-day Saints*, 296.

85. Bigler and Bagley, *The Mormon Rebellion*, 310.

86. "Mormon Affairs: Address of Judge Cradlebaugh, of Utah, on the Condition of Public and Social Life in Utah," *New York Times*, March 21, 1860.

87. Bigler and Bagley, *The Mormon Rebellion*, 332.

88. Poll, "Utah Expedition," 1501.

89. Gustive O. Larson, "Federal Government Efforts to 'Americanize' Utah Before Admission to Statehood," *Brigham Young University Studies Quarterly* 10, no. 2 (1970): 221.

90. Bigler and Bagley, *The Mormon Rebellion*, 345, 351.

91. Bigler and Bagley, *The Mormon Rebellion*, 350.

92. In 1879, the Supreme Court upheld the Morrill Anti-Bigamy Act in *Reynolds v. U.S.*, 98 U.S. 145.

93. Stephen Cresswell, *Mormons and Cowboys, Moonshiners and Klansmen: Federal Law Enforcement in the South and West, 1870–1893* (Tuscaloosa: University of Alabama Press, 2002), 95.

94. Larson, "Federal Government Efforts to 'Americanize' Utah Before Admission to Statehood," 222.

95. Allen and Leonard, *The Story of the Latter-day Saints*, 397.

96. "The Doom of Polygamy," *New York Times*, April 21, 1882.

97. Abraham Lincoln, quoted in Ted Widmer, "Lincoln and the Mormons," *New York Times*, November 17, 2011; Schuyler Colfax, quoted in Larson, "Federal Government Efforts to 'Americanize' Utah Before Admission to Statehood," 222.

98. Rutherford B. Hayes, Fourth Annual Message to Congress, December 6, 1880, American Presidency Project, ed. Gerhard Peters and John T. Woolley, https://www.presidency.ucsb.edu/node/204258.

99. James Garfield, Inaugural Address, March 1881, quoted in Paul M. Holsinger, "Harry M. Teller and the Edmunds-Tucker Act," *Colorado Magazine* 48, no. 1 (1971): 2.

100. Chester A. Arthur, First Annual Message, December 6, 1881, American Presidency Project, ed. Gerhard Peters and John T. Woolley, https://www.presidency.ucsb.edu/node/203844; Chester A. Arthur, Third Annual Message, December 4, 1883, American Presidency Project, ed. Gerhard Peters and John T. Woolley, https://www.presidency.ucsb.edu/node/203861; Chester A. Arthur, Fourth Annual Message, December 1, 1884, American Presidency Project, ed. Gerhard Peters and John T. Woolley, https://www.presidency.ucsb.edu/node/203865. See also Edwin Brown Firmage and Richard Collin Mangum, *Zion in the Courts: A Legal History of the Church of Jesus Christ of Latter-day Saints, 1830–1900* (Champaign: University of Illinois Press, 2001), 198.

101. In *Murphy v. Ramsey* (114 U.S. 15 [1885]), the Supreme Court upheld the Edmunds Act of 1882 as a necessary moral corrective: "For certainly no legislation can be supposed more wholesome and necessary in the founding of a free, self-governing commonwealth, fit to take rank as one of the coordinate States of the Union, than that which seeks to establish it on the basis of the idea of the family, as consisting in and springing from the union for life of one man and one woman in the holy estate of matrimony; the sure foundation of all that is stable and noble in our civilization; the best guaranty of that reverent morality which is the source of all beneficent progress in social and political improvement."

102. Cresswell, *Mormons and Cowboys, Moonshiners and Klansmen*, 97; Krakauer, *Under the Banner of Heaven*, 254.

103. Krakauer, *Under the Banner of Heaven*, 253.

104. In *The Late Corporation of the Church of Jesus Christ of Latter-Day Saints v. United States* (136 [1890]), the Supreme Court upheld the Edmunds-Tucker Act of 1887, which had disincorporated the LDS Church.

105. Krakauer, *Under the Banner of Heaven*, 6–7.

106. Wilford Woodruff, Official Declaration 1, in "Official Declaration," *Deseret Evening News*, September 25, 1890.

107. Benjamin Harrison, Second Annual Message, December 1, 1890, American Presidency Project, ed. Gerhard Peters and John T. Woolley, https://www.presidency.ucsb.edu/node/205158.

108. "Amnesty for the Mormons," *Washington Post*, February 21, 1892.

109. Benjamin Harrison, "Proclamation 346—Granting Amnesty and Pardon for the Offense of Engaging in Polygamous or Plural Marriage to Members of the Church of Latter-Day Saints," January 4, 1893, American Presidency Project, ed. Gerhard Peters and John T. Woolley, https://www.presidency.ucsb.edu/node/205484.

110. *Deseret News*, January 5, 1893, reprinted in *Public Opinion: A Comprehensive Summary of the Press Throughout the World on All Important Current Topics* (Washington, DC: Public Opinion, 1893), 347.

111. *Salt Lake Herald*, January 5, 1893, reprinted in *Public Opinion*, 347.

112. *New York Mail and Express*, January 5, 1893, reprinted in *Public Opinion*, 347.

113. *Washington Star*, January 5, 1893, reprinted in *Public Opinion*, 347.

114. "Utah and Amnesty," *Washington Post*, January 7, 1893.

115. Allen and Leonard, *The Story of the Latter-day Saints*, 396. Clawson had been sentenced to four years in prison and a fine of $800, and he had only four months left in his sentence when he was pardoned.

116. Grover Cleveland, "Proclamation 369—Granting Amnesty and Pardon for the Offenses of Polygamy, Bigamy, Adultery, or Unlawful Cohabitation to Members of the Church of Latter-Day Saints," September 25, 1894, American Presidency Project, ed. Gerhard Peters and John T. Woolley, https://www.presidency.ucsb.edu/node/206350.

117. "Amnesty for Polygamy," *Washington Post*, September 29, 1894.

118. Caleb West, quoted in "Mormons Are Satisfied," *Washington Post*, October 31, 1894.

119. Bigler and Bagley, *The Mormon Rebellion*, 329, 354.

4. THE CIVIL WAR

1. A study conducted in 2012 found that the death toll was likely 20 percent higher, or about 750,000. See Guy Gugliotta, "New Estimate Raises Civil War Death Toll," *New York Times*, April 2, 2012.

2. Douglas L. Wilson, *Lincoln's Sword: The Presidency and the Power of Words* (New York: Vintage, 2006), 147. Although "it is doubtful that Lincoln ever studied the art of persuasion as a formal discipline" (Wilson, *Lincoln's Sword*, 147), some scholars nevertheless claim that his communication embodied many principles of Aristotelian rhetoric.

3. Abraham Lincoln, Temperance Address, February 22, 1842, quoted in Wilson, *Lincoln's Sword*, 146.

4. In contrast to Lincoln's evident faith in second chances, in several private letters he invoked the metaphor of broken eggs to indicate the irreversible violence and damage of war: "Broken eggs can never be mended" (quoted in Wilson, *Lincoln's Sword*, 154–55). And in contrast to the view of Lincoln as forgiving, Adam Gopnik maintains that "Lincoln's genius . . . was never for conciliation but always for drawing the

maximally tough line with minimal outward hysteria" ("Shot of Courage," *New Yorker Magazine*, October 2, 2017).

5. Jonathan Truman Dorris, *Pardon and Amnesty Under Lincoln and Johnson: The Restoration of the Confederates to Their Rights and Privileges, 1861–1898* (1953; reprint, Westport, CT: Greenwood Press, 1977), xvii.

6. Ron Soodalter, "The Limits of Lincoln's Mercy," *New York Times*, February 23, 2012.

7. Soodalter, "The Limits of Lincoln's Mercy."

8. Dorris, *Pardon and Amnesty Under Lincoln and Johnson*, 10.

9. Oath of allegiance, 1862, quoted in Dorris, *Pardon and Amnesty Under Lincoln and Johnson*, 11.

10. Abraham Lincoln, quoted by Schuyler Colfax in *Reminiscences of Abraham Lincoln by Distinguished Men of His Time*, ed. Allen Thorndike Rice (New York: Haskell House, 1971), 341.

11. Abraham Lincoln, quoted in Mark V. Holden, "Clemency Must Play a Pivotal Role in Reversing the 'Tough on Crime Era,'" *University of St. Thomas Law Journal* 16, no. 3 (2019): 369.

12. Soodalter, "The Limits of Lincoln's Mercy." The book *Don't Shoot That Boy! Abraham Lincoln and Military Justice* by Thomas P. Lowry (Boston: De Capo Press, 1999) documents Lincoln's personal involvement in many military justice cases, but it is considered an unreliable source because its author confessed to altering the date of a pardon document at the National Archives in order to promote his narrative.

13. Doris Kearns Goodwin, *Team of Rivals: The Political Genius of Abraham Lincoln* (New York: Simon and Schuster, 2005), 539.

14. Soodalter, "The Limits of Lincoln's Mercy."

15. In addition to political prisoners and Confederates, Lincoln also pardoned Union military deserters in 1865 on the condition that they return to their units.

16. E. Merton Coulter, *The Confederate States of America, 1861–1865* (Baton Rouge: Louisiana University Press, 1950), 94.

17. Dorris, *Pardon and Amnesty Under Lincoln and Johnson*, 86.

18. Dorris, *Pardon and Amnesty Under Lincoln and Johnson*, 87. Given the reverence that is often accorded to Lincoln's Gettysburg Address, it is perhaps ironic that Lincoln said about it, "The world will little note, nor long remember what we say here." As Sam Leith points out, at the time it did not appear that the Gettysburg Address would be the major speech that we now perceive it to be (*Words Like Loaded Pistols: Rhetoric from Aristotle to Obama* [New York: Basic Books, 2012], 140–41).

19. Rick Beard, "Lincoln's 10 Percent Plan," *New York Times*, December 9, 2013.

20. Harold M. Hyman, passage by the editor in *The Radical Republicans and Reconstruction, 1861–1870*, ed. Harold M. Hyman (Indianapolis, IN: Bobbs-Merrill, 1967), 91; Brooks D. Simpson, *The Reconstruction Presidents* (Lawrence: University Press of Kansas, 1998), 37, 61.

21. Abraham Lincoln, "Proclamation 108—Amnesty and Reconstruction," December 8, 1863, American Presidency Project, ed. Gerhard Peters and John T. Woolley,

https://www.presidency.ucsb.edu/node/202362; all subsequent quotations from the proclamation come from this source.

22. Harold M. Hyman, "Civil War Turncoats," *Military Affairs* 22, no. 3 (Autumn 1958): 136.

23. Goodwin, *Team of Rivals*, 589.

24. Joshua Zeitz, "How Democrats Can Learn Hardball from the Republicans of 1861," *Politico*, October 27, 2020.

25. David Herbert Donald, *Lincoln* (New York: Touchstone, 1996), 471–72.

26. Simpson, *The Reconstruction Presidents*, 41.

27. Bruce Levine, *The Fall of the House of Dixie: The Civil War and the Social Revolution That Transformed the South* (New York: Random House, 2013), 191.

28. *Chicago Tribune*, December 15, 1863, quoted in Eric Foner, *The Fiery Trial: Abraham Lincoln and American Slavery* (New York: Norton, 2010), 272.

29. John Hay, quoted in Donald, *Lincoln*, 473.

30. *New York Herald*, December 11, 1863, quoted in Foner, *The Fiery Trial*, 272.

31. John C. Rodrigue, *Lincoln and Reconstruction* (Carbondale: Southern Illinois University Press, 2013), 71–72.

32. William A. Blair, *With Malice Toward Some: Treason and Loyalty in the Civil War Era* (Chapel Hill: University of North Carolina Press, 2014), 196.

33. Jefferson Davis, quoted in James M. McPherson, *Embattled Rebel: Jefferson Davis as Commander in Chief* (New York: Penguin, 2014), 174.

34. Coulter, *The Confederate States of America*, 95.

35. Hyman, "Civil War Turncoats," 138. In a cinematic treatment of the awkward politics of taking the loyalty oath, the Clint Eastwood film *The Outlaw Josey Wales* (1976) depicts Confederate guerillas who decide to lay down their arms and grudgingly take the oath in order to return to their antebellum lives, only to be massacred by Union militants.

36. Coulter, *The Confederate States of America*, 95.

37. Dorris, *Pardon and Amnesty Under Lincoln and Johnson*, xvi–xvii.

38. Abraham Lincoln, "Proclamation 111—Concerning Amnesty," March 26, 1864, American Presidency Project, ed. Gerhard Peters and John T. Woolley, https://www.presidency.ucsb.edu/node/202385.

39. P. S. Ruckman Jr. and David Kincaid, "Inside Lincoln's Clemency Decision Making," *Presidential Studies Quarterly* 29, no. 1 (1999): 84–99, Isaac Arnold quoted on 87.

40. *New York Daily News*, quoted in Ruckman and Kincaid, "Inside Lincoln's Clemency Decision Making," 94, 98 nn. 33 and 34, citing Herbert Mitgang, ed., *Abraham Lincoln: A Press Portrait* (Athens: University of Georgia Press, 1989), 369–71, 379–80.

41. *Spirit of the Times*, quoted in Ruckman and Kincaid, "Inside Lincoln's Clemency Decision Making," 84, 97 n. 36, citing Carl Sandburg, *Abraham Lincoln*, vol. 2 (New York: Harcourt, Brace, 1939), 643.

42. *New York Tribune*, quoted in Ruckman and Kincaid, "Inside Lincoln's Clemency Decision Making," 94, 97 n. 37, citing Mitgang, ed., *Abraham Lincoln*, 364–65.

43. Other Reconstruction actions under Lincoln included his order to seize the estate of Robert E. Lee. The estate was occupied in 1861 and then seized in June 1864 for failure to pay taxes. Later, Lee's son sued and secured $150,000 in compensation. The land was eventually converted into Arlington National Cemetery. Also in 1864, Congress passed the Wade-Davis bill, "making the process of re-entering the Union more difficult than did [the] plan" that Lincoln had promulgated via his proclamation of December 8 because it set the threshold for readmission at 50 percent of the population taking the oath (Coulter, *The Confederate States of America*, 97). Lincoln used a pocket veto to kill the measure, but a similar law passed after his death in 1865.

44. Eric L. McKitrick, *Andrew Johnson and Reconstruction* (New York: Oxford University Press, 1960), 20; James E. Sefton, *Andrew Johnson and the Uses of Constitutional Power* (Boston: Little, Brown, 1980), 97.

45. Sefton, *Andrew Johnson and the Uses of Constitutional Power*, 89.

46. Governor Andrew Johnson, proclamation, January 26, 1864, printed in *New York Times*, February 1, 1864.

47. Sam Elliott, "The 1865 Constitutional Amendments and the Return of Civil Government in Tennessee," Tennessee Bar Association (TBA), *TBA Law Blog*, December 1, 2017, https://www.tba.org/index.cfm?pg=LawBlog&blAction=showEntry&blogEntry=29528.

48. William C. Harris, *With Charity for All: Lincoln and the Restoration of the Union* (Lexington: University Press of Kentucky, 1997), 214–15; Sefton, *Andrew Johnson and the Uses of Constitutional Power*, 97.

49 Andrew Johnson to Indiana delegation, April 21, 1865, quoted in Edward McPherson, *The Political History of the United States of America, During the Period of Reconstruction* (Washington, DC: Philip and Solomons, 1871), 45; all quotations from the speech come from this source.

50. See, for example, Dorris, *Pardon and Amnesty Under Lincoln and Johnson*, 314–15; Thomas B. Alexander, review of *Pardon and Amnesty Under Lincoln and Johnson*, by Jonathan Truman Dorris (University of North Carolina Press, 1953), *Journal of Southern History* 20, no. 2 (May 1954): 278–79; Albert Castel, *The Presidency of Andrew Johnson* (Lawrence: University Press of Kansas, 1979), 50; Martin E. Mantell, *Johnson, Grant, and the Politics of Reconstruction* (New York: Columbia University Press, 1973), 15.

51. Dorris, *Pardon and Amnesty Under Lincoln and Johnson*, 109.

52. James Speed, report, May 1, 1865, quoted in Dorris, *Pardon and Amnesty Under Lincoln and Johnson*, 109.

53. Heather Cox Richardson, *The Death of Reconstruction: Race, Labor, and Politics in the Post–Civil War North, 1865–1901* (Cambridge, MA: Harvard University Press, 2001), 15.

54. Castel, *Presidency of Andrew Johnson*, 26.

55. Andrew Johnson, "Proclamation 134—Granting Amnesty to Participants in the Rebellion, with Certain Exceptions," May 29, 1865, American Presidency Project, ed. Gerhard Peters and John T. Woolley, https://www.presidency.ucsb.edu/node/203492; all quotations from the proclamation come from this source.

56. Jennifer Szalai, "Impeachment, the First Time Around," review of *The Impeachers*, by Brenda Wineapple (Random House, 2019), *New York Times*, May 15, 2019.

57. "General Robert E. Lee's Parole and Citizenship," *Prologue* 37, no. 1 (Spring 2005), https://www.archives.gov/publications/prologue/2005/spring/piece-lee.

58. Kenneth Weisbrode, "An Unlikely Friendship," *New York Times*, June 9, 2014; Sam Hobbs, "Victim of the 'Lost Cause': James Longstreet in the Postwar South," *Traces: UNC–Chapel Hill Journal of History* 2 (Spring 2013): 35–61.

59. Castel, *Presidency of Andrew Johnson*, 26–27.

60. Andrew Johnson, "Speech at St. Louis, September 8, 1866," in *The Papers of Andrew Johnson: August 1866–January 1867*, ed. Paul H. Bergeron (Knoxville: University of Tennessee Press, 1967), 198–99. See also Ronald G. Shafer, " 'A National Disgrace': As Impeachment Hung Over a President's Head, He Went on a Wild Rally Tour," *Washington Post*, January 11, 2020.

61. Andrew Johnson, "Proclamation 167—Offering and Extending Full Pardon to All Persons Participating in the Late Rebellion," September 7, 1867, American Presidency Project, ed. Gerhard Peters and John T. Woolley, https://www.presidency .ucsb.edu/node/201906; all quotations from the proclamation come from this source.

62. Mantell, *Johnson, Grant, and the Politics of Reconstruction*, 37.

63. "Domestic Intelligence," *Harper's Weekly*, September 21, 1867.

64. Dorris, *Pardon and Amnesty Under Lincoln and Johnson*, 308.

65. Andrew Johnson, "Proclamation 170—Granting Pardon to All Persons Participating in the Late Rebellion Except Those Under Indictment for Treason or Other Felony," July 4, 1868, American Presidency Project, ed. Gerhard Peters and John T. Woolley, https://www.presidency.ucsb.edu/node/202903; all quotations from the proclamation come from this source.

66. Castel, *The Presidency of Andrew Johnson*, 198–99.

67. Dorris, *Pardon and Amnesty Under Lincoln and Johnson*, 330. However, as James Alex Baggett notes, in June 1868 "Congress relieved 1,431 individuals of their restrictions under the Reconstruction Acts and the Fourteenth Amendment" (*The Scalawags: Southern Dissenters in the Civil War and Reconstruction* [Baton Rouge: Louisiana State University Press, 2003], 236). In addition, the Amnesty Act of 1872 gave Confederate leaders the right to hold office, notwithstanding the exclusions of the Fourteenth Amendment.

68. Dorris, *Pardon and Amnesty Under Lincoln and Johnson*, 310–11.

69. Dorris, *Pardon and Amnesty Under Lincoln and Johnson*, 310–11.

70. Frank W. Klingberg, review of *Pardon and Amnesty Under Lincoln and Johnson*, by Jonathan Truman Dorris (University of North Carolina Press, 1953), *Mississippi Valley Historical Review* 41, no. 3 (December 1954): 524. The last formal disability was eliminated in 1898.

71. Andrew Johnson, "Proclamation 179—Granting Full Pardon and Amnesty for the Offense of Treason Against the United States During the Late Civil War," December 25, 1868, American Presidency Project, ed. Gerhard Peters and John T. Woolley,

https://www.presidency.ucsb.edu/node/203394; all quotations from the proclamation come from this source.

72. Jefferson Davis, *The Rise and Fall of the Confederate Government* (New York: Appleton, 1881), part 4, chap. 56.

73. David Blight describes three different versions of Reconstruction—and historical views of the Civil War in general—as reconciliationist, white supremacist, and emancipationist. See David W. Blight, *Race and Reunion: The Civil War in American Memory* (Cambridge, MA: Belknap Press of Harvard University Press, 2001).

74. For this view of Reconstruction's failure, see Eric Foner, "Reconstruction Revisited," in "The Promise of American History: Progress and Prospects," *Reviews of American History* 10, no. 4 (December 1982): 82–100. In contrast, Henry Louis Gates Jr. claims that at least the cultural politics of Reconstruction continued after 1877. See Henry Louis Gates Jr., *Stony the Road: Reconstruction, White Supremacy, and the Rise of Jim Crow* (New York: Penguin Press, 2019).

75. Klingberg, review of *Pardon and Amnesty Under Lincoln and Johnson*, 524.

76. Frank W. Klingberg, *The Southern Claims Commission* (New York: Octagon Books, 1978), 89.

77. Dorris, *Pardon and Amnesty Under Lincoln and Johnson*, 330.

78. Baggett, *The Scalawags*, 236.

79. Klingberg, review of *Pardon and Amnesty Under Lincoln and Johnson*, 524.

80. National Constitution Center Staff, "The Pardon of Jefferson Davis and the 14th Amendment," National Constitution Center, October 17, 2018, https://constitutioncenter.org/blog/the-pardon-of-jefferson-davis-and-the-14th-amendment/.

81. William C. Davis, *Look Away! A History of the Confederate States of America* (New York: Free Press, 1992), 424.

82. Terrence McCoy, "They Lost the Civil War and Fled to Brazil: Their Descendants Refuse to Take Down the Confederate Flag," *Washington Post*, July 11, 2020.

83. George Horne, cited in Simon Romero, "A Slice of the Confederacy in the Interior of Brazil," *New York Times*, May 8, 2016.

84. Davis, *Look Away!*, 424. See also Cyrus B. Dawsey and James M. Dawsey, eds., *The Confederados: Old South Immigrants in Brazil* (Tuscaloosa: University of Alabama Press, 1998); Andrew F. Rolle, *The Lost Cause: The Confederate Exodus to Mexico* (Norman: University of Oklahoma Press, 1992); Eugene C. Harter, *The Lost Colony of the Confederacy* (College Station: Texas A&M University Press, 2000); Donald C. Simmons Jr., *Confederate Settlements in British Honduras* (Jefferson, NC: McFarland, 2001); Phil Leigh, "The Confederate Diaspora," *New York Times*, May 14, 2015. Confederate general George Pickett (of Pickett's Charge fame) requested a pardon from Johnson in June 1865 but fled to Canada to avoid possible prosecution for war crimes for having hanged twenty-two Confederate deserters who had joined Union forces. He returned to the United States but was never charged. Ulysses Grant supported Pickett's request for a pardon, but other government officials did not. Nevertheless, Pickett was apparently covered by Johnson's

pardon of December 1868 as well as by later congressional legislation to remove any remaining political disabilities. See "Pickett, George E.," in *The Oxford Encyclopedia of the Civil War*, ed. William L. Barney (Oxford: Oxford University Press, 2001), 240; James O. Hall, "Atonement," *Civil War Times Illustrated* 19, no. 5 (August 1980): 19–21.

85. Leigh, "The Confederate Diaspora."

86. Blight, *Race and Reunion.*

87. John Logan and speaker in Philadelphia, quoted in Nina Silber, *The Romance of Reunion: Northerners and the South, 1865–1900* (Chapel Hill: University of North Carolina Press, 1993), 60.

88. Silber, *The Romance of Reunion*, 61, 94–95.

89. In 2017, Mayor Mitch Landrieu of New Orleans claimed that contemporary controversies about removing Confederate memorials indicated that the country was still working through issues from the Civil War: "Centuries-old wounds are still raw because they never healed right in the first place" (quoted in Olivia B. Waxman, "Why Jefferson Davis Got His U.S. Citizenship Back," *Time*, June 5, 2017).

90. Jimmy Carter, "Department of Defense Remarks and a Question-and-Answer Session with Department Employees," March 1, 1977, American Presidency Project, ed. Gerhard Peters and John T. Woolley, http://www.presidency.ucsb.edu/ws/index.php ?pid=7099. I am indebted to Michelle Belco for apprising me of Carter's remarks to Department of Defense employees on March 1, 1977.

91. Jimmy Carter, "Restoration of Citizenship Rights to Jefferson F. Davis, Statement on Signing S. J. Res. 16 Into Law," October 17, 1978, American Presidency Project, ed. Gerhard Peters and John T. Woolley, http://www.presidency.ucsb.edu/ws/ ?pid=29993. See also National Constitution Center, "The Pardon of Jefferson Davis and the 14th Amendment," October 17, 2018, https://constitutioncenter.org/blog/the -pardon-of-jefferson-davis-and-the-14th-amendment.

92. Francis MacDonnell, "Reconstruction in the Wake of Vietnam: The Pardoning of Robert E. Lee and Jefferson Davis," *Civil War History* 40, no. 2 (June 1994): 119, 132.

5. VIETNAM WAR RESISTERS

1. Stanley Karnow, *Vietnam: A History* (New York: Penguin, 1984), 478. More than three decades later, in 2007, that number had risen to 74 percent. See Jeffrey Jones, "Latest Poll Shows High Point in Opposition to Iraq War," Gallup.com, July 11, 2007, https://news.gallup.com/poll/28099/latest-poll-shows-high-point-opposition-iraq -war.aspx.

2. Karl Marlantes, "Vietnam: The War That Killed Trust," *New York Times*, January 7, 2017.

3. Amy J. Rutenberg, "What Trump's Draft Deferments Reveal," *Atlantic*, January 2, 2019.

4. Amy J. Rutenberg, "How the Draft Reshaped America," *New York Times*, October 6, 2017.

5. Bill Zimmerman, "The Four Stages of the Antiwar Movement," *New York Times*, October 4, 1967.

6. Michael Stewart Foley, "The Moral Case for Draft Resistance," *New York Times*, October 17, 2017.

7. Amy Scott, "Patriots for Peace: People to People Diplomacy and the Anti-war Movement," in *America and the Vietnam War: Re-examining the Culture and History of a Generation*, ed. Andrew Wiest, Mary Kathryn Barbier, and Glenn Robins (London: Routledge, 2009), 124.

8. Richard Nixon, "Address to the Nation on the War in Vietnam," November 3, 1969, American Presidency Project, ed. Gerhard Peters and John T. Woolley, https://www .presidency.ucsb.edu/node/240027.

9. Richard Nixon, "Statement on Campus Disorders," March 22, 1969, American Presidency Project, ed. Gerhard Peters and John T. Woolley, https://www.presidency.ucsb .edu/node/239730.

10. Richard Nixon, "Address to the Nation on the Situation in Southeast Asia," April 30, 1970, American Presidency Project, ed. Gerhard Peters and John T. Woolley, https:// www.presidency.ucsb.edu/node/239701.

11. Richard Nixon, May 1972, quoted in George Lardner Jr., "Nixon Defended Envoy's Groping," *Washington Post*, March 1, 2002.

12 Betty Medsger, *The Burglary: The Discovery of J. Edgar Hoover's Secret FBI* (New York: Vintage, 2014), 442–44.

13. Jack Calhoun, review of *The Vietnam War and the Vietnam Generation*, by Lawrence M. Baskir and William A. Strauss (Knopf, 1978), *Peace and Change* 6, no. 3 (October 1980): 73.

14. In his review of the book *The Vietnam War and the Vietnam Generation* by Baskir and Strauss, who led Ford's clemency program, Jack Calhoun reports, "Of those members of the Vietnam generation opposed to the war, Baskir and Strauss find about 172,000 draft age youth qualified as conscientious objectors, of whom 96,000 completed their civilian alternative service requirements. Although 570,000 young men broke Selective Service laws, only about 210,000 cases were reported to federal prosecutors. The authors estimate an additional 250,000 failed to register with the draft system as required by law.... There were about 1,500,000 incidents of GIs going AWOL for short periods of time and about 500,000 cases of desertion or long-time AWOLs" (73.) According to Warren Hoover of the National Interreligious Service Board for Conscientious Objectors, the groups who in 1973 stood to benefit from amnesty included 60,000 to 100,000 draft resisters and military deserters who were in exile; 80,000 resisters and deserters who were underground in the United States; 10,000 resisters and deserters who were in prison, were currently facing charges in court, or were on probation; 300,000 veterans with less-than-honorable discharges; and an unknown number of civilians charged with various crimes for opposing the

war (Hoover cited in Anthony Ripley, "Amnesty for Draft Resisters Is Expected to Be Divisive Political Issue for Years," *New York Times*, January 30, 1973).

15. William W. Scranton, chairman, *The Report of the President's Commission on Campus Unrest* (Washington, DC: U.S. Government Printing Office, 1970), 174.

16. Ronald Reagan, quoted in Medsger, *The Burglary*, 25.

17. James Rhodes, quoted in Stewart J. Lawrence, "The Unquiet Ghosts of Kent State," *Guardian*, May 4, 2011.

18. David Harris, "I Picked Prison Over Fighting in Vietnam," *New York Times*, June 23, 2017.

19. Medsger, *The Burglary*, 201.

20. Similar CIA programs to spy on domestic critics of the war allegedly included Project RESISTANCE and Project MERRIMAC. See Eugene Phillips, "The Central Intelligence Agency's Surveillance of the New Left," *Review of History and Political Science* 5, no. 2 (December 2017): 1.

21. Medsger, *The Burglary*, 208, 250.

22. Medsger, *The Burglary*, 168, 202–3, 333.

23. Julius Duscha, "Should There Be Amnesty for the War Resister?," *New York Times*, December 24, 1972.

24. Duscha, "Should There Be Amnesty for the War Resister?"

25 Regarding draft evaders who went to Sweden, see Matthew Sweet, *Operation Chaos: The Vietnam Deserters Who Fought the CIA, the Brainwashers, and Themselves* (New York: Holt, 2018).

26. There is much dispute about the numbers of draft dodgers and military deserters who fled to Canada. In 1974, Nixon aid Pat Buchanan estimated the number to be 7,000 to 10,000 (cited in William Borders, "Exiles Are Cool to Amnesty Move," *New York Times*, August 21, 1974). In early 1977, the *New York Times* put the number at 20,000 to 50,000 (Robert Trumbell, "Pardon Brings Cautious Response from Some War Exiles in Canada," *New York Times*, January 23, 1977). The historian John Hagan says it was 50,000, which constituted the "largest political exodus from the United States since the American Revolution" (*Northern Passage: American Vietnam War Resisters in Canada* [Cambridge, MA: Harvard University Press, 2001], 218). In fact, there is a book devoted exclusively to trying to ascertain the correct number of American war resisters in Canada: Joseph Jones, *Contending Statistics: The Numbers for U.S. Vietnam War Resisters in Canada* (Vancouver: Quarter Sheaf, 2005). Jones examines estimates ranging from 20,000 to more than 100,000, and he settles on 60,000 as the best approximation (34). See also James L. Dickerson, *North to Canada: Men and Women Against the Vietnam War* (Westport, CT: Praeger, 1999).

27. Jack Todd, "Remembering the 1975 Fall of Saigon," *Montreal Gazette*, April 30, 2015.

28. Quoted in Kathleen Rodgers, *Welcome to Resisterville: American Dissidents in British Columbia* (Vancouver: University of British Columbia Press, 2014), 29.

29. David S. Surrey, *Choice of Conscience: Vietnam Era Military and Draft Resisters in Canada* (Westport, CT: Praeger, 1982), 167.

30. Craig Allen Smith and Kathy B. Smith, *The White House Speaks: Presidential Leadership as Persuasion* (Westport, CT: Praeger, 1994), 59.

31. Wilfred L. Ebel, "The Amnesty Issue: An Historical Perspective," *Parameters* 4, no. 1 (January 1, 1974): 67–77. Truman issued amnesties regarding military service in 1945, 1946, and 1952.

32. Duscha, "Should There Be Amnesty for the War Resister?"

33. Jason Friedman, "Just a Caretaker?," in *A Companion to Gerald R. Ford and Jimmy Carter*, ed. Scott Kaufman (Hoboken, NJ: Wiley, 2015), 207. But see Sheila Rudy Plaxton, "To Reconcile a Nation: Gerald Ford, Jimmy Carter, and the Question of Amnesty," PhD diss., Queens University, 1995.

34. George McGovern, quoted in Hagan, *Northern Passage*, 154.

35. David Shichor and Donald R. Ranish, "President Carter's Vietnam Amnesty," *Presidential Studies Quarterly* 10 (1980): 444.

36. Renee G. Kasinsky, *Refugees from Militarism: Draft-Age Americans in Canada* (Piscataway, NJ: Transaction, 1976), 243.

37. Amy Swerdlow, *Women Strike for Peace: Traditional Motherhood and Radical Politics in the 1960s* (Chicago: University of Chicago Press, 1993), 183.

38. Arlo Tatum and Henry Steele Commager, testimony, U.S. Senate, Subcommittee on Administrative Practice and Procedure, *Selective Service and Amnesty: Hearing Before the Subcommittee on Administrative Practice and Procedure of the Committee on the Judiciary, U.S. Senate, February 29 to March 1, 1972,* 92nd Cong., 2nd sess. (Washington, DC: U.S. Government Printing Office, 1972), 171, 188–89.

39. Harris, "I Picked Prison Over Fighting in Vietnam."

40. Edward Kennedy, quoted in Julius Duscha, "More Than 50,000 Americans Killed in Vietnam, More Than 300,000 Wounded or Injured, More Than 1,600 P.O.W.'s or M.I.A.'s," *New York Times*, December 24, 1972.

41. Robert F. Froehlke, "A Statement on Amnesty," U.S. House of Representatives, March 11, 1974, box 1, folder "Amnesty—General," Charles E. Goodell Papers, Gerald R. Ford Presidential Library, Grand Rapids, MI, https://www.fordlibrarymuseum.gov/library/document/0193/1505960.pdf.

42. Robert F. Froehlke, quoted in Jules Witcover, "Middle-Road Policy on Amnesty Seen," *Washington Post*, August 26, 1974.

43. Philip Hart, quoted in Calhoun, review of *The Vietnam War and the Vietnam Generation*, 75.

44. Spiro Agnew, quoted in Hagan, *Northern Passage*, 155.

45. Hagan, *Northern Passage*, 155.

46. Richard Nixon, quoted in Duscha, "More Than 50,000 Americans Killed in Vietnam."

47. Dan Rather and Richard Nixon, quoted in Rick Perlstein, *Nixonland: The Rise of a President and the Fracturing of America* (New York: Scribner, 2008), 618, emphasis in original.

48. Ripley, "Amnesty for Draft Resisters Is Expected to Be Divisive Political Issue for Years"; Perlstein, *Nixonland*, 640.

49. Ripley, "Amnesty for Draft Resisters Is Expected to Be Divisive Political Issue for Years."

50. Donald Rumsfeld, *When the Center Held: Gerald Ford and the Rescue of the American Presidency* (New York: Free Press, 2018), 3.

51. John Robert Greene, *The Presidency of Gerald R. Ford* (Lawrence: University Press of Kansas, 1994), 34.

52. Greene, *The Presidency of Gerald R. Ford*, 39.

53. See, for example, Smith and Smith, *The White House Speaks*, 61; and David L. Anderson, "Gerald R. Ford and the Presidents' War in Vietnam," in *Shadow on the White House: Presidents and the Vietnam War, 1945–1975*, ed. David L. Anderson (Lawrence: University Press of Kansas, 1993), 188–89.

54. Richard Norton Smith, comment made in Paul O'Neill, interviewed by Richard Norton Smith, Gerald R. Ford Oral History Project, March 19, 2010. http://geraldrfordfoundation.org/centennial/oralhistory/paul-oneill/.

55. Gerald R. Ford, quoted in Betty Ford and Chris Chase, *The Times of My Life* (New York: Harper Collins, 1978), 164.

56. Greene, *The Presidency of Gerald R. Ford*, 9.

57. Mary E. Stuckey, *Political Rhetoric: A Presidential Briefing Book* (New York: Routledge, 2015), 1.

58. Gerald R. Ford, "Remarks to the Veterans of Foreign Wars Annual Convention, Chicago, Illinois," August 19, 1974, American Presidency Project, ed. Gerhard Peters and John T. Woolley, https://www.presidency.ucsb.edu/node/256148; all quotations from Ford's remarks at the convention come from this source.

59. Gerald R. Ford, Inaugural Address, August 9, 1974, quoted in David Veenstra, "As God Gives Me to See the Right: Gerald Ford, Religion, and Healing After Vietnam and Watergate," *Pro Rege* 43, no. 3 (March 2015): 15.

60. Veenstra, "As God Gives Me to See the Right," 15.

61. Barry Werth, "The Pardon," *Smithsonian*, February 2007.

62. "Amnesty Rejected by VFW," *Baton Rouge Advocate*, August 21, 1974.

63. John P. MacKenzie, "Ford to Get Advice Today on Amnesty," *Washington Post*, August 31, 1974.

64. James Reston Jr., "Limited Amnesty: Not Easy," *New York Times*, September 8, 1974.

65. MacKenzie, "Ford to Get Advice Today on Amnesty."

66. Reston, "Limited Amnesty."

67. Gerald R. Ford, "Proclamation 4311—Granting Pardon to Richard Nixon," September 8, 1974, American Presidency Project, ed. Gerhard Peters and John T. Woolley, https://www.presidency.ucsb.edu/node/256500.

68. Gerald R. Ford, "Remarks on Signing a Proclamation Granting Pardon to Richard Nixon," September 8, 1974, Gerald R. Ford Presidential Library & Museum, https://www.fordlibrarymuseum.gov/library/speeches/740060.asp.

69. Gerald Ford, interviewed by Cokie Roberts, 2004 , clip of Ford making this statement in a tribute program aired one day after Ford died, *President Ford's Life &*

Legacy, NPR, December 27, 2006, https://www.npr.org/templates/story/story.php?storyId=6686363.

70. Joseph Carroll, "Americans Grow to Accept Nixon's Pardon," Gallup.com, May 21, 2001, https://news.gallup.com/poll/3157/americans-grew-accept-nixons-pardon.aspx.

71. Ronald Docksai, quoted in John P. MacKenzie, "Pardon Sparks New Calls for Viet Amnesty," *Washington Post*, September 10, 1974.

72. Gerald R. Ford, "Proclamation 4313—Announcing a Program for the Return of Vietnam Era Draft Evaders and Military Deserters," September 16, 1974, American Presidency Project, ed. Gerhard Peters and John T. Woolley, https://www.presidency.ucsb.edu/node/256605.

73. Gerald R. Ford, "Remarks on Clemency for Vietnam Era Draft Evaders," televised speech, September 16, 1974, Miller Center, https://millercenter.org/the-presidency/presidential-speeches/september-16-1974-remarks-clemency-vietnam-era-draft-evaders.

74. Gerald R. Ford, address at Tulane University Convocation, April 23, 1975, American Presidency Project, ed. Gerhard Peters and John T. Woolley, http://www.presidency.ucsb.edu/ws/?pid=4859.

75. "59% in Poll Favor Amnesty Program Like the Ford Plan," *New York Times*, September 22, 1974.

76. Witcover, "Middle-Road Policy on Amnesty Seen."

77. Nancy Montgomery and Mrs. Clifford Gaddy, quoted in Lawrence Meyer, "Exiles' Families Say Ford Proposal Not True Amnesty," *Washington Post*, September 17, 1974.

78. For a detailed presentation of different reactions to Ford's amnesty program, see Courtney Carver, "To Forgive or Not to Forgive? A Reappraisal of Vietnam War Evaders and Deserters in President Gerald Ford's Clemency Program," master's thesis, University of New Orleans, 2018.

79. Carroll Kilpatrick, "Clemency Offered," *Washington Post*, September 17, 1974.

80. "Vets Group Backs Plan for Amnesty," *Washington Post*, August 29, 1974.

81. Jules Witcover, *Marathon: The Pursuit of the Presidency, 1972–1976* (New York: Viking Press, 1977), 460; Anderson, "Gerald R. Ford and the Presidents' War in Vietnam," 189.

82. Daniel Pollitt and Frank Thompson Jr., "Amnesty: The American Tradition," *Washington Post*, September 19, 1974.

83. Anderson, "Gerald R. Ford and the Presidents' War in Vietnam," 189.

84. "The Vietnam 'Amnesty,'" *Washington Post*, September 18, 1974.

85. American Civil Liberties Union, "The Clemency Program," October 18, 1974, quoted in Kasinsky, *Refugees from Militarism*, 257.

86. Mrs. Douglas Kinsey, quoted in Meyer, "Exiles' Families Say Ford Proposal Not True Amnesty."

87. Steve Grossman, "I Want to Go Home, but . . .," *New York Times*, January 2, 1977.

88. Nora McCabe, "War Resisters' Conference Rejects Ford Amnesty Plan," *Washington Post*, September 22, 1974; Surrey, *Choice of Conscience*, 168.

89. Chair of Presidential Clemency Board, quoted in Bob Kuttner, "Clemency Offer Draws Poor Response," *Washington Post*, November 23, 1974.

90. Kuttner, "Clemency Offer Draws Poor Response."

91. Kasinsky, *Refugees from Militarism*, 259.

92   "Clemency Program May Be Dropped," *New York Times*, December 17, 1976.

93. William C. Westmoreland, "No Pardon for Draft Evaders," *New York Times*, December 12, 1976.

94. Comptroller General of the United States, *Report to the Congress: The Clemency Program of 1974*, 95th Cong., 1st sess. (Washington, DC: U.S. Government Printing Office, January 7, 1977), i.

95. Lou Cannon, "Ford Weighs Amnesty Program," *Washington Post*, December 28, 1976.

96. Dean Hansell, "Amnesty, Discharge Status Upgrading, and Military Deserters Under the Carter Administration: Selective Redemption," *Clearinghouse Review* 11 (1977–1978): 344.

97. Lee Lescaze, "New Vietnam Clemency Proposal Emulates Carter's," *Washington Post*, January 16, 1977.

98. Lawrence Baskir and William Strauss, quoted in Calhoun, review of *The Vietnam War and the Vietnam Generation*, 76.

99. Lawrence M. Baskir and William A. Strauss, *Reconciliation After Vietnam: A Program of Relief for Vietnam-Era Draft and Military Offenders* (Notre Dame, IN: University of Notre Dame Press, 1977), 4.

100. *Georgia Restoration of Rights & Record Relief*, Collateral Consequences Resource Center, updated September 9, 2020, http://ccresourcecenter.org/state-restoration -profiles/georgia-restoration-of-rights-pardon-expungement-sealing/.

101. Jimmy Carter, *Living Faith* (1996; reprint, New York: Three Rivers Press, 2001), 146, 24, 77, 83.

102. "Carter in Action," *National Review*, February 18, 1977.

103. Myra MacPherson, *Long Time Passing: Vietnam and the Haunted Generation* (Bloomington: Indiana University Press, 1984), 350; Witcover, *Marathon*, 357.

104. Tom Wicker, "Clemency: It's Not So Simple," *New York Times*, December 28, 1976.

105. Jimmy Carter, quoted in James Wooten, "Legionnaires Boo Carter on Pardon for Draft Defiers," *New York Times*, August 25, 1976.

106. Helen Dewar, "Legionnaires Boo Carter's Plan to Pardon Draft Evaders," *Washington Post*, August 25, 1976.

107. Jimmy Carter, speech at the American Legion convention, Seattle, August 24, 1976, quoted in Jimmy Carter, *A Government as Good as Its People*, 2nd ed. (Fayetteville: University of Arkansas Press, 1996), 126.

108. Wooten, "Legionnaires Boo Carter on Pardon for Draft Defiers."

109. Witcover, *Marathon*, 526.

110. Wooten, "Legionnaires Boo Carter on Pardon for Draft Defiers"; Witcover, *Marathon*, 526.

111. Carter, speech, American Legion convention, Seattle, August 24, 1976, quoted in Carter, *A Government as Good as Its People*, 127.

112. Witcover, *Marathon*, 526.
113. Bob Dole, quoted in "Ford Opposes Amnesty: Dole," *Chicago Tribune*, August 26, 1976. See also Witcover, *Marathon*, 540–41; Douglas Kneeland, "Dole Attacks Carter on Pardon for Draft Evaders," *New York Times*, August 26, 1976; Dan F. Hahn, "The Rhetoric of Jimmy Carter, 1976–1980," *Presidential Studies Quarterly*, Spring 1984, 267.
114. "In Defense of Jimmy Carter," *Wall Street Journal*, September 2, 1976.
115. Jason Friedman, "Draft Dodger and Deserter Reconciliation, 1972–1977," paper presented at the Peace History Society conference, Mount Pleasant, MI, April 26, 2003.
116. Marvin Kalb and Deborah Kalb, *Haunting Legacy: Vietnam and the American Presidency from Ford to Obama* (Washington, DC: Brookings Institution Press, 2011), 47.
117. Presidential debate, September 23, 1976, Philadelphia, transcript in Gerald R. Ford, *Containing the Public Messages, Speeches, and Statements of the President, 1976–1977*, vol. 3: *July 10, 1976 to January 20, 1977* (Washington, DC: U.S. Government Printing Office, 1979), 2290; subsequent quotations from the debate are on pages 2290–291.
118. Gerald R. Ford, *A Time to Heal* (New York: Harper and Row, 1979), 415–16, quoted in Kalb and Kalb, *Haunting Legacy*, 47.
119. "Carter Aides Widen a Draft Pardon Plan," *New York Times*, December 17, 1976.
120. Wicker, "Clemency."
121. Helen Frazelle and Theresa Cavanaugh, quoted in Sharon Conway, "Families of Vietnam War Victims Divided on Pardon Issue," *Washington Post*, January 17, 1977.
122. Barry W. Lynn, ". . . and the Argument in Favor," *Wall Street Journal*, January 6, 1977.
123. Jimmy Carter, Inaugural Address, January 20, 1977, quoted in "Mr. Carter's Call for Personal and National Humility," *New York Times*, January 23, 1977.
124. Victor Lasky, *Jimmy Carter: The Man and the Myth* (New York: Richard Marek, 1979), 315.
125 Jimmy Carter, "Proclamation 4483—Granting Pardon for Violations of the Selective Service Act, August 4, 1964 to March 28, 1973," January 21, 1977, American Presidency Project, ed. Gerhard Peters and John T. Woolley, https://www.presidency.ucsb.edu/node/243475. See also "Carter's Pardon," *MacNeil/Lehrer Report*, PBS, January 21, 1977, http://www.pbs.org/newshour/bb/asia/vietnam/vietnam_1-21-77 html.
126 "Carter in Action."
127. Jimmy Carter, "Department of Defense Remarks and a Question-and-Answer Session with Department Employees," March 1, 1977, American Presidency Project, ed. Gerhard Peters and John T. Woolley, http://www.presidency.ucsb.edu/ws/index.php?pid=7099. I am indebted to Michelle Belco for apprising me of Carter's remarks to Department of Defense employees on March 1, 1977.
128. Jimmy Carter, interviewed by Brian Williams, March 11, 2006, John F. Kennedy Library and Museum, https://www.jfklibrary.org/events-and-awards/forums/past-forums/transcripts/vietnam-and-the-presidency-introduction-by-caroline-kennedy-and-interview-with-president-jimmy.
129. "Mr. Carter's Call for Personal and National Humility."

130. Louis Harris, "Pardon Criticized," Harris Survey, February 24, 1977; percentages are as given in the poll.
131. "The Pardon Backlash," *Wall Street Journal*, January 25, 1977.
132. Robert D. McFadden, "Pro-Amnesty Groups Offer Praise but Assert That Plan Is Too Limited," *New York Times*, January 22, 1977.
133. "Mr. Carter's Call for Personal and National Humility."
134. Sheila Cavanaugh, quoted in Conway, "Families of Vietnam War Victims Divided on Pardon Issue."
135. Tim Marlow, comment aired in "Carter's Pardon."
136. "Group Wants Carter Ousted from Legion," *New York Times*, January 25, 1977, including quotation from William Rogers.
137. Quoted in Charles Mohr, "10,000 Affected Now," *New York Times*, January 22, 1977.
138. Bob Dole, quoted in McFadden, "Pro-Amnesty Groups Offer Praise but Assert That Plan Is Too Limited."
139. Barry Goldwater, quoted in Burton I. Kaufman, *The Presidency of James Earl Carter* (Lawrence: University Press of Kansas, 1993), 34.
140. "To Fashion a Blanket of Pardon," *New York Times*, January 10, 1974.
141. Elizabeth Holtzman, quoted in "Carter's Pardon."
142. Pat Simon, quoted in Conway, "Families of Vietnam War Victims Divided on Pardon Issue."
143. Corrine Hayword, quoted in Conway, "Families of Vietnam War Victims Divided on Pardon Issue."
144. See George C. Wilson, "Carter Authorizes Military to Review Viet Discharges," *Washington Post*, March 29, 1977.
145. Jimmy Carter, "Veterans Benefits Statement on Signing S. 1307 Into Law," October 8, 1977, American Presidency Project, ed. Gerhard Peters and John T. Woolley, https://www.presidency.ucsb.edu/node/242783.
146. See Lee Lescaze, "Draft Pardon Foes Fail to Obtain Senate Vote," *Washington Post*, January 25, 1977.
147. Jimmy Carter, "Appropriations Bill Statement on Signing H.R. 7556 Into Law," August 3, 1977, American Presidency Project, ed. Gerhard Peters and John T. Woolley, http://www.presidency.ucsb.edu/ws/?pid=7915.
148. Estimates of the numbers of Americans who opted to remain in Canada range from 7,000 (Herbert H. Denton, "They Chose to Remain Despite Amnesty," *Washington Post*, January 1, 1989) to 50,000 (Andrew Glass, "Carter Pardons Draft Dodgers Jan 21 1977," *Politico*, January 21, 2008).
149. Ripley, "Amnesty for Draft Resisters Is Expected to Be Divisive Political Issue for Years."
150. Marlantes, "Vietnam."
151. Ken Burns and Lynn Novick, "Vietnam's Unhealed Wounds," op-ed, *New York Times*, May 29, 2017.
152. Ken Burns and Lynn Novick, dirs., "The Weight of Memory," episode 10 of *The Vietnam War*, PBS (WETA, National Endowment for the Humanities), aired September 28, 2017.

153.   David Greenberg, "The War That Never Ends," review of *The Vietnam War*, by Geoffrey C. Ward (Knopf, 2017), *New York Times Book Review*, September 17, 2017.

154.   U.S. Department of Justice, "Vietnam Era Pardon Instructions," updated March 3, 2016, https://www.justice.gov/pardon/vietnam-war-era-pardon-instructions, emphasis in original.

CONCLUSION

1.   "The Pardon Backlash," *Wall Street Journal*, January 25, 1977.

2.   As the political historian Julian Zelizer notes, "Historians will be cautious about political science claims as to the 'portability' of historical analysis" because historians are more devoted to the idea of "particularity." According to Zelizer, "Historians believe that each moment in history is rather unique since it is produced by a complex mix of forces, individuals, cultures, and institutions that all come together at a single point. Despite the famous mantra about history repeating itself, historians have spent an enormous amount of time showing that, when you get down to the details, each historical moment can only be understood on its own terms" (*Governing America: The Revival of Political History* [Princeton, NJ: Princeton University Press, 2012], 66).

3.   See William J. Novak, "The Myth of the Weak State," *American Historical Review* 113, no. 3 (2008): 752–72; Brian Balogh, *A Government Out of Sight: The Mystery of National Authority in Nineteenth-Century America* (Cambridge: Cambridge University Press, 2009); Desmond King and Robert C. Lieberman, "Ironies of State Building: A Comparative Perspective on the American State," *World Politics* 61 (2009): 547–88; Zelizer, *Governing America*, 95; James T. Sparrow, William J. Novak, and Stephen Sawyer, eds., *Boundaries of the State in U.S. History* (Chicago: University of Chicago Press, 2015).

4.   See Charles Tilly, "Collective Violence in European Perspective," in *Violence in America: Historical and Comparative Perspectives*, ed. Hugh Davis Graham and Ted Robert Gurr, National Commission on the Causes and Prevention of Violence (Washington, DC: U.S. Government Printing Office, 1969), 4–45.

5.   Jeffrey Toobin, "The Trouble with Donald Trump's Clemency and Pardons," *New Yorker*, February 19, 2020.

6.   Gerald R. Ford, "Presidential Remarks for Clemency Board Signings," November 29, 1974, box 6, folder "Goodell—Press Conference, 11/29/74," Charles E. Goodell Papers, Gerald R. Ford Presidential Library, Grand Rapids, MI, https://www.fordlibrarymuseum.gov/library/document/0193/1505998.pdf.

7.   See Andrew Rudalevige, "Executive Orders and Presidential Unilateralism," *Presidential Studies Quarterly* 42, no. 1 (March 2012): 138–60; Matthew Dickinson and Jesse Grub, "The Limits to Power Without Persuasion," *Presidential Studies Quarterly* 46, no. 1 (March 2016): 48–72.

8.   Karlyn Kohrs Campbell and Kathleen Hall Jamieson, *Deeds Done in Words: Presidential Rhetoric and the Genres of Governance* (Chicago: University of Chicago

Press, 1990), 190; Karlyn Kohrs Campbell and Kathleen Hall Jamieson, *Presidents Creating the Presidency: Deeds Done in Words* (Chicago: University of Chicago Press, 2008), 136.

9. Campbell and Jamieson, *Deeds Done in Words*, 168–69; Campbell and Jamieson, *Presidents Creating the Presidency*, 108. See also Craig Allen Smith and Kathy B. Smith, *The White House Speaks: Presidential Leadership as Persuasion* (Westport, CT: Praeger, 1994), 60.

10. Campbell and Jamieson, *Deeds Done in Words*, 170, 4–5; Campbell and Jamieson, *Presidents Creating the Presidency*, 109–10, 7. See also Smith and Smith, *The White House Speaks*, 60.

11. According to Kathleen Dean Moore, "The rhetoric accompanying postwar pardons often bubbles over with reconciliation and healing" (*Pardons: Justice, Mercy, and the Public Interest* [New York: Oxford University Press, 1989], 164).

12. For example, see Christopher S. Kelley, Bryan W. Marshall, and Deanna J. Watts, "Assessing the Rhetorical Side of Presidential Signing Statements," *Presidential Studies Quarterly* 43, no. 2 (June 2013): 274–98.

13. Rogers M. Smith, *Stories of Peoplehood: The Politics and Morals of Political Membership* (Cambridge: Cambridge University Press, 2003), 4–5, 15, 43, 45, 50, 52–53; Rogers M. Smith, *Political Peoplehood: The Roles of Values, Interests, and Identities* (Chicago: University of Chicago Press, 2015), 2, 45. For a broadly similar account of how leaders construct peoplehood, see Joel Migdal, *Boundaries and Belonging: States and Societies in the Struggle to Shape Identities and Local Practices* (Cambridge: Cambridge University Press, 2008).

14. John C. Rodrigue, *Lincoln and Reconstruction* (Carbondale: Southern Illinois University Press, 2013), 69.

15. See, for example, Graham G. Dodds, "Governmental Apologies and Political Reconciliation: Promise and Pitfalls," in *Peacebuilding, Memory, and Reconciliation: Bridging Top-Down and Bottom-Up Approaches*, ed. Bruno Charbonneau and Genevieve Parent (London: Routledge, 2011), 130–45.

16. Moore, *Pardons*, 201.

17. Margaret Atwood, *The Handmaid's Tale* (Toronto: McClellend and Stewart, 1985), 156.

18. This phenomenon might perhaps be understood in terms of the categories discussed in Albert O. Hirschman's classic book *Exit, Voice, and Loyalty* (Cambridge, MA: Harvard University Press, 1970): when the government's policies become onerous, some citizens may give up their blind loyalty and strongly voice their displeasure or even resist the government, and when the government overcomes their resistance and seeks to enforce loyalty on unattractive terms, the aggrieved group may then exit or leave rather than submit.

19. George C. Edwards, *On Deaf Ears: The Limits of the Bully Pulpit* (New Haven, CT: Yale University Press, 2003).

20. An exhaustive list of scholarly rejoinders to Edwards's argument would be quite lengthy, but such works include (in chronological order): Andrew W. Barrett, "Gone Public: The Impact of Going Public on Presidential Legislative Success," *American*

Politics Research 32, no. 3 (2004): 338–70; David Zarefsky, "Presidential Rhetoric and the Power of Definition," *Presidential Studies Quarterly* 34, no. 3 (2004): 607–19; Gary Young and William B. Perkins, "Presidential Rhetoric, the Public Agenda, and the End of Presidential Television's 'Golden Age,'" *Journal of Politics* 67, no. 4 (November 2005): 1190–205; B. Dan Wood, Chris T. Owens, and Brandy M. Durham, "Presidential Rhetoric and the Economy," *Journal of Politics* 67, no. 3 (2005): 627–45; Brandice Canes-Wrone, *Who Leads Whom? Presidents, Policy, and the Public* (Chicago: University of Chicago Press, 2006); John M. Murphy, "Power and Authority in a Postmodern Presidency," in *The Prospect of Presidential Rhetoric*, ed. Martin J. Medhurst and James Arnt Aune (College Station: Texas A&M University Press, 2008), 28–45; Marouf Hasian Jr., "The Return of the Imperial Presidency," in *The Prospect of Presidential Rhetoric*, ed. Medhurst and Aune, 69–98; James A. Aune, "The Econorhetorical Presidency," in *The Prospect of Presidential Rhetoric*, ed. Medhurst and Aune, 46–68; Trevor Parry-Giles, "To Produce a 'Judicious Choice,'" in *The Prospect of Presidential Rhetoric*, ed. Medhurst and Aune, 99–129; Roderick P. Hart, "Thinking Harder About Presidential Discourse: The Question of Efficacy," in *The Prospect of Presidential Rhetoric*, ed. Medhurst and Aune, 238–50; Jeffrey E. Cohen, *Going Local: Presidential Leadership in the Post-broadcast Age* (Cambridge: Cambridge University Press, 2010); Brandon Rottinghaus, *The Provisional Pulpit: Modern Presidential Leadership of Public Opinion* (College Station: Texas A&M University Press, 2010); Mary E. Stuckey, *Political Rhetoric: A Presidential Briefing Book* (New York: Routledge, 2015); Diana C. Mutz, *In-Your-Face Politics: The Consequences of Uncivil Media* (Princeton, NJ: Princeton University Press, 2015); Daniel Q. Gillion, *Governing with Words: The Political Dialogue on Race, Public Policy, and Inequality in America* (Cambridge: Cambridge University Press, 2016); John D. Graham, *Obama on the Home Front: Domestic Policy Triumphs and Setbacks* (Bloomington: Indiana University Press, 2016); Matthew Eshbaugh-Soha, "Presidential Rhetoric, Agency Turnover, and the Importance of Salience to Bureaucratic Leadership," *Social Science Journal* 54, no. 2 (June 2017): 206–15; Amnon Cavari, *The Party Politics of Presidential Rhetoric* (Cambridge: Cambridge University Press, 2017).

21. See, for example, Adam Clymer, "When Presidential Words Led to Swift Action," *Washington Post*, June 8, 2013; Peter Hessler, "Follow the Leader," *New Yorker*, July 24, 2017; and Charles M. Blow, "Trump Savagely Mauls the Language," *New York Times*, July 17, 2017.

22. Indeed, on three occasions over two months in 2017 federal judges used Donald Trump's own words in deciding to rule against his directives on sanctuary cities and foreigners entering the United States. See Sudhin Thanawala, "Another Judge Cites Trump's Comments in Ruling," *Montreal Gazette*, April 27, 2017; Josh Gerstein, "Sparks Fly Over Trump Tweets at Travel Ban Court Arguments," *Politico*, December 8, 2017.

23. Ellaine Kamarck and Christine Stenglein, "How Many Undocumented Immigrants Are in the United States and Who Are They?," Brookings Institution, November 12, 2019, https://www.brookings.edu/policy2020/votervital/how-many-undocumented-immigrants-are-in-the-united-states-and-who-are-they/.

24. Peter L. Markowitz, "Can Obama Pardon Millions of Immigrants?," op-ed., *New York Times*, July 6, 2016; Peter L. Markowitz and Lindsay Nash, "Pardoning Immigrants," *New York University Law Review* 93 (April 2018): 58–106.

25. Susan Hennessey and Benjamin Wittes, *Unmaking the Presidency: Donald Trump's War on the World's Most Powerful Office* (New York: Farrar, Straus and Giroux, 2020), 274.

26. Joseph Story, quoted in Harold J. Krent, "Conditioning the President's Conditional Pardon Power," *California Law Review* 89, no. 6 (December 2001): 1672–673 n. 40.

27 While the post-Nixon fear of political blowback for a pardon might be one reason for the lower rate of pardon issuance today, another might be the rise of harsh penal attitudes per the idea of getting tough on crime. According to Margaret Colgate Love, "Presidential pardoning went into a decline during the Reagan Administration, more sharply during his second term. This is attributable to two relatively new influences in the criminal justice system: the retributivist theory of 'just deserts,' and the politics of the 'war on crime.' The philosophers whose ideas eventually triumphed in the 1984 Sentencing Reform Act took 'a dim view' of pardon" ("Reinventing the President's Pardon Power," American Constitution Society, October, 2007, 6, https://www.acslaw.org/files/Presidential%20Pardons%20Issue%20Brief%20-%20October%202007.pdf). For several years now, however, the zeitgeist appears to have shifted against harsh punishment for criminal convictions, so ideology may no longer be an impediment to issuing more pardons.

28. Love, "Reinventing the President's Pardon Power," 4.

29. Margaret Colgate Love, "The Twilight of the Pardon Power," *Journal of Criminal Law and Criminology* 100, no. 3 (2010): 1193.

30. Marc Miller, quoted in Leon Neyfakh, "The Untapped Power of Presidential Pardons," *Boston Globe*, March 17, 2013.

31. Sari Horwitz, "Obama Grants Final 300 Commutations to Nonviolent Drug Offenders," *New York Times*, January 19, 2017; *New York Times* Editorial Board, "It's Time to Overhaul Clemency," *New York Times*, August 18, 2014; *New York Times* Editorial Board, "President Obama's Last Chance to Show Mercy," *New York Times*, December 6, 2016; *New York Times* Editorial Board, "Mr. Obama, Pick Up Your Pardon Pen," *New York Times*, January 16, 2017.

32. George W. Bush, State of the Union Address, January 20, 2004, White House, https://georgewbush-whitehouse.archives.gov/news/releases/2004/01/20040120-7.html.

APPENDIX

1. By one count, roughly one-third of presidents have issued mass pardons. See Charles Shanor and Marc Miller, "Pardon Us: Systematic Presidential Pardons," *Federal Sentencing Reporter* 13, nos. 3–4 (2000–2001): 139.

2. Mary Kathleen Quigley, "Pardons in Major Cases of Insurrections in Colonial America, 1675–1773," PhD diss., Ohio State University, 1970; Shanor and Miller, "Pardon Us," 140.

3. Wilbur H. Siebert, "George Washington and the Loyalists," *American Antiquarian Society*, April 1933, 38.

4. Siebert, "George Washington and the Loyalists," 43, 47.

5. See Aaron N. Coleman, "Loyalists in War, Americans in Peace: The Reintegration of the Loyalists, 1775–1800," PhD diss., University of Kentucky, 2008; Rebecca Brannon, *From Revolution to Reunion: The Reintegration of South Carolina Loyalists* (Columbia: University of South Carolina Press, 2016).

6. See, for example, F. Forrester Church, "The First American Amnesty Debate: Religion and Politics in Massachusetts, 1783–1784," *Journal of Church and State* 21 (1979): 39–54; Jeffery P. Lucas, "Cooling by Degrees: Reintegration of Loyalists in North Carolina, 1776–1790," master's thesis, North Carolina State University, 2007; Claude Halstead Van Tyne, *The Loyalists in the American Revolution* (New York: Macmillan, 1902), 287.

7. Thomas Jefferson, "Pardon for David Brown," March 12, 1801, and explanatory note, Founders Online, National Archives, https://founders.archives.gov/documents/Jefferson/01-33-02-0209.

8. Gaspar Cusachs, "LaFitte, the Louisiana Pirate and Patriot," *Louisiana Historical Quarterly* 2, no. 7 (1919): 418–38, http://penelope.uchicago.edu/Thayer/E/Gazetteer/Places/America/United_States/Louisiana/_Texts/LHQ/2/4/Lafitte*.html.

9. James Madison, "Proclamation 19—Granting Pardon to Certain Inhabitants of Barataria Who Acted in the Defense of New Orleans," February 6, 1815, American Presidency Project, ed. Gerhard Peters and John T. Woolley, https://www.presidency.ucsb.edu/node/205296.

10. Robert C. Vogel, "Jean Laffite, the Baratarians, and the Battle of New Orleans," *Louisiana History* 41, no. 3 (Summer 2000): 273.

11. Carol Chomsky, "The United States–Dakota War Trials: A Study in Military Injustice," *Stanford Law Review* 43, no. 13 (November 1990): 27.

12. David A. Nichols, *Lincoln and the Indians: Civil War Policy and Politics* (Columbia: University of Missouri Press, 1978), 107.

13. Abraham Lincoln, Second Annual Message to Congress, December 1, 1862, in Presidential Speeches, Miller Center, https://millercenter.org/the-presidency/presidential-speeches/december-1-1862-second-annual-message.

14. Abraham Lincoln and Joseph Holt, quoted in Nichols, *Lincoln and the Indians*, 108.

15. Nichols, *Lincoln and the Indians*, 108.

16. Chomsky, "The United States–Dakota War Trials," 39–40. In March 1866, President Andrew Johnson released the 177 remaining prisoners.

17. Nichols, *Lincoln and the Indians*, 117.

18. Abraham Lincoln, Message to the Senate, December 11, 1862, American Presidency Project, ed. Gerhard Peters and John T. Woolley, https://www.presidency.ucsb.edu/node/202731.

19. Abraham Lincoln, quoted in Nichols, *Lincoln and the Indians*, 94.

20. See Dee Brown, *Bury My Heart at Wounded Knee* (New York: Holt, 1972); Robert Lacy, "Dark Day on the Prairie," *Sewanee Review* 122, no. 2 (Spring 2014): 236–44. In

1987, on the 125th anniversary of the Dakota War, the governor of Minnesota declared a "year of reconciliation."

21. Allen L. Damon, "Amnesty," *American Heritage* 24, no. 6 (October 1973): 8–9, 78–79, Theodore Roosevelt, "Proclamation 483—Granting Pardon and Amnesty to Participants in Insurrection in the Philippines," July 4, 1902, American Presidency Project, ed. Gerhard Peters and John T. Woolley, https://www.presidency.ucsb.edu/node /207304.

22. Marie Gottschalk, *Caught: The Prison State and the Lockdown of American Politics* (Princeton, NJ: Princeton University Press, 2016), 191.

23. David F. Forte, "Writing a Wrong: Woodrow Wilson, Warren G. Harding, and the Espionage Act Prosecutions," *Case Western Law Review* 68 (2018): 1097–151.

24. Patti Iiyama, "Recalling U.S. Detention of Japanese Americans," *Militant* 75, no. 2 (January 17, 2011), https://www.themilitant.com/2011/7502/750258.html. The Civil Liberties Act of 1988 directed the U.S. attorney general to recommend that the president pardon Japanese Americans convicted of violating laws and executive orders related to internment during World War II. No such pardon was issued, but survivors eventually received an apology and compensation. In 1983, during litigation to overturn Fred Korematsu's criminal conviction for defying the internment, the U.S. Justice Department offered him a pardon if he would drop his lawsuit. Korematsu declined, saying the federal government should seek a pardon from Japanese Americans instead: "We should be the ones pardoning the government" (Peter Irons, *Justice at War: The Story of the Japanese American Internment Cases* [Berkeley: University of California Press, 1983], 371).

25. Margaret Colgate Love, "The Twilight of the Pardon Power," *Journal of Criminal Law and Criminology* 100, no. 3 (2010): 1174.

26. Zach Dorfman, "Why Did Obama Free This Terrorist?," *Politico*, January 24, 2017.

27. Eugene M. Wait, *America and the War of 1812* (Commack, NY: Kroshka Books, 1999), 151.

28. Wilfred L. Ebel, "The Amnesty Issue: An Historical Perspective," *Parameters* 4, no. 1 (January 1, 1974): 74–75. Truman issued amnesties regarding military service in 1945, 1946, and 1952.

BIBLIOGRAPHY

Adler, David Gray. "The President's Pardon Power." In *Inventing the American Presidency*, ed. Thomas E. Cronin, 209–35. Lawrence: University Press of Kansas, 1989.

Alden, John R. *George Washington: A Biography*. Baton Rouge: Louisiana State University Press, 1984.

Alexander, Thomas B. Review of *Pardon and Amnesty Under Lincoln and Johnson*, by Jonathan Truman Dorris (University of North Carolina Press, 1953). *Journal of Southern History* 20, no. 2 (May 1954): 278–79.

Alexander, Thomas G. *Brigham Young and the Expansion of the Mormon Faith*. Norman: University of Oklahoma Press, 2019.

Allen, James B., and Glen M. Leonard. *The Story of the Latter-day Saints*. Salt Lake City, UT: Deseret Book, 1976.

Amar, Akhil Reed. *America's Constitution: A Biography*. New York: Random House, 2005.

Anderson, David L. "Gerald R. Ford and the Presidents' War in Vietnam." In *Shadow on the White House: Presidents and the Vietnam War, 1945–1975*, ed. David L. Anderson, 184–207. Lawrence: University Press of Kansas, 1993.

——, ed. *Shadow on the White House: Presidents and the Vietnam War, 1945–1975*. Lawrence: University Press of Kansas, 1993.

Arrington, Leonard J. *Brigham Young: American Moses*. New York: Knopf, 1985.

Atwood, Margaret. *The Handmaid's Tale*. Toronto: McClellend and Stewart, 1985.

Aune, James A. "The Econo-rhetorical Presidency." In *The Prospect of Presidential Rhetoric*, ed. Martin J. Medhurst and James Arnt Aune, 46–68. College Station: Texas A&M University Press, 2008.

Baggett, James Alex. *The Scalawags: Southern Dissenters in the Civil War and Reconstruction*. Baton Rouge: Louisiana State University Press, 2003.

Bagley, Will. *Blood of the Prophets: Brigham Young and the Massacre at Mountain Meadows*. Norman: University of Oklahoma Press, 2012.

——. "President Pardoned All Utahns." *History Matters* blog, February 18, 2001. http://historytogo.utah.gov/salt_lake_tribune/history_matters/021801.html.

Baldwin, Leland D. *Whiskey Rebels: The Story of a Frontier Uprising.* Rev. ed. Pittsburgh: University of Pittsburgh Press, 1968.

Balogh, Brian. *A Government Out of Sight: The Mystery of National Authority in Nineteenth-Century America.* Cambridge: Cambridge University Press, 2009.

Barilleaux, Ryan J. "Foreign Policy and the First Commander in Chief." In *Patriot Sage: George Washington and the American Political Tradition*, ed. Gary L. Gregg and Matthew Spalding, 141–64. Wilmington, DE: ISI Press, 1999.

Barkan, Elazar, and Alexander Karn, eds. *Taking Wrongs Seriously: Apologies and Reconciliation.* Palo Alto, CA: Stanford University Press, 2006.

Barksdale, Kevin T. "Our Rebellious Neighbors: Virginia's Border Counties During Pennsylvania's Whiskey Rebellion." *Virginia Magazine of History and Biography* 111, no. 1 (2003): 5–32.

Barrett, Andrew W. "Gone Public: The Impact of Going Public on Presidential Legislative Success." *American Politics Research* 32, no. 3 (2004): 338–70.

Baskir, Lawrence M., and William A. Strauss. *Reconciliation After Vietnam: A Program of Relief for Vietnam-Era Draft and Military Offenders.* Notre Dame, IN: University of Notre Dame Press, 1977.

Baton Rouge Advocate. "Amnesty Rejected by VFW." August 21, 1974.

Battistella, Edwin. "The Art of the Political Apology." *Politico*, May 7, 2014.

Beard, Rick. "Lincoln's 10 Percent Plan." *New York Times*, December 9, 2013.

Beasley, Vanessa B. "The Rhetorical Presidency Meets the Unitary Executive: Implications for Presidential Rhetoric on Public Policy." *Rhetoric and Public Affairs*, Spring 2010, 7–35.

Belco, Michelle, and Brandon Rottinghaus. *The Dual Executive: Unilateral Orders in a Separated and Shared Power System.* Palo Alto, CA: Stanford University Press, 2017.

Belson, Ken, and Eric Lichtblau. "A Father, a Son, and a Short-Lived Presidential Pardon." *New York Times*, December 25, 2008.

Bennett, Richard E. "Raising Kane." Review of *Liberty to the Downtrodden: Thomas L. Kane, Romantic Reformer*, by Matthew J. Grow (Yale University Press, 2009). *Review of Books on the Book of Mormon* 23, no. 1 (2011): 125–29.

Bigler, David L., and Will Bagley. *The Mormon Rebellion: America's First Civil War, 1857–1858.* Norman: Oklahoma University Press, 2012.

Black, Susan Easton. "Faces Turned West." In Glenn Rawson, Dennis Lyman, and Bryant Bush, *History of the Saints: The Great Mormon Exodus and the Establishment of Zion*, 1–16. American Fork, UT: Covenant Communications, 2014.

Blair, William A. *With Malice Toward Some: Treason and Loyalty in the Civil War Era.* Chapel Hill: University of North Carolina Press, 2014.

Blight, David W. *Race and Reunion: The Civil War in American Memory.* Cambridge, MA: Harvard University Press, 2001.

Blow, Charles M. "Trump Savagely Mauls the Language." *New York Times*, July 17, 2017.

Bogel-Burroughs, Nicholas. "Matt Bevin Drew Outrage Over His Pardons. These Governors Have, Too." *New York Times*, December 21, 2019.

Boorstein, Daniel. *The Americans: The National Experience*. New York: Vintage Books, 1967.

Borders, William. "Exiles Are Cool to Amnesty Move." *New York Times*, August 21, 1974.

Bouton, Terry. *Taming Democracy: "The People," the Founders, and the Troubled Ending of the American Revolution*. New York: Oxford University Press, 2007.

Bowman, Frank O., III. *High Crimes and Misdemeanors: A History of Impeachment for the Age of Trump*. Cambridge: Cambridge University Press, 2019.

Boyd, Steven R. "Hugh Henry Brackenridge, *Incidents of the Insurrection*." In *The Whiskey Rebellion: Past and Present Perspectives*, ed. Steven R. Boyd, 61–76. Westport, CT: Greenwood Press, 1985.

——, ed. *The Whiskey Rebellion: Past and Present Perspectives*. Westport, CT: Greenwood Press, 1985.

Brannon, Rebecca, *From Revolution to Reunion: The Reintegration of South Carolina Loyalists*. Columbia: University of South Carolina Press, 2016.

Bronkhorst, Daan. *Truth and Reconciliation: Obstacles and Opportunities for Human Rights*. Washington, DC: Amnesty International, 1995.

Brooks, Juanita. *The Mountain Meadows Massacre*. Norman: University of Oklahoma Press, 1962.

Brooks, Roy L., ed. *When Sorry Isn't Enough: The Controversy Over Apologies and Reparations for Human Injustice*. New York: New York University Press, 1999.

Brown, Dee. *Bury My Heart at Wounded Knee*. New York: Holt, 1972.

Brown, Ralph Adams. *The Presidency of John Adams*. Lawrence: University Press of Kansas, 1975.

Brown, Richard Maxwell. *Strain of Violence: Historical Studies of American Violence and Vigilantism*. New York: Oxford University Press, 1975.

Brown, Weldon Amzy. "The Howe Peace Commission of 1776." *North Carolina Historical Review* 13, no. 2 (1936): 122–42.

Buffa, D. W. "The Pardon Power and Original Intent." Brookings Institution, July 25, 2018. https://www.brookings.edu/blog/fixgov/2018/07/25/the-pardon-power-and-original -intent/.

Burns, Ken, and Lynn Novick. "Vietnam's Unhealed Wounds." Op-ed. *New York Times*, May 29, 2017.

——, dirs. "The Weight of Memory." Episode 10 of *The Vietnam War*. PBS (WETA, National Endowment for the Humanities), aired September 28, 2017.

Calhoun, Jack. Review of *The Vietnam War and the Vietnam Generation*, by Lawrence M. Baskir and William A. Strauss (Knopf, 1978). *Peace and Change* 6, no. 3 (October 1980): 71–77.

Campbell, Karlyn Kohrs, and Kathleen Hall Jamieson. *Deeds Done in Words: Presidential Rhetoric and the Genres of Governance*. Chicago: University of Chicago Press, 1990.

——. *Presidents Creating the Presidency: Deeds Done in Words*. Chicago: University of Chicago Press, 2008.

Canes-Wrone, Brandice. *Who Leads Whom? Presidents, Policy, and the Public*. Chicago: University of Chicago Press, 2006.

Cannon, Lou. "Ford Weighs Amnesty Program." *Washington Post*, December 28, 1976.

Carroll, Joseph. "Americans Grow to Accept Nixon's Pardon." Gallup.com, May 21, 2001. https://news.gallup.com/poll/3157/americans-grew-accept-nixons-pardon.aspx.

Carter, Jimmy. *A Government as Good as Its People*. 2nd ed. Fayetteville: University of Arkansas Press, 1996.

——. Interviewed by Brian Williams. John F. Kennedy Library and Museum, March 11, 2006. https://www.jfklibrary.org/events-and-awards/forums/past-forums/transcripts/vietnam-and-the-presidency-introduction-by-caroline-kennedy-and-interview-with-president-jimmy.

——. *Living Faith*. 1996. Reprint. New York: Three Rivers Press, 2001.

Carver, Courtney. "To Forgive or Not to Forgive? A Reappraisal of Vietnam War Evaders and Deserters in President Gerald Ford's Clemency Program." Master's thesis, University of New Orleans, 2018.

Castel, Albert. *The Presidency of Andrew Johnson*. Lawrence: University Press of Kansas, 1979.

Cavari, Amnon. *The Party Politics of Presidential Rhetoric*. Cambridge: Cambridge University Press, 2017.

Ceaser, James W., Glen E. Thurow, Jeffrey K. Tulis, and Joseph M. Bessette. "The Rise of the Rhetorical Presidency." *Presidential Studies Quarterly* 11, no. 2 (1981): 158–71.

Chappell, Bill. "Chelsea Manning, Once Sentenced to 35 Years, Walks Free After 7 Years." NPR, May 17, 2017.

Cheney, Kyle. "House Dems Push Legislation to Criminalize Quid-pro-Quo Pardons." *Politico*, July 22, 2020.

Chernow, Ron. *Alexander Hamilton*. New York: Penguin Books, 2004.

Chicago Tribune. "Ford Opposes Amnesty: Dole." August 26, 1976.

Chiou, Fang-Yi, and Lawrence S. Rothenberg. *The Enigma of Presidential Power: Parties, Policies, and Strategic Uses of Unilateral Action*. Cambridge: Cambridge University Press, 2017.

Chomsky, Carol. "The United States–Dakota War Trials: A Study in Military Injustice." *Stanford Law Review* 43, no. 13 (November 1990): 13–95.

Church, F. Forrester. "The First American Amnesty Debate: Religion and Politics in Massachusetts, 1783–1784." *Journal of Church and State* 21 (1979): 39–54.

Church of Jesus Christ of Latter-day Saints. "Plural Marriage in Kirtland and Nauvoo." Gospel Topics, 2016. www.lds.org/topics/plural-marriage-in-kirtland-and-nauvoo?lang=eng.

Civil Rights and Restorative Justice Project, Northeastern University School of Law. "Civil Rights–Related Pardons." N.d. https://crrj.northeastern.edu/home/about-us/pardons/.

Clymer, Adam. "When Presidential Words Led to Swift Action." *Washington Post*, June 8, 2013.

Cohen, Jeffrey E. *Going Local: Presidential Leadership in the Post-broadcast Age*. Cambridge: Cambridge University Press, 2010.

——. *Presidential Responsiveness and Public Policy-Making*. Ann Arbor: University of Michigan Press, 1997.

——. "Presidential Rhetoric and the Public Agenda." *American Journal of Political Science* 39, no. 1 (1995): 87–107.

Coke, Edward. *Institutes of the Laws of England.* Part 3. London: Clarke, 1817.

Coleman, Aaron N. "Loyalists in War, Americans in Peace: The Reintegration of the Loyalists, 1775–1800." PhD diss., University of Kentucky, 2008.

Comptroller General of the United States. *Report to the Congress: The Clemency Program of 1974.* 95th Cong., 1st sess. Washington, DC: U.S. Government Printing Office, January 7, 1977.

Conway, Sharon. "Families of Vietnam War Victims Divided on Pardon Issue." *Washington Post*, January 17, 1977.

Cooke, Jacob E. "The Whiskey Insurrection: A Re-evaluation." *Pennsylvania History*, July 1963, 316–64.

Cooper, Phillip J. *By Order of the President: The Use and Abuse of Executive Direct Action.* Lawrence: University Press of Kansas, 2002.

Corwin, Edward S. *The Constitution and What It Means Today.* Princeton, NJ: Princeton University Press, 1948.

——. *The President: Office and Powers, 1787–1957.* 5th rev. ed. New York: New York University Press, 1984.

Coulter, E. Merton. *The Confederate States of America, 1861–1865.* Baton Rouge: Louisiana University Press, 1950.

Crawley, Peter. "The Constitution of the State of Deseret." *Brigham Young University Studies* 29, no. 4 (Fall 1989): 7–22.

Cresswell, Stephen. *Mormons and Cowboys, Moonshiners and Klansmen: Federal Law Enforcement in the South and West, 1870–1893.* Tuscaloosa: University of Alabama Press, 2002.

Crouch, Jeffrey. *The Presidential Pardon Power.* Lawrence: University Press of Kansas, 2009.

——. "The Toussie Pardon, 'Unpardon,' and the Abdication of Responsibility in Clemency Cases." *Congress & the Presidency* 38, no. 1 (2011): 77–100.

C-SPAN. "National Thanksgiving Turkey Pardon." November 21, 2017. https://www.c-span.org/video/?437626-1/president-trump-pardons-thanksgiving-turkey.

Cusachs, Gaspar. "LaFitte, the Louisiana Pirate and Patriot." *Louisiana Historical Quarterly* 2, no. 7 (1919): 418–38. http://penelope.uchicago.edu/Thayer/E/Gazetteer/Places/America/United_States/Louisiana/_Texts/LHQ/2/4/Lafitte*.html.

Cutler, H. G. "The Nation's First Rebellion." *Magazine of American History with Notes and Queries* 12 (1884): 332–47.

Damon, Allen L. "Amnesty." *American Heritage* 24, no. 6 (October 1973): 8–9, 78–79.

Danver, Steven Lawrence, ed. *Revolts, Protests, Demonstrations, and Rebellions in American History.* 3 vols. Santa Barbara, CA: ABC-CLIO, 2011.

Davidson, Lee. "America's Forgotten War." *Deseret News*, July 9, 2006.

Davis, Jefferson. *The Rise and Fall of the Confederate Government.* New York: Appleton, 1881.

Davis, William C. *Look Away! A History of the Confederate States of America.* New York: Free Press, 1992.

Dawsey, Cyrus B., and James M. Dawsey, eds. *The Confederados: Old South Immigrants in Brazil*. Tuscaloosa: University of Alabama Press, 1998.

Deerman, Gene. Review of *The Mormon Rebellion: America's First Civil War, 1857–1858*, by David L. Bigler and Will Bagley (Oklahoma University Press, 2013). Faculty Research and Creative Activity Paper no. 7. http://thekeep.eiu.edu/sociology_fac/7.

Denton, Herbert H. "They Chose to Remain Despite Amnesty." *Washington Post*, January 1, 1989.

Denton, Robert E., and Dan F. Hehn. *Presidential Communication: Description and Analysis*. Westport, CT: Praeger, 1986.

Dershowitz, Alan. "What's Mercy Got to Do with It?" *New York Times*, July 16, 1989.

Deseret Evening News. "Official Declaration." September 25, 1890.

Dewar, Helen. "Legionnaires Boo Carter's Plan to Pardon Draft Evaders." *Washington Post*, August 25, 1976.

Dickerson, James L. *North to Canada: Men and Women Against the Vietnam War*. Westport, CT: Praeger, 1999.

Dickinson, Matthew. "We All Want a Revolution: Neustadt, New Institutionalism, and the Future of Presidency Research." *Presidential Studies Quarterly* 39, no. 4 (December 2009): 736–70.

Dickinson, Matthew, and Jesse Grub. "The Limits to Power Without Persuasion." *Presidential Studies Quarterly* 46, no. 1 (March 2016): 48–72.

Dodds, Graham G. "Governmental Apologies and Political Reconciliation: Promise and Pitfalls." In *Peacebuilding, Memory, and Reconciliation: Bridging Top-Down and Bottom-Up Approaches*, ed. Bruno Charbonneau and Genevieve Parent, 130–45. London: Routledge, 2011.

——. "Political Apologies and Public Discourse." In *Public Discourse in America: Conversation and Community in the Twenty-First Century*, ed. Judith Rodin and Stephen P. Steinberg, 135–60. Philadelphia: University of Pennsylvania Press, 2003.

——. "Political Apologies and Racial Reconciliation." In *Racism and Justice: Dialogue on the Politics of Inequality and Change*, ed. Sean P. Hier and B. Singh Bolaria, 137–51. Black Wood, NS, Canada: Fernwood Press, 2009.

——. *Take Up Your Pen: Unilateral Presidential Directives in American Politics*. Philadelphia: University of Pennsylvania Press, 2013.

Donald, David Herbert. *Lincoln*. New York: Touchstone, 1996.

Dorfman, Zach. "Why Did Obama Free This Terrorist?" *Politico*, January 24, 2017.

Dorris, Jonathan Truman. *Pardon and Amnesty Under Lincoln and Johnson: The Restoration of the Confederates to Their Rights and Privileges, 1861–1898*. 1953. Reprint. Westport, CT: Greenwood Press, 1977.

Doxtader, Erik. "The Potential of Reconciliation's Beginning: A Reply." *Rhetoric and Public Affairs*, Fall 2004, 378–90.

Duker, William. "The President's Power to Pardon: A Constitutional History." *William and Mary Law Review* 18 (1977): 475–538.

Duscha, Julius. "More Than 50,000 Americans Killed in Vietnam, More Than 300,000 Wounded or Injured, More Than 1,600 P.O.W.'s or M.I.A.'s." *New York Times*, December 24, 1972.

——. "Should There Be Amnesty for the War Resister?" *New York Times*, December 24, 1972.

Ebel, Wilfred L. "The Amnesty Issue: An Historical Perspective." *Parameters* 4, no. 1 (January 1, 1974): 67–77.

Edsall, Thomas B. "The Savage Injustice of Trump's Military Pardons." *New York Times*, December 4, 2019.

Edwards, George C. *On Deaf Ears: The Limits of the Bully Pulpit*. New Haven, CT: Yale University Press, 2003.

Elliott, Sam. "The 1865 Constitutional Amendments and the Return of Civil Government in Tennessee." Tennessee Bar Association (TBA), *TBA Law Blog*, December 1, 2017. https:// www.tba.org/index.cfm?pg=LawBlog&blAction=showEntry&blogEntry=29528.

Ellis, Joseph J. *His Excellency: George Washington*. New York: Knopf, 2005.

Ellwager, Adam. "Apology as *Metanoic* Preference: Punitive Rhetoric and Public Speech." *Rhetoric Society Quarterly* 42, no. 4 (2012): 307–29.

Elsmere, Jane Shaffer. "The Trials of John Fries." *Pennsylvania Magazine of History and Biography* 103, no. 4 (October 1979): 432–45.

Emrich, Cynthia G., Holly H. Brower, Jack M. Feldman, and Howard Garland. "Images in Words: Presidential Rhetoric, Charisma, and Greatness." *Administrative Sciences Quarterly* 26 (2001): 527–57.

Epstein, Kayla. "Defeated GOP Governor Pardoned Violent Criminals in a Spree Lawyers Are Calling an 'Atrocity of Justice.'" *Washington Post*, December 12, 2019.

Eshbaugh-Soha, Matthew. "Presidential Rhetoric, Agency Turnover, and the Importance of Salience to Bureaucratic Leadership." *Social Science Journal* 54, no. 2 (June 2017): 206–15.

Fandos, Nicholas. "House Democrats Advance New Checks on Presidential Pardon Power." *New York Times*, July 23, 2020.

The Federalist Papers. 1787–1788. Avalon Project, Yale Law School. https://avalon.law.yale .edu/subject_menus/fed.asp.

Ferling, John. *John Adams: A Life*. Knoxville: University of Tennessee Press, 1992.

Fielding, Robert Kent. *The Unsolicited Chronicler: An Account of the Gunnison Massacre, Its Causes and Consequences*. Taos, NM: Redwing Book, 1992.

Firmage, Edwin Brown, and Richard Collin Mangrum. *Zion in the Courts: A Legal History of the Church of Jesus Christ of Latter-day Saints, 1830–1900*. Champaign: University of Illinois Press, 2001.

Foley, Michael Stewart. "The Moral Case for Draft Resistance." *New York Times*, October 17, 2017.

Foner, Eric. *The Fiery Trial: Abraham Lincoln and American Slavery*. New York: Norton, 2010.

——. "Reconstruction Revisited." In "The Promise of American History: Progress and Prospects," *Reviews in American History* 10, no. 4 (December 1982): 82–100.

Ford, Betty, and Chris Chase. *The Times of My Life*. New York: Harper Collins, 1978.

Ford, Gerald R. *Containing the Public Messages, Speeches, and Statements of the President, 1976–1977*. Vol. 3: *July 10, 1976 to January 20, 1977*. Washington, DC: U.S. Government Printing Office, 1979.

——. *A Time to Heal*. New York: Harper and Row, 1979.

Ford Foundation. "Vietnam Veterans, Deserters, and Draft-Evaders: The Vietnam Decade." September 1974. https://www.fordlibrarymuseum.gov/library/document/0193/1505994 .pdf.

——. "Vietnam Veterans, Deserters, and Draft-Evaders: A Summer Study." September 1974, II-4, https://www.fordlibrarymuseum.gov/library/document/0067/1562799.pdf

Forte, David F. "Writing a Wrong: Woodrow Wilson, Warren G. Harding, and the Espionage Act Prosecutions." *Case Western Reserve Law Review* 68 (2018): 1097–151.

Foster, Michael A. *Presidential Pardons: Overview and Selected Legal Issues*. Washington, DC: Congressional Research Service, January 14, 2020.

Frank, David A., and Mark Lawrence McPhail. "Barack Obama's Address to the 2004 Democratic National Convention." *Rhetoric and Public Affairs*, Winter 2005, 571–93.

Friedman, Jason. "Draft Dodger and Deserter Reconciliation, 1972–1977." Paper presented at the Peace History Society conference, Mount Pleasant, MI, April 26, 2003.

——. "Just a Caretaker?" *A Companion to Gerald R. Ford and Jimmy Carter*, ed. Scott Kaufman, 196–210. Hoboken, NJ: Wiley, 2015.

Furniss, Norman F. *The Mormon Conflict: 1850–1859*. New Haven, CT: Yale University Press, 1960.

Gates, Henry Louis, Jr. *Stony the Road: Reconstruction, White Supremacy, and the Rise of Jim Crow*. New York: Penguin Press, 2019.

Georgia Restoration of Rights & Record Relief. Collateral Consequences Resource Center, updated September 9, 2020. http://ccresourcecenter.org/state-restoration-profiles /georgia-restoration-of-rights-pardon-expungement-sealing/.

Gerstbauer, Loramy. *U.S. Foreign Policy and the Politics of Apology*. London: Routledge, 2016.

Gerstein, Josh. "House Democrats Ask Judge to Reject Arpaio Pardon." *Politico*, September 27, 2017.

——. "Sparks Fly Over Trump Tweets at Travel Ban Court Arguments." *Politico*, December 8, 2017.

Gillion, Daniel Q. *Governing with Words: The Political Dialogue on Race, Public Policy, and Inequality in America*. Cambridge: Cambridge University Press, 2016.

Gitterman, Daniel. *Calling the Shots: The President, Executive Orders, and Public Policy*. Washington, DC: Brookings Institution Press, 2017.

Glass, Andrew. "Carter Pardons Draft Dodgers Jan 21 1977." *Politico*, January 21, 2008.

Goodwin, Doris Kearns. *Team of Rivals: The Political Genius of Abraham Lincoln*. New York: Simon and Schuster, 2005.

Gopnik, Adam. "Shot of Courage." *New Yorker Magazine*, October 2, 2017.

Gottschalk, Marie. *Caught: The Prison State and the Lockdown of American Politics*. Princeton, NJ: Princeton University Press, 2016.

Graham, Hugh Davis, and Ted Robert Gurr, eds. *Violence in America: Historical and Comparative Perspectives*. National Commission on the Causes and Prevention of Violence. Washington, DC: U.S. Government Printing Office, 1969.

——, eds. *Violence in America: Historical and Comparative Perspectives*. Rev. ed. Thousand Oaks, CA: Sage, 1979.

Graham, John D. *Obama on the Home Front: Domestic Policy Triumphs and Setbacks*. Bloomington: Indiana University Press, 2016.

Gramlich, John, and Kirsten Bialik. "Obama Used Clemency Power More Often Than Any President Since Truman." Pew Research Center, January 20, 2017.

Grann, David. *Killers of the Flower Moon: The Osage Murders and the Birth of the FBI*. New York: Vintage, 2017.

Greenberg, David. "The War That Never Ends." Review of *The Vietnam War*, by Geoffrey C. Ward (Knopf, 2017). *New York Times Book Review*, September 17, 2017.

Greene, John Robert. *The Presidency of Gerald R. Ford*. Lawrence: University Press of Kansas, 1994.

Greenspan, Stephen. "Posthumous Pardons in American History." Death Penalty Information Center, March 2011.

Greenstein, Fred I. *Inventing the Job of President: Leadership Style from George Washington to Andrew Jackson*. Princeton, NJ: Princeton University Press, 2009.

——. "Presidential Difference in the Early Republic: The Highly Disparate Leadership Styles of Washington, Adams, and Jefferson." *Presidential Studies Quarterly* 36, no. 3 (September 2006): 373–90.

Gregg, Gary L. "The Symbolic Dimensions of the First Presidency." In *Patriot Sage: George Washington and the American Political Tradition*, ed. Gary L. Gregg and Matthew Spalding, 165–98. Wilmington, DE: ISI Books, 1999.

Gregg, Gary L., and Matthew Spalding, eds. *Patriot Sage: George Washington and the American Political Tradition*. Wilmington, DE: ISI Books, 1999.

Grossman, Steve. "I Want to Go Home, but. . . ." *New York Times*, January 2, 1977.

Grow, Matthew F., and Ronald W. Walker, eds. *The Prophet and the Reformer: The Letters of Brigham Young and Thomas L. Kane*. New York: Oxford University Press, 2015.

Gugliotta, Guy. "New Estimate Raises Civil War Death Toll." *New York Times*, April 2, 2012.

Gurr, Ted Robert. *Political Rebellion: Causes, Outcomes, and Alternatives*. London: Routledge, 2015.

——. *Violence in America: Protest, Rebellion, Reform*. Thousand Oaks, CA: Sage, 1989.

Hafen, LeRoy, and Ann Woodbury Hafen, eds. *Mormon Resistance: A Documentary Account of the Utah Expedition, 1857–1858*. Lincoln: University of Nebraska Press, 2005.

Hagan, John. *Northern Passage: American Vietnam War Resisters in Canada*. Cambridge, MA: Harvard University Press, 2001.

Hahn, Dan F. "The Rhetoric of Jimmy Carter, 1976–1980." *Presidential Studies Quarterly*, Spring 1984, 265–88.

Hall, James O. "Atonement." *Civil War Times Illustrated* 19, no. 5 (August 1980): 19–21.

Hamilton, Alexander. *Selected Writings and Speeches of Alexander Hamilton*. Ed. Morton J. Frisch. Washington, DC: AEI Press, 1985.

Hansell, Dean. "Amnesty, Discharge Status Upgrading, and Military Deserters Under the Carter Administration: Selective Redemption." *Clearinghouse Review* 11 (1977–1978): 344–51.

Hansen, Lorin K. "Voyage of the *Brooklyn*." *Dialogue: A Journal of Mormon Thought* 21 (Autumn 1988): 47–72.

Harper's Weekly. "Domestic Intelligence." September 21, 1867.

Harris, David. "I Picked Prison Over Fighting in Vietnam." *New York Times*, June 23, 2017.

Harris, Louis. "Pardon Criticized." Harris Survey, February 24, 1977.

Harris, William C. *With Charity for All: Lincoln and the Restoration of the Union*. Lexington: University Press of Kentucky, 1997.

Hart, Roderick P. *The Sound of Leadership: Presidential Communication in the Modern Age*. Chicago: University of Chicago Press, 1987.

——. "Thinking Harder About Presidential Discourse: The Question of Efficacy." In *The Prospect of Presidential Rhetoric*, ed. Martin J. Medhurst and James Arnt Aune, 238–50. College Station: Texas A&M University Press, 2008.

Harter, Eugene C. *The Lost Colony of the Confederacy*. College Station: Texas A&M University Press, 2000.

Hartley, William G. "Exodus from Nauvoo." In Glenn Rawson, Dennis Lyman, and Bryant Bush, *History of the Saints: The Great Mormon Exodus and the Establishment of Zion*, 17–32. American Fork, UT: Covenant Communications, 2014.

Hasian, Marouf, Jr. "The Return of the Imperial Presidency." In *The Prospect of Presidential Rhetoric*, ed. Martin J. Medhurst and James Arnt Aune, 69–98. College Station: Texas A&M University Press, 2008.

Hatch, John B. "Dialogic Rhetoric in *Letters Across the Divide*: A Dance of (Good) Faith Toward Racial Reconciliation." *Rhetoric and Public Affairs*, Winter 2009, 482–532.

——. "The Hope of Reconciliation: Continuing the Conversation." *Rhetoric and Public Affairs*, Summer 2006, 259–77.

——. "Reconciliation: Building a Bridge from Complicity to Coherence in the Rhetoric of Race Relations." *Rhetoric and Public Affairs*, Winter 2003, 737–64.

Hemel, Daniel, and Richard Posner. "If Trump Pardons, It Could Be a Crime." *New York Times*, July 21, 2017.

Hennessey, Susan, and Benjamin Wittes. *Unmaking the Presidency: Donald Trump's War on the World's Most Powerful Office*. New York: Farrar, Straus and Giroux, 2020.

Herbers, Hon. "Ford Gives Pardon to Nixon, Who 'Regrets My Mistakes.'" *New York Times*, September 9, 1974.

Hessler, Peter. "Follow the Leader." *New Yorker*, July 24, 2017.

Hill, Kim Quaile. "The Policy Agendas of the President and the Mass Public." *American Journal of Political Science* 42, no. 4 (1998): 1328–334.

Hill, Marvin S., and James B. Allen. Introduction to *Mormonism and American Culture*, ed. Marvin S. Hill and James B. Allen, 1–10. New York: Harper and Row, 1972.

——, eds. *Mormonism and American Culture*. New York: Harper and Row, 1972.

Hirschman, Albert O. *Exit, Voice, and Loyalty*. Cambridge, MA: Harvard University Press, 1970.

Hobbs, Sam. "Victim of the 'Lost Cause': James Longstreet in the Postwar South." *Traces: UNC-Chapel Hill Journal of History* 2 (Spring 2013): 35–61.

Hobbes, Thomas. *Leviathan*. Ed. Richard Tuck. Cambridge: Cambridge University Press, 1996.

Hofstadter, Richard. "Reflections on Violence in the United States." In *American Violence: A Documentary History*, ed. Richard Hofstadter and Michael Wallace, 3–43. New York: Knopf, 1970.

Hofstadter, Richard, and Michael Wallace, eds. *American Violence: A Documentary History*. New York: Knopf, 1970.

Hogeland, William. *The Whiskey Rebellion: George Washington, Alexander Hamilton, and the Frontier Rebels Who Challenged America's Newfound Sovereignty*. 2006. Reprint. New York: Simon and Schuster, 2010.

Holden, Mark V. "Clemency Must Play a Pivotal Role in Reversing the 'Tough on Crime Era.'" *University of St. Thomas Law Journal* 16, no. 3 (2019): 358–72.

Holsinger, Paul M. "Harry M. Teller and the Edmunds-Tucker Act." *Colorado Magazine* 48, no. 1 (1971): 1–14.

Hoover, Michael. "The Whiskey Rebellion." Alcohol and Tobacco, Tax and Trade Bureau, U.S. Department of the Treasury, August 21, 2014. https://www.ttb.gov/public -information/whiskey-rebellion.

Horwitz, Sari. "Obama Grants Final 300 Commutations to Nonviolent Drug Offenders." *New York Times*, January 19, 2017.

Howell, William G. *Power Without Persuasion: The Politics of Direct Presidential Action*. Princeton, NJ: Princeton University Press, 2003.

Hunter, J. Michael, ed. *Mormons and Popular Culture: The Global Influence of an American Phenomenon*. Vol. 1. Santa Barbara, CA: Praeger, 2013.

——. "Preface and Acknowledgments." In *Mormons and Popular Culture: The Global Influence of an American Phenomenon*, vol. 1, ed. J. Michael Hunter, vii–viii. Santa Barbara, CA: Praeger, 2013.

Hyman, Harold M. "Civil War Turncoats." *Military Affairs* 22, no. 3 (Autumn 1958): 134–38.

——, ed. *The Radical Republicans and Reconstruction, 1861–1870*. Indianapolis, IN: Bobbs-Merrill, 1967.

Ifft, Richard A. "Treason in the Early Republic: The Federal Courts, Popular Protest, and Federalism During the Whiskey Insurrection." In *The Whiskey Rebellion: Past and Present Perspectives*, ed. Steven R. Boyd, 165–82. Westport, CT: Greenwood, 1985.

Iiyama, Patti. "Recalling U.S. Detention of Japanese Americans." *Militant* 75, no. 2 (January 17, 2011). https://www.themilitant.com/2011/7502/750258.html.

Irons, Peter. *Justice at War: The Story of the Japanese American Internment Cases*. Berkeley: University of California Press, 1983.

Johansen, Jerald Ray. *After the Martyrdom: What Happened to the Family of Joseph Smith?* Springville, UT: Cedar Fort, 1997.

Johnson, Andrew. "Speech at St. Louis, September 8, 1866." In *The Papers of Andrew Johnson: August 1866–January 1867*, ed. Paul H. Bergeron, 192–201. Knoxville: University of Tennessee Press, 1967.

Jones, Jeffrey. "Latest Poll Shows High Point in Opposition to Iraq War." Gallup.com, July 11, 2007. https://news.gallup.com/poll/28099/latest-poll-shows-high-point-opposition-iraq -war.aspx.

Jones, Joseph. *Contending Statistics: The Numbers for U.S. Vietnam War Resisters in Canada*. Vancouver: Quarter Sheaf, 2005.

Kalb, Marvin, and Deborah Kalb. *Haunting Legacy: Vietnam and the American Presidency from Ford to Obama*. Washington, DC: Brookings Institution Press, 2011.

Karmarck, Elaine, and Christine Stenglein. "How Many Undocumented Immigrants Are in the United States and Who Are They?" Brookings Institution, November 12, 2019. https://www.brookings.edu/policy2020/votervital/how-many-undocumented-immigrants-are-in-the-united-states-and-who-are-they/.

Karnow, Stanley. *Vietnam: A History*. New York: Penguin, 1984.

Kasinsky, Renee G. *Refugees from Militarism: Draft-Age Americans in Canada*. Piscataway, NJ: Transaction, 1976.

Kaufman, Burton I. *The Presidency of James Earl Carter*. Lawrence: University Press of Kansas, 1993.

Keane, Jonathan. "History of an American Uprising." Review of *The Whiskey Rebellion*, by William Hogeland (Scribner, 2006). World Socialist website, October 5, 2006. http://www.wsws.org/articles/2006/oct2006/whis-005.shtml.

Keen, Judy. "Bush Grants Pardons Less Than Predecessors." *USA Today*, December 30, 2005.

Kelley, Christopher S., Bryan W. Marshall, and Deanna J. Watts. "Assessing the Rhetorical Side of Presidential Signing Statements." *Presidential Studies Quarterly* 43, no. 2 (June 2013): 274–98.

Kilpatrick, Carroll. "Clemency Offered." *Washington Post*, September 17, 1974.

King, Desmond, and Robert C. Lieberman. "Ironies of State Building: A Comparative Perspective on the American State." *World Politics* 61 (2009): 547–88.

Klingberg, Frank W. Review of *Pardon and Amnesty Under Lincoln and Johnson*, by Jonathan Truman Dorris (University of North Carolina Press, 1953). *Mississippi Valley Historical Review* 41, no. 3 (December 1954): 523–24.

——. *The Southern Claims Commission*. New York: Octagon Books, 1978.

Kneeland, Douglas. "Dole Attacks Carter on Pardon for Draft Evaders." *New York Times*, August 26, 1976.

Kobil, Daniel T. "The Quality of Mercy Strained." *Texas Law Review* 69 (1991): 569–641.

Kotlowitz, Alex. "A Quarter of a Century Behind Bars, for a Crime He Didn't Commit." Review of *Ghost of the Innocent Man: A True Story of Trial and Redemption*, by Benjamin Rachlin (Little, Brown, 2017). *New York Times Book Review*, October 27, 2017.

Krakauer, John. *Under the Banner of Heaven: A Story of Violent Faith*. New York: Anchor Books, 2003.

Krent, Harold J. "Conditioning the President's Conditional Pardon Power." *California Law Review* 89, no. 6 (December 2001): 1665–720.

Krom, Cynthia L., and Stephanie Krom. "The Whiskey Tax of 1791 and the Consequent Insurrection: 'A Wicked and Unhappy Tumult.'" *Accounting Historians Journal* 40, no. 2 (December 2013): 91–114.

Kurland, Philip B., and Ralph Lerner, eds. *The Founders' Constitution*. Chicago: University of Chicago Press, 1987. https://press-pubs.uchicago.edu/founders/.

Kuttner, Bob. "Clemency Offer Draws Poor Response." *Washington Post*, November 23, 1974.

Lacy, Robert. 2014. "Dark Day on the Prairie." *Sewanee Review* 122, no. 2 (Spring 2014): 236–44.

Lamar, Howard R. *The Far Southwest, 1846–1912*. Rev. ed. Albuquerque: University of New Mexico Press, 2000.

Lardner, George, Jr. "Nixon Defended Envoy's Groping." *Washington Post*, March 1, 2002.

Larson, Gustive O. "Federal Government Efforts to 'Americanize' Utah Before Admission to Statehood." *Brigham Young University Studies Quarterly* 10, no. 2 (1970): 218–32.

Lasky, Victor. *Jimmy Carter: The Man and the Myth*. New York: Richard Marek, 1979.

Laurie, Clayton D., and Robert H. Cole. *The Role of Federal Military Forces in Domestic Disorders, 1877–1945*. Washington, DC: Center of Military History, 1997.

Lawrence, Adam. "Does It Really Matter What Presidents Say? The Influence of Presidential Rhetoric on the Public Agenda, 1946–2002." Paper presented at the American Political Science Association conference, Boston, 2002.

Lawrence, Stewart J. "The Unquiet Ghosts of Kent State." *Guardian*, May 4, 2011.

Lazare, Aaron. *On Apology*. New York: Oxford University Press, 2005.

Leigh, Phil. "The Confederate Diaspora." *New York Times*, May 14, 2015.

Leith, Sam. *Words Like Loaded Pistols: Rhetoric from Aristotle to Obama*. New York: Basic Books, 2012.

Lescaze, Lee. "Draft Pardon Foes Fail to Obtain Senate Vote." *Washington Post*, January 25, 1977.

——. "New Vietnam Clemency Proposal Emulates Carter's." *Washington Post*, January 16, 1977.

Lessa, Francesca, and Leigh A. Payne. *Amnesty in the Age of Human Rights Accountability*. Cambridge: Cambridge University Press, 2012.

Levine, Bruce. *The Fall of the House of Dixie: The Civil War and the Social Revolution That Transformed the South*. New York: Random House, 2013.

Lieberman, Robert C., and Suzanne Mettler. *Four Threats: The Recurring Crises of American Democracy*. New York: St. Martin's, 2020.

Lim, Elvin T. *The Anti-intellectual Presidency: The Decline of Presidential Rhetoric from George Washington to George W. Bush*. New York: Oxford University Press, 2008.

Lind, Jennifer. "Apologies in International Relations." *Security Studies* 18, no. 3 (2009): 517–56.

——. *Sorry States: Apologies in International Politics*. Ithaca, NY: Cornell University Press, 2008.

Lloyd, R. Scott. "1856 Election Sowed the Seeds of Utah War, Y. Scholar Says." *Deseret News*, June 30, 2012.

——. "Former Missouri Governor Honored for Rescinding Mormon 'Extermination Order.'" *Deseret News*, May 31, 2010.

——. "Pioneer Women Left Accounts of Hardships Suffered in 'Move South' During Utah War." Church of Jesus Christ of Latter-Day Saints, 2016. https://www.lds.org/church /news/pioneer-women-left-accounts-of-hardships-suffered-in-move-south-during -utah-war?lang=eng.

Love, Margaret Colgate. "Of Pardons, Politics, and Collar Buttons: Reflections on the President's Duty to Be Merciful." *Fordham Urban Law Journal* 27, no. 5 (2000): 1483–513.

——. "Reinventing the President's Pardon Power." American Constitution Society, October 2007. https://www.acslaw.org/wp-content/uploads/old-uploads/originals/documents/Presidential%20Pardons%20Issue%20Brief%20-%20October%202007.pdf.

——. "The Twilight of the Pardon Power." *Journal of Criminal Law and Criminology* 100, no. 3 (2010): 1169–212.

Lu, Catherine. *Justice and Reconciliation in World Politics.* Cambridge: Cambridge University Press, 2017.

Lucas, Jeffery P. "Cooling by Degrees: Reintegration of Loyalists in North Carolina, 1776–1790." Master's thesis, North Carolina State University, 2007.

Lynn, Barry W. ". . . and the Argument in Favor." *Wall Street Journal*, January 6, 1977.

MacDonnell, Francis. "Reconstruction in the Wake of Vietnam: The Pardoning of Robert E. Lee and Jefferson Davis." *Civil War History* 40, no. 2 (June 1994): 119–33.

MacKenzie, John P. "Ford to Get Advice Today on Amnesty." *Washington Post*, August 31, 1974.

——. "Pardon Sparks New Calls for Viet Amnesty." *Washington Post*, September 10, 1974.

MacKinnon, William P. "'Full of Courage': Thomas L. Kane, the Utah War, and BYU's Kane Collection as Lodestone." *Brigham Young University Studies* 48, no. 4 (2009): 89–119.

——. *At Sword's Point, Part 1: A Documentary History of the Utah War to 1858.* Norman: University of Oklahoma Press, 2008.

MacNeil/Lehrer Report. "Carter's Pardon." PBS, January 21, 1977. http://www.pbs.org/newshour/bb/asia/vietnam/vietnam_1-21-77 html.

MacPherson, Myra. *Long Time Passing: Vietnam and the Haunted Generation.* Bloomington: Indiana University Press, 1984.

Maier, Pauline. "Popular Uprisings and Civil Authority in Eighteenth-Century America." *William and Mary Quarterly* 27 (1970): 3–35.

Mantell, Martin E. *Johnson, Grant, and the Politics of Reconstruction.* New York: Columbia University Press, 1973.

Markowitz, Peter L. "Can Obama Pardon Millions of Immigrants?" Op-ed. *New York Times*, July 6, 2016.

Markowitz, Peter L., and Lindsay Nash. "Pardoning Immigrants." *New York University Law Review* 93 (April 2018): 58–106.

Marlantes, Karl. "Vietnam: The War That Killed Trust." *New York Times*, January 7, 2017.

Mason, David Vaughn. *Brigham Young: Sovereign in America.* London: Routledge, 2014.

Massachusetts Historical Society. "'This Convulsed Commonwealth': Daniel Shays Attempts to Call a Truce During Shays' Rebellion, the Agrarian Revolt Named for Him." Massachusetts Historical Society, May 2013. http://www.masshist.org/object-of-the-month/may-2013.

Mayer, Kenneth R. *With the Stroke of a Pen: Executive Orders and Presidential Power.* Princeton, NJ: Princeton University Press, 2001.

McCabe, Nora. "War Resisters' Conference Rejects Ford Amnesty Plan." *Washington Post*, September 22, 1974.

McCoy, Terrence. "They Lost the Civil War and Fled to Brazil: Their Descendants Refuse to Take Down the Confederate Flag." *Washington Post*, July 11, 2020.

McCullough, David. *John Adams*. New York: Simon and Schuster, 2001.

McDonald, Forrest. *Alexander Hamilton: A Biography*. New York: Norton, 1979.

——. *The Presidency of George Washington*. Lawrence: University Press of Kansas, 1974.

McFadden, Robert D. "Pro-Amnesty Groups Offer Praise but Assert That Plan Is Too Limited." *New York Times*, January 22, 1977.

McKitrick, Eric L. *Andrew Johnson and Reconstruction*. New York: Oxford University Press, 1960.

McPherson, Edward. *The Political History of the United States of America, During the Period of Reconstruction*. Washington, DC: Philip and Solomons, 1871.

McPherson, James M. *Embattled Rebel: Jefferson Davis as Commander in Chief*. New York: Penguin, 2014.

Medhurst, Martin J., and James Arnt Aune, eds. *The Prospect of Presidential Rhetoric*. College Station: Texas A&M University Press, 2008.

Medsger, Betty. *The Burglary: The Discovery of J. Edgar Hoover's Secret FBI*. New York: Vintage, 2014.

Messing, Noah A. "A New Power? Civil Offenses and Presidential Clemency." *Buffalo Law Review* 64, no. 4 (2016): 661–743.

Meyer, Lawrence. "Exiles' Families Say Ford Proposal Not True Amnesty." *Washington Post*, September 17, 1974.

Migdal, Joel S. *Boundaries and Belonging: States and Societies in the Struggle to Shape Identities and Local Practices*. Cambridge: Cambridge University Press, 2008.

Miller, John C. *Alexander Hamilton and the Growth of the New Nation*. New York: Harper and Row, 1964.

Minow, Martha. *Between Vengeance and Forgiveness: Facing History After Genocide and Mass Violence*. Boston: Beacon, 1998.

——. *When Should Law Forgive?* New York: Norton, 2019.

Mitgang, Herbert, ed. *Abraham Lincoln: A Press Portrait*. Athens: University of Georgia Press, 1989.

Mohr, Charles. "10,000 Affected Now." *New York Times*, January 22, 1977.

Moore, Kathleen Dean. *Pardons: Justice, Mercy, and the Public Interest*. New York: Oxford University Press, 1989.

Morgan, Ruth. *The President and Civil Rights: Policy-Making by Executive Order*. New York: St. Martin's, 1970.

Murphy, John M. "Power and Authority in a Postmodern Presidency." In *The Prospect of Presidential Rhetoric*, ed. Martin J. Medhurst and James Arnt Aune, 28–45. College Station: Texas A&M University Press, 2008.

Mutz, Diana C. *In-Your-Face Politics: The Consequences of Uncivil Media*. Princeton, NJ: Princeton University Press, 2015.

National Constitution Center Staff. "The Pardon of Jefferson Davis and the 14th Amendment." National Constitution Center, October 17, 2018. https://constitutioncenter.org/blog/the-pardon-of-jefferson-davis-and-the-14th-amendment/.

National Review. "Carter in Action." February 18, 1977.

Necker, Jacques. *On Executive Power in Great States*. Ed. Aurelian Craiutu. Indianapolis, IN: Liberty Fund, 2020.

Nelson, Michael, ed. *The Evolving Presidency: Landmark Documents*. 6th ed. Washington, DC: Congressional Quarterly Press, 2019.

Neustadt, Richard E. *Presidential Power: The Politics of Leadership from FDR to Carter*. 1960. Reprint. New York: Wiley, 1980.

Newman, Paul Douglas. "Fries's Rebellion and American Political Culture, 1798–1800." *Pennsylvania Magazine of History and Biography* 119, nos. 1–2 (January–April 1995): 37–73.

——. *Fries's Rebellion: The Enduring Struggle for the American Revolution*. Philadelphia: University of Pennsylvania Press, 2004.

New York Times. "59% in Poll Favor Amnesty Program Like the Ford Plan," September 22, 1974.

——. "Carter Aides Widen a Draft Pardon Plan." December 17, 1976.

——. "Clemency Program May Be Dropped." December 17, 1976.

——. "The Doom of Polygamy." April 21, 1882.

——. "Group Wants Carter Ousted from Legion." January 25, 1977.

——. "The Moral Injury of War Crimes Pardons." November 24, 2019.

——. "Mormon Affairs: Address of Judge Cradlebaugh, of Utah, on the Condition of Public and Social Life in Utah." March 21, 1860.

——. "Mr. Carter's Call for Personal and National Humility." January 23, 1977.

——. "The President and His Power to Pardon." May 19, 2019.

——. "To Fashion a Blanket of Pardon." January 10, 1974.

New York Times Editorial Board. "It's Time to Overhaul Clemency." *New York Times*, August 18, 2014.

——. "Mr. Obama, Pick Up Your Pardon Pen." *New York Times*, January 16, 2017.

——. "The Perils of a Pardon for Joe Arpaio." *New York Times*, August 24, 2017.

——. "President Obama's Last Chance to Show Mercy." *New York Times*, December 6, 2016.

Neyfakh, Leon. "The Untapped Power of Presidential Pardons." *Boston Globe*, March 17, 2013.

Nichols, David A. *Lincoln and the Indians: Civil War Policy and Politics*. Columbia: University of Missouri Press, 1978.

Nobles, Gregory H. "Historians Extend the Reach of the American Revolution." In *Whose American Revolution Was It?*, ed. Alfred F. Young and Gregory H. Nobles, 135–256. New York: New York University Press, 2011.

Nobles, Melissa. *The Past Is Present: Official Apologies and Multicultural Citizenship*. Cambridge: Cambridge University Press, 2007.

Novak, Andrew. *Comparative Executive Clemency: The Constitutional Pardon Power and the Prerogative of Mercy in Global Perspective*. London: Routledge, 2015.

Novak, William J. "The Myth of the Weak State." *American Historical Review* 113, no. 3 (2008): 752–72.

NPR. "President Ford's Life & Legacy." December 27, 2006. https://www.npr.org/templates /story/story.php?storyId=6686363.

———. "Reversal of Presidential Pardon Analyzed." December 25, 2008. https://www.npr.org/templates/story/story.php?storyId=98711226.

O'Neill, Paul. Interviewed by Richard Norton Smith. Gerald R. Ford Oral History Project, Gerald R. Ford Foundation, March 19, 2010. http://geraldrfordfoundation.org/centennial/oralhistory/paul-oneill/.

Parry-Giles, Trevor. "To Produce a 'Judicious Choice.'" In *The Prospect of Presidential Rhetoric*, ed. Martin J. Medhurst and James Arnt Aune, 99–129. College Station: Texas A&M University Press, 2008.

Perlstein, Rick. *Nixonland: The Rise of a President and the Fracturing of America*. New York: Scribner, 2008.

Pfiffner, James. "The President's Broad Power to Pardon and Commute." Heritage Foundation, July 9, 2007.

Pfleger, Birte. Review of *Fries's Rebellion*, by Paul Douglas Newman (University of Pennsylvania Press, 2004). *Pennsylvania Magazine of History and Biography*, July 2006, 336–37.

Phillips, Eugene. "The Central Intelligence Agency's Surveillance of the New Left." *Review of History and Political Science* 5, no. 2 (December 2017): 1–10.

"Pickett, George E." In *The Oxford Encyclopedia of the Civil War*, ed. William L. Barney, 240. Oxford: Oxford University Press, 2001.

Plaxton, Sheila Rudy. "To Reconcile a Nation: Gerald Ford, Jimmy Carter, and the Question of Amnesty." PhD diss., Queens University, 1995.

Poll, Richard D. "Utah Expedition." In *Encyclopedia of Mormonism*, ed. Daniel H. Ludlow, 1500–502. New York: Macmillan, 1992.

Poll, Richard D., and Ralph W. Hansen. "Buchanan's Blunder." *Military Affairs* 25, no. 3, part 1 (Autumn 1961): 121–31.

Pollitt, Daniel, and Frank Thompson Jr. "Amnesty: The American Tradition." *Washington Post*, September 19, 1974.

Prologue. "General Robert E. Lee's Parole and Citizenship." 37, no. 1 (Spring 2005). https://www.archives.gov/publications/prologue/2005/spring/piece-lee.

Public Opinion: A Comprehensive Summary of the Press Throughout the World on All Important Current Topics. Washington, DC: Public Opinion, 1893.

Quandt, Katie Rose. "The Largest Commutation in U.S. History." *Slate*, November 8, 2019.

Quigley, Mary Kathleen. "Pardons in Major Cases of Insurrections in Colonial America, 1675–1773." PhD diss., Ohio State University, 1970.

Rawson, Glenn, Dennis Lyman, and Bryant Bush. *History of the Saints: The Great Mormon Exodus and the Establishment of Zion*. American Fork, UT: Covenant Communications, 2014. [With chapters by Susan Easton Black, William G. Hartley, and Ronald W. Walker.]

Reston, James, Jr. "Limited Amnesty: Not Easy." *New York Times*, September 8, 1974.

Rice, Allen Thorndike, ed. *Reminiscences of Abraham Lincoln by Distinguished Men of His Time*. New York: Haskell House, 1971.

Richards, Leonard L. *Shays's Rebellion: The American Revolution's Final Battle*. Philadelphia: University of Pennsylvania Press, 2003.

Richardson, Heather Cox. *The Death of Reconstruction: Race, Labor, and Politics in the Post–Civil War North, 1865–1901*. Cambridge, MA: Harvard University Press, 2001.

Ridgway, Whitman H. "Fries in the Federalist Imagination: A Crisis of Republican Society." *Pennsylvania History* 67, no. 1 (Winter 2000): 141–60.

Ripley, Anthony. "Amnesty for Draft Resisters Is Expected to Be Divisive Political Issue for Years." *New York Times*, January 30, 1973.

Roberts, David. "The Brink of War." *Smithsonian*, June 2008.

Rodgers, Kathleen. *Welcome to Resisterville: American Dissidents in British Columbia*. Vancouver: University of British Columbia Press, 2014.

Rodrigue, John C. *Lincoln and Reconstruction*. Carbondale: Southern Illinois University Press, 2013.

Rodrigues, Ricardo Jose Pereira. *The Preeminence of Politics: Executive Orders from Eisenhower to Clinton*. New York: LFB Scholarly, 2007.

Rolle, Andrew F. *The Lost Cause: The Confederate Exodus to Mexico*. Norman: University of Oklahoma Press, 1992.

Romero, Simon. "A Slice of the Confederacy in the Interior of Brazil." *New York Times*, May 8, 2016.

Rose, Thomas, ed. *Violence in America: A Historical and Contemporary Reader*. New York: Random House, 1969.

Rottinghaus, Brandon. *The Provisional Pulpit: Modern Presidential Leadership of Public Opinion*. College Station: Texas A&M University Press, 2010.

Rozell, Mark J. "The Presidential Pardon Power: A Bibliographic Essay," *Journal of Law and Politics* 5, no. 2 (Winter 1989): 459–67.

Ruckman, P. S., Jr. "'Last-Minute' Pardon Scandals: Fact and Fiction." Paper presented at the Midwest Political Science Association conference, Chicago, April 2004.

——. "Presidential Character and Executive Clemency: A Reexamination." *Social Science Quarterly* 76, no. 1 (March 1995): 213–21.

——. "The Study of Mercy: What Political Scientists Know (and Don't Know) About the Pardon Power." *University of St. Thomas Law Review* 9 (2012): 783–868.

Ruckman, P. S., Jr., and David Kincaid. "Inside Lincoln's Clemency Decision Making." *Presidential Studies Quarterly* 29, no. 1 (1999): 84–99.

Rudalevige, Andrew C. "Executive Orders and Presidential Unilateralism." *Presidential Studies Quarterly* 42, no. 1 (March 2012): 138–60.

Rumsfeld, Donald. "How the Nixon Pardon Tore the Ford Administration Apart." *Politico*, May 20, 2018.

——. *When the Center Held: Gerald Ford and the Rescue of the American Presidency*. New York: Free Press, 2018.

Rutenberg, Amy J. "How the Draft Reshaped America." *New York Times*, October 6, 2017.

——. "What Trump's Draft Deferments Reveal." *Atlantic*, January 2, 2019.

Sammin, Kyle. "Why We Should Amend the Constitution to Restrict the President's Power to Pardon." *Federalist*, February 8, 2019.

Sandburg, Carl. *Abraham Lincoln*. Vol. 2. New York: Harcourt, Brace, 1939.

Sanford, Melissa. "Illinois Tells Mormons It Regrets Expulsion." *New York Times*, April 8, 2004.

Sarat, Austin, and Nasser Hussain, eds. *Forgiveness, Mercy, and Clemency*. Palo Alto, CA: Stanford University Press, 2008.

Scanlon, Donna. "The Whiskey Rebellion." Library of Congress, Business Reference Services, December 2009. https://www.loc.gov/rr/business/businesshistory/August/whiskeyrebellion.html.

Schama, Simon. "Mourning in America; a Whiff of Dread for the Land of Hope." *New York Times*, September 15, 2002.

Schindler, Harold. *In Another Time: Sketches of Utah History*. Logan: Utah State University Press, 1998.

——. "Utah War Broke Hold Mormons Had on Utah Centennial: Dark Time in Utah History." *Salt Lake Tribune*, July 23, 1995.

Schubert, Glendon A. *The Presidency in the Courts*. Minneapolis: University of Minnesota Press, 1956.

Scott, Amy. "Patriots for Peace: People to People Diplomacy and the Anti-war Movement." In *America and the Vietnam War: Re-examining the Culture and History of a Generation*, ed. Andrew Wiest, Mary Kathryn Barbier, and Glenn Robins, 121–42. London: Routledge, 2009.

Scranton, William W., chairman. *The Report of the President's Commission on Campus Unrest*. Washington, DC: U.S. Government Printing Office, 1970.

Sefton, James E. *Andrew Johnson and the Uses of Constitutional Power*. Boston: Little, Brown, 1980.

Shafer, Ronald G. "'A National Disgrace': As Impeachment Hung Over a President's Head, He Went on a Wild Rally Tour." *Washington Post*, January 11, 2020.

Shane, Scott. "For Ford, Pardon Decision Was Always Clear-Cut." *New York Times*, December 29, 2006.

Shanor, Charles, and Marc Miller. "Pardon Us: Systematic Presidential Pardons." *Federal Sentencing Reporter* 13, nos. 3–4 (2000–2001): 139–46.

Sharp, James Roger. "The Whiskey Rebellion and the Question of Representation." In *The Whiskey Rebellion: Past and Present Perspectives*, ed. Steven R. Boyd, 119–34. Westport, CT: Greenwood Press, 1985.

Shichor, David, and Donald R. Ranish. "President Carter's Vietnam Amnesty." *Presidential Studies Quarterly* 10 (1980): 443–50.

Shogan, Colleen. *The Moral Rhetoric of American Presidents*. College Station: Texas A&M University Press, 2006.

Siebert, Wilbur H. "George Washington and the Loyalists." *American Antiquarian Society*, April 1933, 34–48.

Silber, Nina. *The Romance of Reunion: Northerners and the South, 1865–1900*. Chapel Hill: University of North Carolina Press, 1993.

Simmons, Donald C., Jr. *Confederate Settlements in British Honduras*. Jefferson, NC: McFarland, 2001.

Simpson, Brooks D. *The Reconstruction Presidents*. Lawrence: University Press of Kansas, 1998.

Skowronek, Stephen. *The Politics Presidents Make: Leadership from John Adams to George Bush*. Cambridge, MA: Harvard University Press, 1993.

Slaughter, Thomas P. *The Whiskey Rebellion: Frontier Epilogue to the American Revolution*. New York: Oxford University Press, 1986.

Smith, Craig Allen, and Kathy B. Smith. *The White House Speaks: Presidential Leadership as Persuasion*. Westport, CT: Praeger, 1994.

Smith, Elbert B. *The Presidency of James Buchanan*. Lawrence: University Press of Kansas, 1975.

Smith, Page. *John Adams*. Vol. 2. New York: Doubleday, 1962.

Smith, Rogers M. *Political Peoplehood: The Roles of Values, Interests, and Identities*. Chicago: University of Chicago Press, 2015.

——. *Stories of Peoplehood: The Politics and Morals of Political Membership*. Cambridge: Cambridge University Press, 2003.

Soodalter, Ron. "The Limits of Lincoln's Mercy." *New York Times*, February 23, 2012.

Sparrow, James T., William J. Novak, and Stephen Sawyer, eds. *Boundaries of the State in U.S. History*. Chicago: University of Chicago Press, 2015.

Stenhouse, Thomas B. H. *The Rocky Mountain Saints: A Full and Complete History of the Mormons*. New York: Appleton, 1873.

Stuckey, Mary E. *Defining Americans: The Presidency and National Identity*. Lawrence: University Press of Kansas, 2004.

——. *Political Rhetoric: A Presidential Briefing Book*. New York: Routledge, 2015.

——. *The President as Interpreter-in-Chief*. Chapel Hill: University of North Carolina Press, 1991.

Surrey, David S. *Choice of Conscience: Vietnam Era Military and Draft Resisters in Canada*. Westport, CT: Praeger, 1982.

Sweet, Matthew. *Operation Chaos: The Vietnam Deserters Who Fought the CIA, the Brainwashers, and Themselves*. New York: Holt, 2018.

Swerdlow, Amy. *Women Strike for Peace: Traditional Motherhood and Radical Politics in the 1960s*. Chicago: University of Chicago Press, 1993.

Szalai, Jennifer. "Impeachment, the First Time Around." Review of *The Impeachers*, by Brenda Wineapple (Random House, 2019). *New York Times*, May 15, 2019.

Taub, Amanda. "The Word May Be Toxic, but Amnesty Is Everywhere." *New York Times*, October 15, 2017.

Tavuchis, Nicholas. *Mea Culpa: A Sociology of Apology and Reconciliation*. Palo Alto, CA: Stanford University Press, 1991.

Taylor, Alan. *American Revolutions: A Continental History, 1750–1804*. New York: Norton, 2016.

Thanawala, Sudhin. "Another Judge Cites Trump's Comments in Ruling." *Montreal Gazette*, April 27, 2017.

Thomas, Kenneth R., ed. "Pardons and Reprieves." In *The Constitution of the United States of America: Analysis and Interpretation*, 510–17. Washington, DC: Congressional Research Service, June 28, 2012. http://law.justia.com/constitution/us/article-2/16-pardons-and-reprieves.html.

Thrush, Glenn. "Clinton's '08 Slaps Still Sting Obama." *Politico*, August 1, 2013.

Tilly, Charles. "Collective Violence in European Perspective." In *Violence in America: Historical and Comparative Perspectives*, ed. Hugh Davis Graham and Ted Robert Gurr, 4–45. National Commission on the Causes and Prevention of Violence. Washington, DC: U.S. Government Printing Office, 1969.

Todd, Jack. "Remembering the 1975 Fall of Saigon." *Montreal Gazette*, April 30, 2015.

Toobin, Jeffrey. "The Trouble with Donald Trump's Clemency and Pardons." *New Yorker*, February 19, 2020.

Trumbell, Robert. "Pardon Brings Cautious Response from Some War Exiles in Canada." *New York Times*, January 23, 1977.

Tulis, Jeffrey. *The Rhetorical Presidency*. Princeton, NJ: Princeton University Press, 1987.

Tullidge, Edward W. *The History of Salt Lake City and Its Founders*. Salt Lake City, UT: E. W. Tullidge, 1886.

Tumulty, Karen. "More on Pardons." *Time*, December 25, 2008.

U.S. House of Representatives, Committee on Government Reform. *Justice Undone: Clemency Decisions in the Clinton White House*. House Report 107-454, 107th Cong., 2nd sess., May 14, 2002. Washington, DC: U.S. Government Printing Office, 2002.

U.S. House of Representatives, Subcommittee on Courts, Civil Liberties, and the Administration of Justice. *Amnesty: Hearings Before the Subcommittee on Courts, Civil Liberties, and the Administration of Justice, Committee on the Judiciary, House of Representatives, March 8, 11, and 13, 1974*. 93rd Cong., 2nd sess. Washington, DC: U.S. Government Printing Office, 1974.

——. *Information on H.R. 9568: The Vietnam Era Reconciliation Act*. 94th Cong., 1st sess. Washington, DC: U.S. Government Printing Office, October 1975.

U.S. National Park Service. "Whiskey Rebellion." Friendship Hill National Historical Site, Pennsylvania, February 26, 2015. https://www.nps.gov/frhi/learn/historyculture/whiskeyrebellion.htm.

U.S. Senate, Subcommittee on Administrative Practice and Procedure. *Selective Service and Amnesty: Hearing Before the Subcommittee on Administrative Practice and Procedure of the Committee on the Judiciary, U.S. Senate, February 29 to March 1, 1972*, 92nd Cong., 2nd sess. Washington, DC: U.S. Government Printing Office, 1972.

Van Tyne, Claude Halstead. *The Loyalists in the American Revolution*. New York: Macmillan, 1902.

Veenstra, David. "As God Gives Me to See the Right: Gerald Ford, Religion, and Healing After Vietnam and Watergate." *Pro Rege* 43, no. 3 (March 2015): 12–18.

Vogel, Robert C., "Jean Laffite, the Baratarians, and the Battle of New Orleans." *Louisiana History* 41, no. 3 (Summer 2000): 261–76.

Volokh, Eugene. "If You're Pardoned, Can You Be Compelled to Testify About Your Crime?" *Washington Post*, June 2, 2017.

Wait, Eugene M. *America and the War of 1812*. Commack, NY: Kroshka Books, 1999.

Waldrep, Christopher, and Michael Bellesiles, eds. *Documenting American Violence: A Sourcebook*. New York: Oxford University Press, 2006.

——. Introduction to *Documenting American Violence*, ed. Christopher Waldrep and Michael Bellesiles, 3–10. New York: Oxford University Press, 2006.

Walker, Ronald W. "'Deseret' and Utah's Early Governments." In Glenn Rawson, Dennis Lyman, and Bryant Bush, *History of the Saints: The Great Mormon Exodus and the Establishment of Zion*, 181–96. American Fork, UT: Covenant Communications, 2014.

——. "'Proud as a Peacock and Ignorant as a Jackass': William W. Drummond's Unusual Career with the Mormons." *Journal of Mormon History* 42, no. 3 (July 2016): 1–34.

Wall Street Journal. "In Defense of Jimmy Carter." September 2, 1976.

——. "The Pardon Backlash." January 25, 1977.

Warber, Adam L. *Executive Orders and the Modern Presidency.* Boulder, CO: Lynne Rienner, 2006.

Washington Post. "Amnesty for the Mormons." February 21, 1892.

——. "Amnesty for Polygamy." September 29, 1894.

——. "Mormons Are Satisfied." October 31, 1894.

——. "Utah and Amnesty." January 7, 1893.

——. "Vets Group Backs Plan for Amnesty." August 29, 1974.

——. "The Vietnam 'Amnesty.'" September 18, 1974.

Waxman, Olivia B. "Why Jefferson Davis Got His U.S. Citizenship Back." *Time*, June 5, 2017.

Weisbrode, Kenneth. "An Unlikely Friendship." *New York Times*, June 9, 2014.

Werth, Barry. "The Pardon." *Smithsonian*, February 2007.

Westmoreland, William C. "No Pardon for Draft Evaders." *New York Times*, December 12, 1976.

Weyeneth, Robert R. "The Power of Apology and the Process of Historical Reconciliation." *Public Historian* 23, no. 3 (Summer 2001): 9–38.

Whelan, Frank. "Angry Taxpayers, U.S. Clashed in Fries Rebellion." *Morning Call*, November 25, 1984.

Whitmore, Connor K., and Preston Boggs. *Rebellions of the United States.* North Charleston, SC: CreateSpace Independent Publishing Platform, 2016.

Wicker, Tom. "Clemency: It's Not So Simple." *New York Times*, December 28, 1976.

Widmer, Ted. "Lincoln and the Mormons." *New York Times*, November 17, 2011.

Williams, Carol. "End-of-Term Clemency Is a Centuries-Old, Often Vilified Tradition." *Los Angeles Times*, January 10, 2011.

Williams, Raymond T. "A Simple Twist of the Wrist: Presidential Use of Executive Orders and Proclamations in Times of Crisis, 1861–2012." PhD diss., University of Maryland, 2017.

Wilson, Douglas L. *Lincoln's Sword: The Presidency and the Power of Words.* New York: Vintage, 2006.

Wilson, Frederick T. *Federal Aid in Domestic Disturbances, 1787–1903.* Washington, DC: U.S. Government Printing Office, 1903.

Wilson, George C. "Carter Authorizes Military to Review Viet Discharges." *Washington Post*, March 29, 1977.

Wilson, Kirt H. "Is There Interest in Reconciliation?" *Rhetoric and Public Affairs*, Fall 2004, 367–77.

Witcover, Jules. *Marathon: The Pursuit of the Presidency, 1972–1976*. New York: Viking Press, 1977.

——. "Middle-Road Policy on Amnesty Seen." *Washington Post*, August 26, 1974.

Wood, B. Dan, Chris T. Owens, and Brandy M. Durham. "Presidential Rhetoric and the Economy." *Journal of Politics* 67, no. 3 (2005): 627–45.

Wooten, James. "Legionnaires Boo Carter on Pardon for Draft Defiers." *New York Times*, August 25, 1976.

Young, Eugene. "Revival of the Mormon Problem." *North American Review* 168, no. 509 (April 1899): 476–89.

Young, Gary, and William B. Perkins. "Presidential Rhetoric, the Public Agenda, and the End of Presidential Television's 'Golden Age.'" *Journal of Politics* 67, no. 4 (November 2005): 1190–205.

Zarefsky, David. "Presidential Rhetoric and the Power of Definition." *Presidential Studies Quarterly* 34, no. 3 (2004): 607–19.

Zeitz, Joshua. "How Democrats Can Learn Hardball from the Republicans of 1861." *Politico*, October 27, 2020.

Zelizer, Julian E. *Governing America: The Revival of Political History*. Princeton, NJ: Princeton University Press, 2012.

Zimmerman, Bill. "The Four Stages of the Antiwar Movement." *New York Times*, October 4, 1967.

Zug, Charles U. "Daniel Shays and the Question of Oligarchy at the Founding." Paper presented at the American Political Science Association conference, Boston, 2018.

INDEX

GPSR Authorized Representative: Easy Access System Europe, Mustamäe tee
50, 10621 Tallinn, Estonia, gpsr.requests@easproject.com

www.ingramcontent.com/pod-product-compliance
Lightning Source LLC
Chambersburg PA
CBHW022139020426
42334CB00015B/973

9 780231 200790